OUTLINE GRAMMAR

OF

THE ∞' (KHÂMTÎ) LANGUAGE

AS SPOKEN BY THE KHÂMTÎS RESIDING IN THE NEIGHBOURHOOD OF SADIYA

OUTLINE GRAMMAR

OF

THE ∞' (KHÂMTÎ) LANGUAGE

AS SPOKEN BY THE KHÂMTÎS RESIDING IN THE NEIGHBOURHOOD OF SADIYA

J. F. NEEDHAM

GYAN

Published by

GYAN

Gyan Publishing House
5, Ansari Road
Daryaganj, New Delhi-110002
Phone: 011-47034999, 9811692060
E-mail: books@gyanbooks.com

Distribution Network
gyanbooks.com
India, USA, Canada, UK, Australia

ISBN: 978-93-6780-215-1 (HB)

First Published, 1894

2nd Impression 2024

Printed at: Gyan Press, Delhi.

OUTLINE GRAMMAR OFTHE ∞' (KHÂMTÎ) LANGUAGE
Author: J. F. NEEDHAM

OUTLINE GRAMMAR

OF

THE ထ' (KHÂMTÎ) LANGUAGE

AS SPOKEN BY THE KHÂMTÎS RESIDING IN THE NEIGHBOURHOOD OF SADIYA,

WITH

ILLUSTRATIVE SENTENCES, PHRASE-BOOK AND VOCABULARY

BY

J. F. ṆEEDHAM,
Assistant Political Officer, Sadiya.

RANGOON:

PRINTED BY THE SUPERINTENDENT, GOVERNMENT PRINTING, BURMA.

1894.

PREFACE.

THE Khâmtîs residing within British territory (chiefly up the Tengapani) on our north-east frontier are a small, well-behaved, and industrious community, numbering about 2,000 souls.

They call themselves တႝ (Tai), and their forefathers came to Assam over 100 years ago from the country known to us as Bôr or great Khâmtî, a valley of considerable extent lying high up the Irrawaddy, in latitude 27° and 28° north (eastward of Sadiya).

The Bôr Khâmtîs likewise call themselves *Tai*, and they are supposed to number about 20,000. They speak of their country as မိင်ၶံတီ (Müng Khâmtî) = "country of the Khâmtîs," and two derivations of the word Khâmtî have been given me: (1) It means "tied to spot," from ၶံ (khâm) = to stick, adhere to, remain where placed, &c., and တီ (tî) = spot, place. The Bôr Khâmtîs having numerous slaves who, it is alleged, would bolt *en masse* if an opportunity offered itself, are afraid to move about; (2) Khâmtî means "golden locality," from ၶံ (khâm = gold and တီ (tî) = spot, place.

A legend exists that a tree of iron grew in their country which yielded golden fruit; that their enemies fearing they (Bôr Khâmtîs) would become inordinately rich by means of this tree sent a demon to devour them; that this demon took up his abode in the said gold-yielding tree and as he threatened to annihilate them they were compelled, in self-defence, to fell the tree in order to kill him, it being too high to admit of their doing so in any other way. The legend says the tree was felled by means of fire and the demon was then destroyed.

This တ (Tai) family to quote from the Rev. J. N. Cushing's introduction to his revised grammar of the Shan* language, dated Rangoon, the 14th October 1887, a copy of which I received in May last from Captain Dun, of the Intelligence Branch of the Quartermaster-General's Department, "comprises several divisions, namely, the Siamese, Laos, Lau, "Burmese-Shan, Tai Mau or Tai Khe (Chinese-Shan), "Khâmtî, and Ahom, and their original home was, without doubt Southern China, whence the different divisions "migrated at various times as internal dissentions or the outside pressure of the conquering Chinese drove them forth;" and Dr. Cushing is of opinion "that it extends from the Gulf "of Siam northward into Yunnan, and thence westward to "Assam;" also "that the language of the different divisions "of the တ family come from a common source," but "in "process of time the speech of each division was not only "modified by the inevitable changes arising from a separate "life as a people, but was considerably affected by the language of the people among whom it settled," and I find these latter remarks applicable to the language treated in this little work.

Khâmtî undoubtedly comes from the same source as the Shan language treated in the Rev. Dr. Cushing's work, though almost all the words found in use in Khâmtî are quite different from those in use among Dr. Cushing's Shans. The (Khâmtî) alphabet resembles the Shan, though there is a marked difference in the formation of a few of the letters.

The character is not difficult, but the various tones met with in the language are very puzzling.

By finely modulated intonation sounds organically the same are often made to express totally different ideas; thus, to give a single illustration there are no less than six words

---

* *Khâmtîs* call the Shans တလူင (Tai lông) or great Tais.

written ၵႆ (khai), but each one expresses a different meaning according to the tone in which it is uttered, namely,—

ၵႆ = ill;
ၵႆ = sell;
ၵႆ = buffalo;
ၵႆ = egg;
ၵႆ = go, depart;
ၵႆ = tell, inform.

Khâmtî is written from left to right and allows of little or no separation between the words.

With a few exceptions words are spelt as pronounced. I have purposely written the words in this little work much further apart than is usual in order to give a transliteration below each.

One noticeable peculiarity about Khâmtî writing is the use of a large black dot in the formation of the letters. The dots given by me in this work are much smaller than those usually seen in books, though not much smaller than those made by ordinary writers, as will be seen from the following specimen writing.

SADIYA:
The 10th August 1890.

J. NEEDHAM,
Assistant Political Officer.

PART I.

The Alphabet.

The Khâmtî alphabet consists of nine vowels and 17 consonants.

The names and powers of the vowels are as follows:—

အ = *a* short, as in America.

အႃ = *â* long, as in father as ႁႃ = (hâ) 5.

အိ = *i* (1) short, as in lip; as တိၼ် = (tin) leg.

(2) short *e*, as in met; as ပိၼ် = (pen) able.

(3) *i* in French word elite; as တိၵျႃ = (tikhyâ) different.

(4) *ey* in they; as သိင် = (sêng) diamond.

ႁိင် = (hêng) dry. လိမ် = (lêm) look.

အီ = *î* long, as in police; as ပီ = (pî) year.

အု = *u* (1) short, *oo* in good; as ၵုမ် = (khum) bitter.

(2) long *oo* in loot; as ထုင် = (thûng) custom.

(3) long *ô* in pope; as လုမ် = (lôm) wind.

အူ = *û* as *oo* in too; as အႃမူ = (â mû) work.

အေ = *e* in eh!; as လေ = (lê) lick; ၶေ = (khê) net.

အႆ = *i* in shine; as တႆ = (tai) die, but it often has a broader sound as ၶႆ (khâi) buffalo.

အေႃ = *aw* short, as *o* in often; as ၵေႃ = (kaw); and also—

(2) long *ô* as in potato; as ပေႃ = (pô) father ၵေႃ = (kô) fear.

Note.—Although some of the vowels represent two, three, and sometimes four distinctly different sounds, there is nothing to guide one in pronouncing them until one has mastered the language and understands the meaning of each word as one reads it. For instance: တိၼ် (tin), a leg, may be (to a beginner) tin, ten, tîn, or tên!

Diphthongs.

ဢွ် = *au*, like sound of *ow* in how; as ဢွ် = (au) take;
ပွ် = (pau) blow.

ဢိူဝ် = (1) *ĭ û*; as ဢိူဝ် = (î û) call, give alarm.
(2) *ĭ au*; as သိူဝ် = (siau) seize, lay hold of.
(3) *i ó*; as ၶိူဝ် = (khiô) a tooth.

ဢူဝ် = *ó* long, as in pope; as တူဝ် = (tô) body.
ဢိုဝ် = *ü*, like *u* in fur; as ယိုဝ် = (yü) shoot.

Note.—This diphthong is extensively used in the formation of words, while ဢိူဝ် is not often met with. When used as a negative verbal particle ဢိုဝ် = *ü* has the sound of *ün* (French *n*); as ဢိုဝ်ပိၼ် = *ün* pen, not able. The sound of *ün*, however, is so very nearly like an initial *n alone*, that I have transliterated ဢိုဝ် (the negative prefix particle) *n'* throughout this work.

ဢွႆ = *oi*, as in boil; as ႁွႆ = (hoi) hang, suspend;
ပွႆ = (poi) send; ၼွႆ = (noi) hill, mountain.

Note.—To the *o* in *oi* a very slight sound of *w* is occasionally added.

ဢိုႆ = *aü* or *aeü*; as သိုႆ = (saü) fill, put into.

The Vowel symbols and their positions with reference to a Consonant are given below.

Vowel.	Symbol.	Position.
အာ	ာ	after.
အိ	ိ	above.
အီ	ီ	above.
အု	ု	below.
အူ	ူ	below.
အေဳ	ေ ဳ	before, above.
အဲ	ဲ	above.
အော	ေ ာ	before, after.
အို	ို	above, below.
အိဝ်	ိ ဝ် ...	above, after.
အူဝ်	ူဝ်	below, after.
အိုဝ်	ို ဝ်	above, below, after.
အွဲ	ွဲ	below, above.
အှံ	ှံ	below, above.

Note.—The vowel အ (*a*) is inherent in every consonant and therefore has no distinctive symbol.

Consonants.

The names and powers of the consonants are—

က=*k* as in king.

ၶ=*kh* like Bengali খ.

င=*ng* when final as in king. It is initial in a few words; as ငႝ = (ngai) now ငု = (ngô) cow.

ꩡ=*ch* as in chair; as ꩡိမ် = (cham) track. In a few words it is pronounced like a တ (t) as ႁိတ် = (het) do.

Note.—There is no *ch* in Shan, but they have an aspirated *s*, which I do not find used in Khâmtî.

ꩬ= *s* like Bengali স. This letter is written ꩬ in Shan.

ꩥ= *ny*. Sometimes, however, this letter is pronounced as *n*, at others *y* only; as ၶိꩥ် = (khên) more; ꩥုꩻ = (nôy) tire.

တ=*t* like the Bengali ত; as တိၼ် = (tin) leg.

ထ= *th* Bengali থ; as ထိမ် = (thim) throw stone.

ၼ = *n* }
ပ = *p* } as in English.

ၽ= *ph* an aspirated *p*, made ၽ in Shan.

မ = *m*
ယ= *y*
ရ = *r* as in English.
လ = *l* interchangeable with ၼ (n).
ဝ = *w*
ႁ= *h* made *p* in Shan.

There are no representatives of *b*, *d*, *f*, *g* or *j* in Khâmtî.

Compound Consonants.

These are formed by combining one or more of the letters under symbolic forms with simple consonants as follows :—

Letter.	Symbol.	Combined with က = k	Power.	Examples.
ယ (y)	ျ	ကျ	kya	မျက် = (meyk) carry (on shoulder).
ရ (r)	ြ	ကြ	kra	တြာ = (tra) rupee.
ဝ (w)	ွ	ကွ	kaw*	မွက် = (m a k) a "chûnga."
ဝ ယ (w) (y)	ျွ	ကျွ	kyaw†	အာကျွင် (â k y â n g) purport.

Combination of Vowels with Consonants.

The consonants combine with the vowels according to the following table :—

Vowel.	Symbol.	Examples showing consonants combined with vowels.
အာ	ာ	ကာ နာ = (kâ nâ) before.
အိ	ိ	ကိန် = (kin) eat.
အီ	ီ	ပီ = (pi) a year.
အု	ု	ယုံ = (yum) credit, believe.
အူ	ူ	ဖူက် = (phûk) bind, fasten.
အေ	ေ	မေ် = (mê) mother.
အဲ	ဲ	ပဲ = (paï run away).
အော	ော	ပော = (pò) beat.
အွ်	ွ်	ကွ် = (kau) I.
အိဝ်	ိ ဝ်	ချိဝ် = (cheô) quickly.
အူဝ်	ူ ဝ်	ငူဝ် = (ngò) cow.
အိုဝ်	ို ဝ် ...	ထိုန် = (thün) jungle.
အွ်	ွ်	ပွ် = (pau) blow.
အှွ်	ှွ်	မှွ် = (maü) you.

* *Aw* like *a* in ball. I have marked this letter *ă* throughout this work.
† *Yaw* I have marked *yă*.

The compound initial consonants unite with only a portion of the vowel sounds, but I know too little of the language at present to be able to state which vowel sound each compound initial consonant unites with.

Final Consonants.

When a consonant is deprived of its inherent vowel ဢ (*a*) it becomes final in the syllable. The absence of the inherent vowel ဢ (*a*) is denoted by the mark (်) placed above the consonant thus, ၵူၼ် (kôn) man ; ပိၼ် = (pen) able.

If this sign is doubled it denotes the repetition of the word, as ၶၼ်် = (khan khan) quickly. Khâmtîs often add several of these final signs thus, Similarly the repetition of words ending with a vowel may be indicated by doubling the vowel thus,—

မႃႃ = mâ mâ ; ၼိိ = nî nî, or ၼီီ = nî nî ; လွႆႆ = loi loi, &c.

The final consonants are nine in number, namely,—

ၵ	င	ꩡ	ꩥ	တ	ၼ	ပ	မ and	ဝ
k	ng	ch	ny	t	n	p	m	w

Final consonants modify the sound of the preceding vowels; but in closed syllables vowels are not written and there is no rule of any sort to guide one in their pronunciation, for instance :—

တင် = (tang) with, or (tâng) a road.

မၵ် = (mak) fruit, or (mâk) cut (with "dao," &c.)

ယပ် = (yap) difficult, or (yâp) sew.

မၼ် = (man) he, or (mân) a village.

ဝၼ် = (wan) sun, or (wân) sweet.

ႁင် = (hang) for, or (hâng) necessary.

ၶၼ် = (khan) about, or (khân) a hatchet.

လိၼ် = (lin) a foot, or (len) run.

လိင် = (ling) a monkey, or (leng) a bullock cart.

ထႅံ = (them) pour in water, or ထိံ (thim) throw stone.
&c., &c., &c.

To the final consonants should be added (ံ) and (ႅံ).

(ံ) is placed over the consonant with which it is combined and has the power of a final မ (m); as ၼံ = (nam) water; ၵႂႃံ * = (khâm) language.

If the mark (ံ) be doubled it denotes the repetition † of the word, as ၼံံ = (nam nam) many; (ႅံ) is placed over the consonant with which it is combined and has the power of ိမ (im), as တႅံ = (tem) ‡ write; ၵႅံ = (kem) keep.

Note.—Both the above might be written တိမ်ၵိမ်, but the abbreviated form is usually adopted.

The Tones of the Khâmtî Language.

As this little work has been compiled merely as a help to future officers desirous of learning the language from a *native* and not to enable the student to acquire a mere *book* knowledge of it, I do not think it necessary to make any elaborate remarks on the tones of the language or to devise some system of diacritical marks by which, at the best, they might only be *tolerably correctly* learnt.

I submit that they can only be correctly learnt from a *native, i.e.,* by constantly conversing with him. Even if I devised a plan for approximately representing the tone re-

---

* This is one of the instances where words are not spelt as pronounced. This word is written *khwâm*, but pronounced *khâm*.

† ေ and ႃ (*a*) may also be doubled to denote repetition; ေ is doubled by putting an extra mark thus, ေေ or ေေ and *a* by merely doubling ႃ thus, ႃႃ

‡ This is the second sound of *i*, *vide* page 1 *ante*.

quired for each word in a combination spelt alike but used to express totally different meanings which, with my limited knowledge of the language would, I submit, be impossible—and I explained by the further use of diacritical marks the different vowel sounds (*vide* page 2 *ante*) met with in open syllables—the student who wished to acquire a mere book knowledge of the language would still be wholly in the dark as to the vowel sounds in closed syllables (*vide* pages 6 and 7 *ante*).

I may add that three of the tones commonly heard are very marked and not difficult to acquire, namely,—

(i) the natural pitch of the voice with a rising inflection at the end, as ဖ႑ (mâ) dog; ဖူ = (mû) pig;

(ii) the falling tone, as ဖ႑ = (mâ) come; and

(iii) an abrupt termination of the voice, or a sudden cessation of it at the end of a word, as ဖ႑ (mâ) a horse.

Punctuation.

The mark || denotes the close of a sentence, but no other marks of punctuation exist.

PART II ACCIDENCE.

I. Nouns.

1.—Gender.

1. The genders are two only, masculine and feminine. Inanimate nouns having no formal distinction of gender.

2. Gender in the case of human beings is usually distinguished by distinct terms, as—

Masculine.	*Feminine.*
ပေႃ (pô) * *or* ၸဝ်ႈ (chau) = father.	မႄႈ (mê) = mother.
ပူႇထဝ်ႈ (pû thau) = old man.	ယႃႇထဝ်ႈ (yâ thau)=old woman.
ပႃႈၸၢႆး (pâ chai) = male.	ပႃႈယိင်း (pâ ying) = female.
လုၵ်ႈၸၢႆး (lûk chai) = son.	လုၵ်ႈသၢဝ် (lûk sau)=daughter.
ၽူဝ် (phô) = husband.	မေႊ (mê) = wife.
ပီႈၸၢႆး (pî chai)=brother (elder).	ပီႈသၢဝ် (pî sau) = sister (elder).
ၼွင်ႉၸၢႆး (nâng chai) = brother (younger).	ၼွင်ႉသၢဝ် (nâng sau) = sister (younger).

3. Occasionally the word ပႃႈၸၢႆး (pâ chai) = male for the masculine and ပႃႈယိင်း (pâ ying) = female for the feminine is either prefixed or added to the noun, as—

Masculine.	*Feminine.*
တူဝ်ဢွၼ်ႇပႃႈၸၢႆး (tô ån pa chai) = child male, *or* ပႃႈၸၢႆးတူဝ်ဢွၼ်ႇ (pa chai tô ån) = male child.	တူဝ် ဢွၼ်ႇ ပႃႈ ယိင်း (tô ån pâ ying) = child female.
ၶႃႈပႃႈၸၢႆး (khâ pa chai)=slave male.	ၶႃႈ ပႃႈ ယိင်း (khâ pâ ying) = slave female.

4. Gender in the case of the inferior animals is distin-

* *Pô* is used by equals; *chau* in addressing a superior.

guished by the suffix ထုၵ် (thük) for the masculine and မေ (mê) for the feminine, as—

Masculine.	*Feminine.*
မႃ=(mâ) dog မႃထုၵ် =dog, male.	မႃမေ = (mâ mê) dog, female.
လိင်=(ling) monkey လိင် do= monkey, male.	လိင်မေ = (ling mê) monkey, female.
ငဝ် = (ngô)* ox, cow ငဝ် do = male.	ငဝ်မေ = (ngô mê) female.

5. Gender in the case of birds (feathered tribe generally) is distinguished by the suffix ၽူ (phû) for the masculine and မေ (mê) for the feminine, as—

Masculine.	*Feminine.*
ၵႆ (kai) = fowl — ၵႆၽူ	— ၵႆမေ
ႏွၵ်ယူင် (nôk yûng) — ယူင်ၽူ = peacock.	— ယူင်မေ

2.—Number.

The Khâmtî noun admits of no plural form. When it is required to be indicated in order to avoid ambiguity, the suffix ၶဝ် (khau), † third person plural of personal pronouns, is used, as—

Examples.

ဢႃ ၼႆ ငဝ် ၵဝ်။
â[1] nai ngô[2] kau[3] } This[1] cow[2] (is) mine[3].

ဢႃ ၼၼ်း ၶဝ် ငဝ် မၼ်း။
â nan[1] khau[2] ngô man.[3] } Those[1] cows[2] (are) his[3].

3.—Case.

The accidence of case are expressed by means of particles which sometimes follow, at others precede, the nouns they serve to qualify.

---

* *Ngô* is equivalent to the Assamese *garû* meaning an animal, male or female, of the bovine genus.

† *Khau* is generally used in conjunction with *nai*, the demonstrative pronoun, as *the* pigs=*mû nai khau*. If *khau* was used alone, *mû khau* would mean their pigs; *nai*, therefore, is used for *emphasis and recognition.*

1. The nominative is the noun in its natural state and does not require the aid of a particle, as—

Examples.

မႃ ၼႆ * ၶႆ ဢူ ‖ mâ nai khai û 2 1 4 3	The dog is sick. 1 2 3 4
သိူဝ် ၵပ် † ငူဝ် ယဝ်ႉ ‡ sü kâp ngô yau 1 2 3 2	(A) tiger killed (a) cow. 1 2 3
မႃ ၼိၼ် ၵၢင် ဝၼ်း ၼၢၼ် ဢူ ‖ mâ nin kâng wan nân û 1 3 2	Jackals sleep (in the) day time. 1 2 3

2. The expression of the genitive case depends on the juxtaposition of the two substantives, in which the *latter* is understood to be in the genitive case.

Examples.

လဵပ် သိူဝ် lep sü 2 1	A tiger's claw. 1 2
ပိၵ်း ၼူၵ်း pik nôk 2 1	A bird's wing. 1 2
ၼိူဝ်ႉ ၸၢင်ႉ ၶဵင် ဢူ nü châng kheng û 2 1 4 3	Elephant's flesh is hard. 1 2 3 4

3. The dative, accusative, and locative cases are marked by the particle suffix မႆ (mai), as—

Examples.

ၵူၼ်း မႆ (*or* ၵူၼ်း alone) ႁွင်ႉ တႃ ¶ kôn mai hâng tâ 3 2 1	Call (to) the man. 1 2 3
ဝၼ်း ၼိုင်ႈ ပႃ လင် ၼေႃ ဝႃ ပႃ လင် သႃ မႆ wan lüng Pâ lang nô wâ Pâ lang sa mai 2 1 3 4 6 5	One day Pâlangnô said to Pâlangsa 1 2 3 4 5 6

---

* *Nai* is the demonstrative pronoun, used here for emphasis and recognition.
† *Kâp* means to bite, but as tigers cause death by biting, it means here kill.
‡ *Yau* is a completive verbal particle, it belongs here to *kâp*; *kâp yau u* = killed.
¶ *Tâ* is the imperative tense suffix.

ၵွ် မႆ ငိုၼ် ပၵ်ႉ လိုင် ၵူ ႁႂ် မႃ။ *† kau mai ngün pâk lüng **kû haü mâ** 9 8 10 12 11 7 မိုၼ် ၼႆ ပႃ လင် သႃ ပႃ လင် ၼေႃ မႆ **mü nai** Pâ lang sâ Pâ lang nô mai 13 14 17 16 ငိုၼ် ပၵ်ႉ လိုင် * ၵူ ႁႂ် ၵႃ ‡ ။ ngün pâk lüng **kû haü kâ** 18 20 19 15	lend to me rupees 7 8 9 10 one hundred. 11 12 Then Pâlangsâ gave 13 14 15 to Pâlangnô 16 17 rupees one hun- 18 19 20 dred.
ၵွ် မႆ ႁႂ် မႃ kau mai **haü mâ** 3 2 1	Give (it) to me. 1 2 3
ၽႃ ¶ ၼႆ ၼဵတ်ႉ မႆ ဝႆ တႃ phâ nai net mai **wai tâ** 3 2 5 4 1	Put the cloth in (the) 1 2 3 4 sun. 5
မႂ် သိုဝ် မႆ ယိုဝ် ၵႃ ၵေႃ § maü sü mai yü kâ kê 2 5 4 3 1	Did you shoot the 1 2 3 4 tiger? 5
ၼူ ႁူ မႆ ၶွ် ‖ ယွ် nû hû mai khau yau 1 4 3 2	The mouse **has enter-** 1 2 **ed** (into) the hole. 3 4
ၼမ် မႆ ပႃ ယင် ဢူ nam mai pâ **yang û** 4 3 2 1	**There are** fish in the 1 2 3 river. 4

4. Sometimes the particle တီ (tî), equivalent to the English *to*, is used either with or without မႆ (mai) to form the dative case, as—

Examples.

ၵွ် **တီ ၸွ် မႃ ႁႃ** မႆ ** ဝႃ ၵႃ။ kau **ti Chau mâ hâ mai** wâ kâ 1 3 2	I told to **Chau mâ hâ.** 1 2 3

* *Kû haü* is a compound verb; *kû*=loan; *haû*=give.
† *Ma* is the imperative suffix.
‡ *Ka* is the past tense suffix.
¶ *Nai* is the demonstrative pronoun, used here like our definite article.
§ *Kê* is the interrogative particle.
‖ *Yau* is a verbal tense suffix denoting the completion of an act.
** *Mai* is the accusative case postposition.

တီ ပိတ် ၼႆ* ၶွ မႆ† ၼမ် ႁိူ တႃ။
tî pet nai khau mai nam haü tâ — Give to the ducks water.

or / *or*

ပိတ်‡ *or* ၼႆ ၶွ† မႆ ၼမ် ႁိူ တႃ။
pet nai khau mai nam haü tâ — Give the ducks water.

5. The ablative case *prefix* particle is လုၵ် (lûk), used in conjunction with the *suffix* particle မႆ (mai), as—

Examples.

ၵွ လုၵ် ထိုၼ် မႆ ၼႆ ယွ‡
kau lûk thün mai nai yau — I got (it) from the jungle

လုၵ် ႁူ မၵ် ၸႃ မႆ လိုတ် ဢွၵ် ၵႃ။
lûk hû mak châ mai lüt åk kâ — Blood flowed from the bullet hole.

လုၵ် လုၵ်** သိုၵ် မႆ ဢႃပွတ်†† ပႆ ယွ။
lûk lûk sük mai Abor pai yau — The Abor ran away from the sepoy.

6. The instrumental case particle is ဢွ (au) = *with instrument prefixed* to the noun, as—

Examples.

ၼိုဝ် မႆ‡‡ ဢွ ႁွၵ် ဢွ တႆ တႃ။
nü mai au håk au tai tâ — Kill the deer with a spear.

မၼ် မၢၼ် မႆ‡‡ ဢွ ၾႆ သတ် ၵႃ။
man mân mai au phai såt kâ — He destroyed the village with fire.

---

* *Nai* is the demonstrative pronoun, used here for emphasis and recognition. *Pet khau* alone might mean their ducks.

† *Mai* is the accusative case postposition.

‡ *Yau* is a completive verbal particle.

** *Lûk* is a prefix particle denoting the agent and is equivalent to our final syllable *er* in such words as *worker*, *sinner*, &c. *Sûk* means war; *so lûk sük* means a fighter, sepoy.

†† *P* is used here as the Khâmtis have no *b*.

‡‡ *Mai* is the accusative case suffix.

မၼ် မၼ် မႆ* ဢဝ် မႆ ထွင် ပေႃ ၵႃ။
man [1] man mai [3] au [4] mai tau [5] po kâ [2] — He [1] beat [2] him [3] with [4] a stick [5].

4. *II.—Adjectives.*

1. Comparison is made by adding the adverb လိုမ်သီ † (lüm sî), apparently equivalent to our adverb *than*, to the adjective in its positive form, as—

Examples.

သုင်	လိုမ်	သီ	ႁိုၼ်	Higher [1] than [2] the house [3]
sûng [1]	lüm [2]	si	hün [3]	
ၵၢတ်	လိုမ်	သီ	ၼမ်	Colder [1] than [2] water. [3]
kat [1]	lüm [2]	sî	nam [3]	

ၸၢင်	ယႂ်	လိုမ်	သီ	ၶႂၢႆ	(An) elephant [1] (is) larger [2] than [3] a buffalo. [4]
châng [1]	yaü [2]	lüm [3]	sî	khâi [4]	

ၵုၼ်	ဢၼ်	ၼႆ	ထဝ်	လိုမ်	သီ	ၵုၼ်	ဢၼ်	ၼၼ်	This [1] man [2] (is) older [3] than [4] that [5] man. [6]
kôn [2]	â [1]	nai [1]	thau [3]	lüm [4]	sî	kôn [6]	â [5]	nan [5]	

2. The comparative degree may likewise be made by using ၶဵၼ် (khen) = *more* either in conjunction with မႆ (mai) *or* လိုမ် သီ (lüm sî), as—

Examples.

ၵုၼ် ဢၼ် ၼႆ မႆ‡ ၵုၼ် ဢၼ် ၼၼ် ၶဵၼ် ထဝ်။
kôn [6] â nai [5] mai kôn [2] â nan [3] khen [4] thau [3] — That [1] man [2] (is) older [3] than [4] this [5] man. [6]

---

* *Mai* is the accusative case suffix.

† *Sî* is the participal suffix, which is likewise used as an adverbial suffix.

‡ *Mai* is the ablative case particle *kon â nai mai*, meaning from this man.

ၵုၼ် ဢႃ ၼႆ ၶိုၼ် ထဝ် လိုမ် သီ
kôn â nai khen thau lüm sî
2 1 3 4

ၵုၼ် ဢႃ ၼၼ်၊
kôn â nan
6 5

This man (is) older than that man.
1 2 3 4 5 6

ၵဝ် မႆ ႁိုဝ် ဢၼ်* ၶိုၼ် ယႂ် လိုမ် သီ
kaü mai hü an khen yaü lüm sî
2 3 4 5 6 7

ဢႃ ၼၼ် ဢဝ် မႃ တႃ၊
â nan au mâ tâ
8 1

Give me (a larger boat than that) boat which more large than that.
1 2 3 4 5 6 7 8

ၽႃ ဢၼ်† ၶိုၼ် ၼီ လိုမ် သီ ၽႃ
phâ ân khen ni lüm sî phâ
1 2 3 4 5 6

မၼ် ၵဝ် မႆ ၽုၼ် လိုင်‡ ႁႂ် မႃ။
man kau mai phûn lüng haü mâ
7 8 9 10

Give me a better cloth than his; cloth which more good than cloth his me one give.
1 2 3 4 5 6 7 8 9 10

4. The superlative degree is formed by using the adjective တင်မိုင် (tâng müng) = *all* either with or without တီ = (tî) *to* prefixed, as—

Examples.

ႁိုၼ်† ဢၼ် ၶိုၼ် ယႂ် လိုမ် သီ
hün an khen yaü lüm sî
1 2 3 4 5

တင် မိုင် ၼႆ¶ လုမ် ၵႃ။
tâng müng nai lôm kâ
6 7

The largest house fell; house which more large than all fell.
1 2 3 4 5 6 7

သႃ လတ် ဢႃ ၼႆ ၼီ လိုမ် တီ တင် မိုင်
sâ lat â nai nî lüm tî tâng müng
3 1 2 4

This is the best gun of all. Literally, gun this good than (=better) to all or than all.
1 2 3 4

---

* *An* is the relative pronoun which.

† These are relative clauses.

‡ *Phûn* is a numeral expletive; ႁိုင်, is an abbreviation for *lüng*=one.

¶ *Nai* is the demonstrative pronoun, used here for emphasis and recognition.

5. The adjective generally *follows* a substantive, as—

Examples.

ႁိုဝ် ၽေ *or* ႁိုဝ် ဢၼ်* ၽေ။
hü phê *or* hü an phe
(hü phê: —, 1; hü an phe: 1, 2, 3)
A broken boat; boat which broken.
(broken 1, boat 2; boat 1, which 2, broken 3)

ၵုၼ် ႁဵင် *or* ၵုၼ် ဢၼ် * ႁဵင်။
kôn hêng *or* kôn an hêng
(kôn hêng: 2, 1; kôn an hêng: 1, 2, 3)
A strong man; man who (is) strong.
(strong 1, man 2; man 1, who 2, strong 3)

ၼမ် လိုၵ်
nam lük (2, 1)
deep water. (deep 1, water 2)

ႁိုဝ် ယႂ်
hü yaü (2, 1)
a large boat. (large 1, boat 2)

ၵုၼ် သုင်
kôn sûng (2, 1)
a tall man. (tall 1, man 2)

သဝ် ယၢဝ်
sau yau (2, 1)
a long post. (long 1, post 2)

မႃ ဢွၼ် ဢၼ် † ၽိုၵ် ဢႃ လိုင်။
mâ ån an phük â lüng (1, 2, 3, 4, 5)
A small white dog;
dog small which white one. (dog 1, small 2, which 3, white 4, one 5)

ၵဝ် ၶႆ ႁေ‡ ၶႆ ထိုၵ် လူင်
kau khâi he khâi thük lông (1, 7, 5, 7, 6, 4)
တူဝ် လိုင် ႁၼ် ၵႃ။
tô lüng han kâ (—, 3, 2)
I saw a large wild male buffalo.
(I 1, saw 2, a 3, large 4, wild 5, male 6, buffalo 7)

---

* These are relative clauses.

† *An* is the relative pronoun.

‡ *Khâi he* = wild buffalo. *Khâi thük* = male buffalo.

5.—*Numeral Adjectives.*

1. The numerals from 1 to 10 are—

၁ = လိုင် (lüng) ...	... 1	၆ = ႁုၵ် (hôk) ...	6
၂ = သွင် (sång) ...	... 2	၇ = ၸိတ် (chet) ...	7
၃ = သံ (sâm) ...	... 3	၈ = ပိတ် (pet) ...	8
၄ = သိ (sî) ...	... 4	၉ = ၵွ် (kau) ...	9
၅ = ႁႃ (hâ) ...	... 5	၁၀ = သိပ်လိုင် (sip lüng)	10

After which the cardinals are repeated and compounded, as—

သိပ် ဢိတ် * (sip et) ...	11	သိ သိပ် (sî sip) ...	40
သိပ် သွင် (sip sång, &c.)...	12	သိ သိပ် လိုင် (sî sip lüng, &c.) ...	41
သွ် *or* သွ် လိုင် (sau *or* sau lüng) ...	20	ႁႃ သိပ် (hâ sip) ...	50
သွ် ဢိတ် * (sau et)	21	ႁႃ သိပ် လိုင် (hâ sip lüng)	51
သွ် သွင် (sau sång, &c.) ...	22	ႁႃ သိပ် သွင် (hâ sip sång, &c.)	52
သံ သိပ် (sâm sip) ...	30	ႁုၵ် သိပ် (hôk sip) ...	60
သံ သိပ် လိုင် (sâm sip lüng)	31	ၸိတ် သိပ် (chet sip) ...	70
သံ သိပ် သွင် (sâm sip sång)	32	ပိတ် သိပ် (pet sip) ...	80
		ၵွ် သိပ် (kau sip) ...	90

ပၵ် လိုင် (pâk lüng)	100
သွင် ပၵ် (sang pâk, &c.)... ...	200
ႁိင် (heng)	1,000
သွင် ႁိင် (sång heng, &c.) ...	2,000
မုၼ် (mûn)	10,000
သိၼ် (sen)	100,000

2. To the numeral လိုင် = (lüng) (1) the particle ဢႃ = (â) is prefixed to denote a *single* one, but ဢႃလိုင် = (â lüng) is usually written in an abbreviated form thus, ဢႃလိူ. This word is often used like our indefinite article *a*, or, in the sense

* As *lüng* = one is used with *sip* and *sau* to denote a full ten and twenty, *et* is used to make eleven and twenty-one.

of *a certain one.** The particle ဢၼ် = *an* is suffixed to the remaining numerals, and is equivalent to the Assamese *tâ*.

It (*an*) is a numeral particle, used in enumerating *things* generally.

3. Numeral particles are common in Khâmtî. A few of those most commonly used are given below :—

ကုဝ် (= kô) is the numeral particle applied to human beings.

တုဝ် (= tô) is the numeral particle applied to animals and birds.

ၽုၼ် (= phun) is the numeral particle applied to clothes and fishing nets.

ႁွႝ (=hôy) is the numeral particle applied to boats, brass, 'goti,' 'batis,' eggs, and round things generally.

လိဝ် *or* လိမ် (= lem) is the numeral particle applied to knives, boats, spears, posts, and things with length generally.

လံ (= lam) is the numeral particle applied to bamboos.

လွၵ် (= lau) is the numeral particle applied to guns.

လင် (= lang) is the numeral particle applied to houses.

လင် (= lâng) is the numeral particle applied to plates.

သဵၼ် (= sen) is the numeral particle applied to rings, also pieces of sewing thread cut into lengths.

မႂ် *or* မင် (= maü *or* mâng) is the numeral particle applied to leaves, the latter also used with paper.

တွၼ် (= tân) is the numeral particle applied to *pieces* of anything.

Examples.

(Illustrating how numeral particles are used in conversation.)

ကုၼ် သိပ် ကုဝ် မႃ ႁဵတ်† ဢႃ မူႉ
kôn sip kô mâ het â mû — Ten men (have) come to work.

(Numbering in the original: kôn [2] sip kô [1] mâ [3] het [4] â mû [5]; Ten [1] men [2] come [3] to [4] work [5].)

* As ကုၼ် ဢႃ လိူင် = (kôn alüng) a certain man.

† *Het* means literally to do, make, hence *het â mû* = to work.

ႁိုဝ် မႆ့ သွင် ၵုဝ် ယင် ယူ။
hü [5] mai sång kô [3] yang [1] û [2]

There [1] are [2] two [3] (men) in the boat [5].

ၵႂ် ၼိုဝ် သံ တုဝ် ယိုဝ် ၵႃ။
kau [1] nü [4] sâm [3] tô yü kâ [2]

I [1] shot [2] three [3] deer [4].

မၼ်း ၵႆ့ သိပ် သွင် တုဝ် ႁင် ၶႆ့ ယင် ယူ
man [1] kai sip sång [4] tô [3] hang [5] khai [6] yang û [2]

He [1] has [2] twelve [3] fowls [4] for [5] sale [6].

ဢႃ ၼႆ့ သံ တုဝ် ငုဝ် ၵႂ်
â nai [1] sâm tô [2] ngô [3] kau [4]

These [1] three [2] cows [3] (are) mine [4].

မူ သွင် တုဝ် ပေ ယႃ ၸဵတ် တုဝ် ဢႂ် မႃ တႃ *
mû [3] sång tô [2] pê yâ [5] chet tô [5] au mâ tâ [1]

Bring [1] two [2] pigs [3] (and) seven [4] goats [5].

ၵႂ် မႆ့ ၽႃ သံ ၽုၼ် ႁႂ် မႃ †
kau mai [2] phâ [4] sâm phûn [3] haü mâ [1]

Give [1] me [2] three [3] cloths [4].

ၽႃ ႁူဝ် ႁႃ ၽုၼ် ၼႆ့ ႁင် ၶႃ မႂ်
phâ hô [3] hâ phûn [2] nai [1] hang [4] khâ [6] maü [5]

These [1] five [2] 'pugris' [3] (are) for [4] your [5] slaves [6].

မႂ် ၽႃ ၼွႆ့ ၵေႃ ႁႃ ၽုၼ် ၶႃ ၼႆ့ ၵေ ‡
maü [1] phâ [3] noi kaw [4] hâ phun [5] khâ nai kê [2]

Do you want five dhoties also.

---

* *Mâ tâ* = imperative mood suffixes.

† Here *mâ* alone is used for the imperative, *tâ* being understood.

‡ *Khâ nai* = verbal noun from root verb *khâ* = wish, want, &c.; *kê* = interrogative particle.

မၵ် ၸႃ ပိတ် ႁွႆ ၼႆ ထိ လွမ်
mak châ pet hoy nai n' lâm
3 2 1 4 5
These eight bullets (are) not round.
1 2 3 4 5

ၵႆ ဢႃ ၼႆ ၼိုၼ် ၼႆ မႆ* ၶႆ
kai â nai nün nai mai khai
2 1 9 8 7
သၢဝ် ႁႃ ႁွႆ ၶႆ ၵႃ
sau hâ hoy khai kâ
5 6 4 3
This fowl has laid twenty-five eggs this month.
1 2 3 4 5 6 7 8 9

ၵဝ် ႁၵ် သီ လဵမ် တီ သိုဝ် ၼမ် †
kau hâk sî lem tî sü nam
1 5 4 2 3
I will buy four spears.
1 3 5 4 2

မၼ်း ႁိုဝ် သွင် လဵမ် ၶႆ ၵႃ
man hü sång lem khai kâ
1 5 4 3 2
He has sold two boats.
1 2 3 4 5

ၵဝ် သီ လတ် ႁႃ လဝ် ယင် ဢူ
kau sî lat hâ lau yang û
1 4 3 2
I have five guns.
1 2 3 4

မၢၼ်း ၼႆ မႆ* ႁိုၼ်း သိပ် လင် ၼႆ
mân nai mai hün sip lang nai
2 1 6 5 4
ယင် ဢူ
yang . û
3
This village has only ten houses.
1 2 3 4 5 6

4. The numeral always *precedes* the noun it qualifies, except in cases where a numeral particle is used when it *follows* the noun, as—

---

* *Mai* is the locative case particle; *nün nai mai* meaning during this month, and *mân nai mai* = in this village.

† *Nam* is an assertive particle.

Examples.

† သံ ၶိုၼ်
sâm khün (1, 2) } = three nights. (1, 2)

သွင် ပီ
sång pî (1, 2) } = two years. (1, 2)

သံ ၵုၼ်
sâm kôn (1, 2) } = three men. (1, 2)

သိပ် ဝၼ်
sip wan (1, 2) } = ten days. (1, 2)

ၵုၼ် သံ ၵုဝ်
kôn sâm kô (2, 1) } = three men. (1, 2)

ႁိုၼ် ႁႃ လင်
hün hâ lang (2, 1) } = five houses. (1, 2)

ၶႆ သဝ် ႁွႆ
khai sau hoy (2, 1) } = twenty eggs. (1, 2)

5. The adverbial numeral *once* is made by prefixing the particle ပွၵ် (= påk), *or* ပၼ် (= pân), *or* လၵ် * (= låk to the numeral လိုင် (=lüng) 1, and the remainder by *subjoining* the numerals သွင် =(sång) 2, သံ = (sâm) 3, &c., to ပွၵ်, *or* ပၼ်, *or* လၵ်, as—

ပွၵ် လိုင်
påk lüng } =once.

သွင် ပွၵ်
sång påk } =twice.

သံ ပွၵ်
sâm påk } =thrice.

---

* လၵ် is oftener used with the numeral လိုင် than with the others.

မႂ် တပ် * သေလႃတီယႃ မႆ maü tâp Sadiya mai ၵီ ပွၵ် ၵႃ မႃ kê påk kâ mâ	How many times have you been to Sadiya ?
ၵဝ် သိပ် ပွၵ် ၵႃ မႃ kau sip påk kâ mâ	I have been ten times.
ၼိၼ် ၼႆ သီ ပွၵ် ထဝ် တႃ nin nai sî påk thau tâ	Plough the land four times.

Ordinals.

The ordinal of လုင် = (lüng) *one* is ဢၼ် တင် = (ån tâng) *first*, but no other ordinals are to be found in Khâmtî. Their place is supplied by the adjectives ထတ် = (that) *next*, and ၵႃလင် = (kâ lang) *last*, or by using a participle, as—

Examples.

ဢၼ် တင် ယိုဝ်† ၼႆ မႃ‡ ထုၵ် ån tâng yü nai mâ thôk ထတ် ၼႆ ယို ထုၵ် ၵႃ တိၼ် that nai yü thôk kâ tin ၼိုဝ် မႆ ၵႃ လင် ယိုဝ်† ၼႆ nü mai kâ lang yü nai ထုၵ် ၵႃ တွင် မႆ thôk kâ tång mai	(My) first shot missed. The second hit (the) deer in the leg (and) the third one in (the) stomach.

---

* တပ် = (tâp) town. It is always prefixed to the names of our stations.

† *Yü nai* = shot and is the past participle passive of the root verb *yü* to shoot.

‡ *Mâ* is a negative prefix particle ; *mâ thôk* = not hit.

6. *III.—Pronouns.*

1. There are four kinds of pronouns in Khâmtî, namely, prsonal, relative, interrogative, and adjective.

6.—*Personal Pronouns.*

Singular.

Nom.	ꩦွ် = (kau) ... I	ꩫုိ = (maü) ... you	မꩫ် = (man) ... him.
Dat. and Acct.	ꩦွ် မႝ =(kau mai) to me—me	ꩫုိ မႝ = (maü mai) to you—you	မꩫ် မႝ = (man mai) to him—him.
Poss.	ꩭင် ꩦွ် = (khång kau) mine	ꩭင် ꩫုိ = (khång maü) ... yours	ꩭင် မꩫ် = (khång man) ... his.
Abl.	လုꩦ် ꩦွ် မႝ=(lûk kau mai) from me	လုꩦ် ꩫုိ မႝ = (lûk maü mai) from you	လုꩦ် မꩫ် မႝ = (lûk man mai) from him.

Plural.

Nom.	တူ *or* ꩭွ် = (tû *or* hau) we	ꩬူ = (sû) ... you	ꩭွ် = (khau) *or* မꩫ် ꩭွ် = (man khau) they.
Dat. and Acct.	တူ မႝ = (tû mai) to us—us	ꩬူ မႝ = (sû mai) to you—you	ꩭွ် မႝ = (khau mai to = them.
Poss.	ꩭင် တူ = (khång tû) ours	ꩭင် ꩬူ = (khång sû) ... yours	ꩭင် ꩭွ် = (khång khau) theirs.
Abl.	လုꩦ် တူ မႝ = (lûk tû mai) from us	လုꩦ် ꩬူ မႝ = (lûk sû mai) from you	လုꩦ် ꩭွ် မႝ = (lûk khau mai) from them.

Note.—The genetive case is not marked by a particle, but by juxtaposition of the pronoun to the noun, as— ၽႃ ၵဝ် = (phâ kau) *cloth my* မႃ မၼ်း = (mâ man) *dogs his, &c.*

ၸဝ် (chau) is added to the *second* and *third* person, *singular* and *plural* of the personal pronouns, as a mark of *respect* when an inferior addresses a superior, as— မႂ် ၸဝ် (maü chau) = *you* မၼ်း ၸဝ် (man chaü) = *he*, &c.

တူ (tû) means I and another, or others, *with* the speaker and does *not* include *the person spoken to.* It is equivalent to the Assamese *âmár lô ké.*

ႁဝ် (hau) means *we*, and is used like our English word.

ႁႃ (hâ) means *both of us, i.e.*, we two *only.*

ႁၢင် ၶိုၼ် (hâng khü) means *both*, I and another *only.*

သၢင် ၶိုၼ် (sång khü) means *both* (you two) and is used in speaking *to* two persons.

သၢင် ၶႃ (sâng khâ) *or* ၼိုင် ၶႃ (n' khâ) means *both* (they two) and is used in speaking *of* two persons.

တင် သၢင် (tang sâng) means *both, i.e.*, the one and the other.

သင် (sang), a particle denoting an *hypothesis*, is often used with the personal pronouns as an *emphatic* particle, as—

မႂ် သင်	ဝႃ ၵႃ	
maü sang	wâ kâ	you said (it).
1	2	1 2

ၶဝ် သင်	ဝႃ	ႁဵတ်း	
khau sang	wâ	het	they must do (it).
1	2	3	1 2 3

2. The reflective pronoun is ပႃ ၸဝ် (pâ chau = self, as—

Examples.

မႂ် ပႃ ၸဝ်	ႁဵၵ်*	တႃ"	
maü pâ chau	het	tâ	Do (it) yourself.
2	1		1 2

---

* ၵ် (ch) used instead of တ် *vide* footnote, page 3 *ante.*

Reciprocal or mutual action is expressed by the suffix particle ကၼ် (kan) as the following words show :—

ၼၼ် ကၼ် (nan kan) = quarrel.

ပုပ် ကၼ် (pô kan) = fight, literally mutual striking.

ႁုမ် ကၼ် (hom kan) = together.

ႁၵ် ကၼ် (hâk kan) = mutual love, liking.

တု ကၼ် *or* တု တု ကၼ် { (tû kan) (tû tû kan) } = alike, same.

7.—Relative Pronouns.

1. The relative pronoun is ဢၼ် (an) — *who*, *what*, or *which*, according to the connection. It is *affixed* to its antecedent, as—

Examples.

ၽႃ ဢၼ် တိုၼ် * phâ (1) an (2) tün (3) } The (torn cloth) cloth (1) which (2) torn (3).

ႁိုဝ် ဢၼ် ၸုမ် hü an chôm } The boat (1) which (2) sunk (3).

တူဝ်ဢွၼ် † ပႃ ၸၢႆ ဢၼ် တိၼ် ႁၢၼ် tô ăn (1) pâ chai (2) an tin hăn (3) } The boy (1) who (2) (is) lame (3).

ၵူၼ် ဢၼ် ယိုဝ် ၼိုၼ် ၼႆ ‡ kôn (1) an (2) yü (3) nü (4) nai } The man (1) who (2) shot (3) the deer (4).

ၵူၼ် ဢၼ် မႃ ငႃ မႃ ၼႆ ‡ ၽႂ် kôn (2) an (3) mâ ngâ (5) mâ (4) nai phaü (1) } Who (1) is the man (2) who (3) came (4) yesterday (5)?

2. Relative clauses may likewise be construed by using the interrogative or indefinite pronouns, as—

---

* *Tün* is the bare root of the verb *phâ an tün*, therefore, means literally cloth which tear.

† *Tô ăn* = child ; *pâ chai* = male.

‡ *Nai* participial suffix. *Yü nai* and *mâ nai* are verbal nouns ; *kôn an yü nü nai* = deer-shooting man. *Kôn an mâ ngâ mâ nai*= the yesterday-coming man

Examples.

တုၵ် ဢွၼ် * ပႃ ၸႆ ၽဝ် † ၽိတ် ၵေႃ †
tô ån pâ chai phaü phet kaw
2 1 3 1
မၼ် မႆ ‡ ဝႃ ပေႃ
man mai wâ pô
4 5 6

Whatever boy has lied he must (be) beaten.
1 2 3 4 5 6

Relative clauses of *time*, *place*, and *manner*.

မိုဝ် မႂ် ယတ် ¶ သီ လတ် ယွၵ် ¶ ၼႆ
mü maü sat sî lat yau nai
2 3 4 3
ၵွၵ် မႆ လွၵ် တႃ
kau mai lau tâ
6 5

When you have loaded (your) gun tell me.
1 2 3 4 5 6

ၼိုဝ် ဢႃ လႂ် မႆ § ယင် ၵွၵ် မႆ ‖ ၸိ တႃ
nü a laü mai yang kau mai chî tâ
4 3 5 2 1

Show me where the deer are.
1 2 3 4 5

ၼိုဝ် မႃ လႂ် ** ႁၼ် ဢူ ** ၵေႃ ၵွၵ် ယိုဝ် ဢူ
nü mâ laü han û kaw kau yü û
3 1 2 1 4 5

Whenever (I) see a deer I shoot (it).
1 2 3 4 5

ၽုၼ် တုၵ် ၵႃ ယေ †† ၼမ် လွင် ဢူ
phôn tôk kâ yê nam lång û
2 3 1 4 5

When rain falling the rivers rise.
1 2 3 4 5

ၵႃ ပႃ လႂ် ဢူ ၵေႃ မႂ် တီ ႁၼ် ၼမ် ၼႆ
kâ pâ laü û kaw maü tî han nam nai
2 1 2 1 3 4 5 6 7

Wherever (you) go you will see water only.
1 2 3 4 5 6

---

* *Tô ån* = child ; *pâ chai* = male.

† *Phaü* = who ; *kaw* = even ; *phaü kaw* = whatever.

‡ *Mai* = accusative case, postposition. *Man mai wâ pô* = him must beat.

¶ *Sat yau nai* means finished loading. *Yau* is a particle directing the completion of an act.

§ *A laü mai* = literally in which place.

‖ *Mai* = accusative case, postposition.

** *Mâ laü* must be read with *kaw*.

†† *Kâ yê* is a conditional participial suffix. *Ma phôn tôk nai* would be more correct.

ႁိုဝ် ၼိုဝ် သီ* ႁဵတ် ဢူ ၵေႃ ယိုဝ် ၼီ
hü nü sî het û kaw n' nî — However (you) do it, it (will) not (be) well.
(1) (2) (2) (3) (4) — (1) (2) (3) (5)

8. *Interrogative Pronouns.*

ၽႂ် = (phaü) Who ?

declined like personal pronouns.

Examples.

(Illustrating how used.

မႂ် မႆ ၽႂ် ပေႃ ၵႃ
maü mai phaü pô kâ — Who struck you ?
(3) (1) (2) — (1) (2) (3)

မႂ် ၽႂ် မႆ ပေႃ ၵႃ
maü phaü mai pô kâ — Whom did you strike ?
(3) (1) (4) (2) — (1) (2) (3) (4)

မႂ် ၽႂ် မႆ ႁႂ် ၵႃ
maü phaü mai haü kâ — To whom did you give it ?
(4) (2) (1) (5) (3) — (1) (2) (3) (4) (5)

မႂ် လုၵ် ၽႂ် မႆ ၼႆ မႃ
maü lûk phaü mai nai mâ — From whom did you get (it) ?
(4) (1) (2) (5) (3) — (1) (2) (3) (4) (5)

ၵႃ သင် = (kâ sang) what ?
ဢႃ လႂ် = (â laü) which ? — not declined.

Examples.

(Illustrating how used.)

ဢႃ ၼႆ ၵႃ သင်
â nai kâ sang — What (is) this ?
(2) (1) — (1) (2)

မႂ် ၶႃ† ၼႆ ၵႃ သင်
maü khâ nai kâ sang — What (do) you want ?
(2) (3) (1) — (1) (2) (3)

---

* *Hü nü* or *hî lü* = how, in what manner ; and the *sî* is the participial suffix, also used with adverbs, *het û kaw* = do even so ; *hü nü sî het û kaw* means literally, however, do even.

† ၶႃ (*Khâ*) wish, desire, a root verb, with *nai* the participial suffix, added. *Khâ nai* is here a verbal noun.

ကွ်ၢ် တီ ႁဵတ် ကႃ သင်
kau tî het kâ sang
3 2 4 1 — What shall I do ?
(What 1, shall 2, I 3, do 4)

ၽႃ ကွ်ၢ် ဢႃ လႆ
phâ kau â laü
3 2 — 1 — Which (is) my cloth ?
(Which 1, my 2, cloth 3)

မႂ် လုၵ် ႁိုဝ် ဢႃလႆ မႆ*
maü lûk hü âlaü mai
5 1 3 2 1
ဢွ်ၢ် ကႃ
au kâ
6 6 — From which boat did you take (it) ?
(From 1, which 2, boat 3, did 4, you 5, take 6)

Sometimes ႁိုဝ် = *hü* is used for the English interrogative *what* ? as—

Examples.

မၼ်း ဝႃ ႁိုဝ်
man wâ hü
2 3 1 — What (is) he saying ?
(What 1, he 2, saying 3)

ပဵၼ် ႁိုဝ် ကႃ
pen hü ka — What (is) the matter ? (What 1, matter 2)
What has happened ?
Assamese *ki hŏl* ?

ၸိုဝ် မႂ် ဝႃ † ႁိုဝ်
chü maü wâ hü
3 2 — 1 — What (is) your name ?
(What 1, your 2, name 3)

ဢၼ် ၼင် ႁိုဝ် = an nang ‡ hü
or
ဢၼ် ၼႃ ႁိုဝ် = an na hü
— Is used apparently as an adjective in the sense *what sort*, or *kind of ?*

Examples.

မႂ် ဢႃမူ ၼင် ႁိုဝ် ႁဵတ် ပဵၼ်
maü âmû nang hü het pen
4 2 1 5 3 — What kind of work can you do ?
(What kind of 1, work 2, can 3, you 4, do 5)

---

* *Mai* belongs to *lûk* ; *lûk mai* meaning from out.

† ဝႃ = (*wâ*) say ; *chü maü wâ hü* means name your say what ?

‡ *Nang* means like. *An* is the relative pronoun.

မၼ်း ၵုၼ်း ဢၼ်း ၼင် ႁိုဝ် — What sort of a man (is) he?
man kôn an nang hü
3 2 1 — 1 2 3

ၵွႝ တီ ၸိုဝ် လၢ ဢၼ်း ၼင် ႁိုဝ် — What kind of cloth shall I buy?
4 3 5 2 1 — 1 2 3 4 5

ၶႃ လႆႈ = khâ laü, or ၵီ = kî = how much, many.

Examples.

(Illustrating how used.)

ၶွႝ သၢၼ်း ၶႃ လႆႈ ယင် ဢူ — How much rice is there.
khau sân khâlaü yang û
2 1 3 — 1 2

မႆႉ ယင် ႁုင် ၶႃ လႆႈ မၢၵ်ႇ ၵႃ — How much rubber have you cut.
maü yang hûng khâlaü mâk kâ
3 2 1 4 — 1 2 4 3 4

ၾုၼ်း ၵီ ဝၼ်း* တွၵ်ႇ ၵႃ — How many days did it rain?
phôn ki wan tôk kâ
4 1 2 3 — 1 2 3

မႆႉ ႁိုဝ် ၶႃ လႆႈ† ၶႃ ၼႆ — How many boats do you require?
maü hü khalaü khânai
or
မႆႉ ႁိုဝ် ၵီ‡ ႁွႆ ၶႃ ၼႆ†
maü hü kî hôy khâ nai
— 1 2 3 4

မႆႉ ၼိုဝ် ၶႃ လႆႈ ႁၢၼ်း ၵႃ — How many deer did you see?
maü nü khalaü han kâ
4 2 1 5 3 — 1 2 4 5

မႃ လႆႈ = (mâ laü) *When?*

Examples.

(Illustrating how used.)

မႆႉ မႃ လႆႈ ႁၢၼ်း ၼႃ ၵႃ — When were you born in Khâmtî? When did you see face?
maü mâ laü han nâ kâ
3 1 4 5 2 — 1 2 3 4 5

---

* *Tôk* means to fall from above. *Phôn tôk*=to rain.

† *Khâ nai* is a verbal noun=wanting, requiring.

‡ *Hôy* is a numeral particle.

ကွ် မႃ လွ် တီ ႁိတ်
kau [3] mâ [1] laü [2] tî het [4] — When [1] shall [2] I [3] do [4] (it)?

မွ် မႃ လွ် တီ ပတ်* ၶွ်
maü [3] mâ [1] laü tî [2] pat khau [4] — When [1] will [2] you [3] reap [4] (your) dhân [4]?

ADJECTIVE PRONOUNS.

The adjective pronouns are of three kinds, namely, possessive, demonstrative, and indefinite.

The Possessive.

These are made by merely affixing the personal pronouns to the nouns, as—

Examples.

မႃ ကွ် တိၼ်း ႁၢၼ်း
mâ [2] kau [1] tin hân [3] — My [1] horse [2] (is) lame [3].

ဢႃ ၼႝ ပီ သွ်† မွ် ၵေး‡
â nai [2] pî sau [4] maü [3] kê [1] — Is [1] this [2] your [3] sister [4]?

ၶႝ မၼ်း မႝ¶ ကွ် ႁၢၼ်း ၵႃ
khâi [4] man mai [3] kau [1] han [2] kâ — I [1] saw [2] his [3] buffalo [4].

ႁိုဝ် တူ ႁူဝ် ဢူ
hü [2] tû [1] hô [4] û [3] — Our [1] boat [2] is [3] leaking [4].

မၼ်း ၶွ် ပတ် ၶွ် ၶွ် ပႃ ၸွ်§ ဢူ
man [1] khau [6] pat khau [3] khau [4] pâ [5] chau [2] û — They [1] are [2] reaping [3] their own [5] paddy [6].

ယေ ၶွ် ၶွ် မႝ ၵႃ။
yê khau [1] khau [2] mai kâ [3] — Their granaries were burnt. Granaries [1] their [2] burnt [3].

* *Pat*=cut; *khau*=dhân; *pat khau*=reap.

† *Pí sau*=*elder* sister.

‡ *Kê*=interrogative particle.

¶ *Man mai*=accusative case of *man*.

§ *Pat khau khau pâ chau û* = their own paddy.

9.—*Demonstrative Pronouns.*

The *demonstrative pronouns* are—

ဢႃ ၼႆ (â nai) *or* ဢၼ် ၼႆ (an nai)—this person or thing, *present* or *near*.

ဢႃ ၼၼ် (â nan)
or
ဢၼ် မၼ် ၼႆ (an man nai) } —— that person *or* thing, *distant*.

The plural is found by suffixing ၶဝ် (khau) the third person plural of the personal pronouns, as—

Examples.

ၵူၼ်	ၼႆ	ၶဝ်။	These people.
kôn	nai	khau	1 2
2	1		

ပေ	ယႃ	ၼၼ်	ၶဝ်	Those goats.
pê	yâ	nan	khau	1 2
	2	1		

Examples.

(Illustrating how demonstrative pronouns are used.)

မႃ	ဢႃ	ၼႆ	တိၼ်	ႁၢၼ်	This horse (is) lame.
mâ	â	nai	tin	han	1 2 3
2	1		3		

ႁိူဝ်	ဢႃ	ၼႆ	တဵမ်*	ၸႂ်	ဢူ။†	This boat is full.
hü	â	nai	tem tem	chaü	û	1 2 3 4
2		1	4	3		

ၶႆ	ဢႃ	ၼႆ	ၶွင်‡	ၵူၼ်	ဢႃ
khâi	â	nai	khâng	kôn	â
3	2			5	
			ၼၼ်	ၵေႃး§	
			nan	kê	
			4	1	

Is this buffalo that man's? 1 2 3 4 5

ၵူၼ်	ဢႃ	ၼၼ်	ႁူ	ၼွၵ်။	That man (is) deaf.
kôn	â	nan	hü	nôk	1 2 3
2		1	3		

---

* The doubling of the final mark (်) denotes the repetition of the word.

† *Chaü û* is the substantive verb.

‡ *Khâng* is a particle denoting ownership, *vide* page 23 *ante*, when it appears among the personal pronouns.

§ *Kê* is the interrogative particle.

ဢႃ ၼၼ်ႉ ၵႃ သင်။
â nan kâ sang
2 1
} What (is) that?
1 2

ငေႃ ဢႃ ၼၼ်ႉ ၶဝ် ႁေႃ တႃ။
ngô â nan khau ho ta
3 2 1
} Drive away those cows.
1 2 3

သင် (sang) a particle denoting ***hypothesis*** is often added to these pronouns as well as to the personal pronouns, as—

Examples.

ၵူၼ်း ဢႃ ၼႝ သင် ဢိုဝ် * ၼီ
kôn â nai sang n' nî
1 2 3 4
} This man (is) not good,
1 2 3 4.

10.—Indefinite Pronouns.

The following is a list of the indefinite pronouns most commonly used in conversing :—

ၽႂ် † ၵႝ=(phaü kai) any one, some one.

ၽႂ် ၵေႃ ဢိုဝ် * ယင်
phaü kaw n' yang
1 2 4 3
} =no body (literally who even exist not).
1 2 3 4

ၵႃ သင် ၵေႃ * ဢိုဝ်ယင်
kâ sang kaw n'yang
} = nothing (literally what even exists not).
1 2 3 4

ၵမ် ၽင် or ဢႃ လိူင် ‡ ဢႃ လိူင် ‡
kam phâng âlüng âlüng
} = some (âlüng âlüng = one one).

This pronoun (*some*) may likewise be made by *prefixing* ယေႝ = *yé* to a numeral particle *repeated*, or to a noun *repeated*, as—

---

* This is the diphthong *â* mentioned at page 2 *ante*, used here as a negative particle.

† *Kai* is a particle expressive of doubt.

‡ လိူင် the abbreviation for *lüng* = one, mentioned at pages 17 and 18 *ante*.

ယေဝ် ကုဝ် ကုဝ် } = *some men* ကုဝ် (kô)
yê kô kô } being the numeral expletive used with human beings.

ယေဝ် တုဝ် တုဝ် } = *some animals* တုဝ်
yê tô tô } numeral expletive used with animals.

ယေဝ် တိ တိ } = *some places* တိ (tî)
yê tî tî } = a place, spot.
&c., &c.,

ၼမ် * = (nam nam) many, much.

or ကွႝ ကွင် = (koi kâng) heap, mass.

ၶိုၼ် ၼႃ ကွ် *or* } (khün nâ kau) } = more, and
ၶိုင် ၼင် ကွ် } (khün nang kau) }

တင် မိုင် = (tang müng) = all.

ကူ = (kû) ... each

ကႃ = (kâ) ... } as much as, as many as

made by using the interrogative pronouns in conjuction with ေကႃ (kaw) = even, and } whatever, whoever.

Examples.

(Illustrating how Indefinite Pronouns are used.)

ၹႂ် ကႝ† ပိ လတ် ကွ် လၵ် ကႃ } Some one has stolen my gun.
phaü kai sî lat kau lâk kâ }

(1: phaü kai — Some one; 2: kâ — has; 3: lâk — stolen; 4: kau — my; 5: lat — gun.)

ကွ်† ကႝ မႃ ေကဝ်‡ } (Has) any one come?

(1: ကွ်† ကႝ — any one; 2: ေကဝ်‡ — come.)

ကွ် ၹႂ် မႝ § ေကႃ ၼိုဝ် ¶ ႁၼ် } I saw nobody. *In Khâmti*—I who even not see (any one even).
kau phaü mai kaw n' han }

(1: kau — I; 2: phaü mai kaw — who even; 3: n' han — not see.)

* Mark (°) doubled shows word is to be repeated, *vide* page *ante.*

† *Kai* is a particle denoting probability like the Assamese *bá.*

‡ *Kê* is the interrogative particle.

§ *Mai* is the accusative case suffix.

¶ This is the diphthong used as a negative particle.

ၽႂ် ၵေႃ ဢိုဝ်* ဝႃ phaü kaw n' wâ	Nobody said so. *In Khâmtî*— Who even not said.
မိုဝ် ၵွႆ မႆ ၵႃ ယင် ၵေႃ mü(6) kau(5) mai(4) kâsang kaw(3) ဢိုဝ်* ယင် n'(2) yang(1)	(I)[1] have[2] nothing[3] in my hand. Literally hand[1] my[2] in[3] what[4] even[5] not[6] exists.
ၵုၼ်း ယေ ၵေႃ† ၼီ ဢူ kôn(2) yê kô kô(1) nî(4) û(3) ယေ ၵေႃ† ဢိုဝ်‡ ၼီ yê kô kô n'(6) nî	Some(1) men(2) are(3) good(4) some(5) bad(6).
ၽုၼ်း ၵမ် ၽၢင် ၽုမ် ဢူ§ phûn(2) kam phång(1) phûm(3) û ၵမ် ၽၢင် ၽူ ဢူ§ kam phång(4) phû(5) û	Some(1) woods(2) sink,(3) some(4) float(5).
ၶုၼ်း ၼင် ၵွႆ ၵွႆ မႆ khün nang kau(4) kau(3) mai(2) ႁႂ် မႃ¶ haü mâ(1)	Give(1) (to)(2) me(3) more(4).
ယေ‖ ၶွႆ မၼ်း မႆ ၶွႆ yê khau(7) man(6) mai(5) khau(4) ၵွႆ ၵၢင် ယင် ဢူ koi kång(3) yang(1) û(2)	There(1) is(2) a quantity(3) of paddy(4) in(5) his(6) granary(7).

---

* This is the diphthong used as a negative particle.

† Sign (‾) over final consonant denotes word is to be repeated.

‡ Diphthong *ü* used as a negative particle, *vide* page 2 *ante*.

§ *Û* = present tense suffix.

¶ *Mâ* = imperative suffix, first person.

‖ *Yê* means a store-house ; *yê khau* store-house of paddy.

တိက်မၼ် မႝ ငိုၼ် ကွႝ ကွင် ယင် ဢူ
tek man mai ngün koi kång yang û
6 5 4 3 2 1

There are heaps of rupees in his box.
1 2 3 4 5 6

ထိုၼ် မႝ ၼုဝ် ၼံ* ယင် ဢူ
thün mai nü {nam nam} yang û
5 4 3 2 1

There are many deer in the jungle.
1 2 3 4 5

ကွၼ် ကူ ကေႃ† မႝ ကႃ ၼီ ၸၼ်* ႁၢဝ်တႃ
kôn kû kô kô mai kâ nî {chån chån} haü tâ
4 3 3 2 6 5 1

Give to each man a little opium.
1 2 3 4 5 6

ကႃ မႝဝ် ပိၼ် ၼႝ‡ ၵိၼ် တႃ
kâ maü pen nai kin tâ
2 3 4 1

Eat as much as you can.
1 2 3

ကွၼ် ကႃ မႝဝ် ၼႝ ၼႝ‡ ဢဝ် မႃ
kôn kâ maü nai nai au mâ
3 2 4 5 1

Bring as many men *as* you get.
1 2 3 4 5

ပႃ ယိင် တင် မိုင် ၶေႃ ပင် ဢူ
pâ ying tang müng khô pång û
1 2 3 4 5

All the women have goitre.
In Khamti—
Women all neck swell are.
1 2 3 4 5

11.—Verbs.

Auxiliary Verbs.

ယင် (yang)
ၸႝဝ် (chaü)
ဢူ (û)
All signify *to be*.

ယင် (yang) signifies *to be, to have, possess, to exist.* In affirmative sentences it is used conjointly with ဢူ (û), but when used *negatively* ဢူ (û) is dropped. ယင် (yang) is equivalent to the Singpho auxiliary verb 'ngâ,' but it (ယင်) has no *past* tense.

* Mark (°) and (ᐣ) doubled denotes that the words are to be repeated, *vide* page *ante*.

† *Kô* is a numeral particle applied to human beings.

‡ *Pen nai* and *nai nai* are verbal nouns.

Examples.

(Illustrating how used.)

ႏွ် မ် မှ်ု ယင် ဢူ noi mai môy yang û 4 3 3 1	There is snow on the hill. 1 3 4
ႏွ် မ် မှ်ု ꩫိုဝ် ယင် (*or* မႃ ယင်) noi mai môy n' yang mâ yang 5 4 2 2 1 2 1	There is no snow on the hill 1 2 3 4 5
ꩫီ ကွ် ယင် ဢူ nî kau yang û 2 1 3	I have debts. *In Khâmti*— My debts exist. 1 2 3
မꩫ်း ꩫံ မ် ယင် ဢူ man nam mai yang û 1 4 3 2	He is in (the) water. 1 2 3 4
မꩫ်း ꩫံ မ် ꩫိုဝ်ယင် (*or* မႃယင်) man nam mai n' yang (mâ yang) 1 5 4 3 2 3 2	He is not in (the) water. 1 2 3 4 5
ကွ် ႏွင် ꩡ် ယင် ဢူ kau nâng chai yang û 1 3 2	I have (a) brother. 1 2 3
or ႏွင် ꩡ် ကွ် ယင် ဢူ nâng chai kau yang û 2 1 3	* My brother exists. 1 2 3
ကွ် ႏွင် ꩡ် ꩫိုဝ်ယင် or မႃ ယင် kau nâng chai n' yang mâ yang 1 4 3 2 3 2	I have no brother. 1 2 3 4
ကွ် ꩭိင် ယင် ဢူ kau heng yang û 1 3 2	I possess strength. 1 2 3
ကွ် ꩭိင် ꩫိုဝ်ယင် (*or* မႃ ယင်) kau heng n' yang mâ yang 1 4 2 3 2 3	I do not possess strength. 1 2 3 4
ꩬိုဝ် ꩫ်† လုꩀ် ꩬွင် တုဝ်‡ ယင် ဢူ sü nai lûk sâng tô yang û 2 1 5 4 3	The tiger has two cubs. 1 2 3 4 5

* This is the construction most used.
† *Nai* is the demonstrative pronoun used here for emphasis and recognition.
‡ *Tô* is a numeral particle applied to animals.

ꩡွ် (chaü) signifies *to be*, and is used like the Assamese *hoi*, but it has no *past* tense. When used *affirmatively* it requires ဢူ (û) suffixed, but when used *negatively* the ဢူ (û) is dispensed with, as—

Examples.

ဢႃ ၼႝ ငုဝ် ꩡွ် ဢူ
â nai ngô chaü û — This is a cow.

ဢႃ ၼႝ ငုဝ် ဢိုဝ် ꩡွ်
â nai ngô n' chaü — This is not a cow.

မꩫ် ꩮုꩫ် မႃ ၼီ ꩡွ် ဢူ
man kôn mâ nî chaü û — He is a bad (not good) man.

ၼံ (nam) is used as a verb of *certainty* or *affirmation*, and is equivalent to the Singpho *rè*, as—

Examples.

ꩮွ် ꩭႃ ꩮုꩫ် မꩫ် ꩡၢင် ꩭံ ၼံ
kau khâ kôn mân chảng khâm nam — I slave (am) a Chảng khâm (villager) village man.

ꩡွ် တီ ꩮွ် မႝ ꩮူ မိုဝ် ꩡႃ
chau ti kau mai kû mü châ
ꩭိုꩫ် ၼႃ ꩮွ် ပေႃ၊ ꩮွ် ꩭႃ
khün nâ kau pô kau khâ
တင် မꩫ် ဢူ မႃ ပိꩫ်။ လႝ ပိုဝ် ၼႝ ယီ
tang man û mâ pen lai pü nai sî
ပႝ မႃ * တႃ တီ ꩭႃ ၼံ။
pai mâ kâ tî khâ nam — Chautî always scold and beats me. I slave cannot remain with him, therefore (I) have run away.

---

* *Pai mâ* is a compound verb; *pai* = run away, bolt, and *mâ* = come. *Pai ma* is, therefore, a compound verb.

မၼ် ၵုၼ် တႝ လုင် * ၼံ †
man kôn Tai lông nam
1 3 2
} He (is) a Shan man.
1 2 4

မႃ ၼႝ ၽုၼ် တိ တုၵ် ၼံ †
mâ nai phôn tî tôk nam
5 1 2 4 3
} Rain will certainly fall today.
1 2 3 4 5

ၼံ (nam) is not used *interrogatively* like the Singpho *rĕ*, nor can it be used in a *negative* sense.

ယူ (û) means *to be, remain,* and is used as an auxiliary with all *root* verbs, as well as with ယင် (yang) and ၸႂ် (chaü), as—

Examples.

ၵဝ် ႁင် တႝ ငုဝ် ႁႃ တုဝ် ‡ တိ
kau hâng tai ngô hâ tô tî
1 4 3 6 5 10

တိ ၵျႃ ¶ မႝ ယူ ႁၼ် ၵႃ
tî khy â
tî khy â } mai û han kâ
9 8 7 3

} I saw the dead bodies of five cows lying in different places.
1 2 3 4 5 6 7 8 9 10

မိုဝ် ၼၼ် မိုဝ် ၵဝ် ယူ တပ် တိပြူ
mü nan mü kau û tâp Dibrû
1 2 3 4 6 5

မႝ § ၵဝ် လုၵ် တိမ် ‖ ၽႃ ၼႃ ၵၼ်
mai kau lûk tim phâ nâ kan
4 7 10 9 8

တႝ ၵုဝ် ၵုၼ် ႁုမ် ** ၽၼ် မႃ ယင်
tai kô kôn hôm phan mâ yang
12 15 13 14 11

} Previously when I (was) staying (in) Dibrughur I (was) like an orphan child (as I was) without a companion of same caste man.
1 2 3 4 5 6 7 8 9 10 11 12 13 14 15

---

* Khâmtis call the Shans *Tailông* or great Shans.

† *Nam* here is used as an assertive particle.

‡ *Tô* is a numeral expletive.

¶ The doubling of the vowel denotes that the word is to be repeated.

§ This *nai* belongs to the root verb *û*; *û nai* is a verbal noun.

‖ *Tim* is usually spelt တိမ် ‖

** *Hôm* means literally together.

ၼံ လွင် ဢူ }
nam[1] lång[3] û[2] } The river[1] is[2] rising[3].

မၼ် ၼွၼ် ဢူ }
man[1] nån[3] û[2] } He[1] is[2] sleeping[3].

ၵႃ ၼင် ဢူ }
phâ[1] nang[3] û[2] } It is thundering.
In Khamti—
Heavens[1] are[2] rumbling[3].

ဢူ (û), like the Singpho *dai*, also serves as a connective between the nominative and its qualifying adjective, as—

Examples.

မၵ် ၸႃ လွံ ဢူ }
mak chå[1] lâm[3] û[2] } Bullets[1] are[2] round[3].

ၵုၺ် * ဢွၼ် ဢူ }
kûy[1] ôn[3] û[2] } Cotton[1] is[2] soft[3].

လိၵ် ႁိင် ဢူ }
lek[1] heng[3] û[2] } Iron[1] is[2] hard[3].

Negation with the substantive verbs ယင် (*yang*) and ၸွႆ (chaü) is made by *prefixing* the particles မႃ (mâ) or ဢိုၼ် † (*ün* written by me *n'*).

မႃ ယင် (mâ yang) *or* ဢိုၼ် ယင် (n'yang) means *does not exist, is not to be found*, or *obtained*, while မႃ ၸွႆ (mâ chaü) or ဢိုၼ် ၸွႆ (n'chaü) simply means *is not*.

Examples.

မၼ် မႆ ဢိုၼ် ယင် (*or* မႃ ယင်) }
man[1] mai[4] n'[3] yang[2] mâ[3] yang[2] } He[1] is[2] not[3] here[4].

ၵဝ် ၵုၼ် ထဝ် ဢိုၼ် ၸွႆ }
kau[1] kon[5] thau[4] n'[3] chaü[2] } I[1] am[2] not[3] an old[4] man[5].

---

* Pronounced *gui*.

† This is the diphthong mentioned at page 2 *ante*.

မၼ် ၵႃ ဢိုၼ် ၸႂ် man khâ n'chaü 1 4 3 2	He is not a slave. 1 2 3 4
ၵဝ် ၼွင် သဝ် ဢိုၼ် ယၢင် kau nâng sau n'yang 1 4 3 2	I have no sister. 1 2 3 4
ၶဝ် ၵူၼ်* တႝ ၶၢင် ဢိုၼ် ၸႂ် khau kôn tai khâng n'chaü 1 4 3 2	They are not neighbours. 1 2 3 4
မိုဝ် ၵဝ် မႝ ၵႃ သၢင် ၵေႃ mü kau mai kâ sang kaw 7 6 5 1 2 ဢိုၼ် ယၢင် n'yang 4 3	There is nothing in my land. *In Khâmti*— Anything even exists not in 1 2 3 4 5 my hand. 6 7
မၼ် မႝ ဢိုၼ် ယၢင် man mai n'yang 1 4 3 2	He is not here. 1 2 3 4

COJUGATIONAL EXAMPLE.

Root verb ၵိၼ် = (kin) to take food, or liquid, Assamese *khau.*

Indicative Mood.

Present Tense.

The bare root of the verb is used to form this tense.

Present Definite.

The present definite is formed adding ဢူ (û) to the root, as—

Singular.	*Plural.*
ၵဝ် ၵိၼ် ဢူ = I am eating. kau kin û — 1 3 2 / 1 2 3	တူ ၵိၼ် ဢူ = we are eating. tû kin û — 1 3 2 / 1 2 3
မႂ် ၵိၼ် ဢူ = you are eating. maü kin û — 1 3 2 / 1 2 3	သူ ၵိၼ် ဢူ = you are eating. sû kin û — 1 3 2 / 1 2 3
မၼ် ၵိၼ် ဢူ = he is eating. man kin û — 1 3 2 / 1 2 3	ၶဝ် ၵိၼ် ဢူ = they are eating. khau kin û — 1 3 2 / 1 2 3

* *Kôn taikhâng* means literally near people, namely, *kôn* = person; *taikhang* = near.

This tense may also be used by adding ယိ = (sì) participial suffix to the root followed by ယင် (yang), as—

မၼ် ကိၼ် ယိ ဢူ man kin sì û 1 3 2	He is eating (and not yet risen). 1 2 3

Past Tense.

The past tense suffix is ကႃ (kâ), though မႃ (mâ) is often used to mark it. In some cases one, in some the other, is the right suffix to use, and it is extremely puzzling to know when to use which, and I can give no rule to be of use as a guide.

Singular.	*Plural.*
ကဝ် ကိၼ် ကႃ = I ate. kau kin kâ 1 2	တူ ကိၼ် ကႃ = we ate. tû kin kâ 1 2
မႂ် ကိၼ် ကႃ = thou didst eat. maü kin kâ 1 2 3	သူ ကိၼ် ကႃ = you ate. sû kin kâ 1 2
မၼ် ကိၼ် ကႃ—he did eat. man kin kâ 1 2 3	ၶဝ် ကိၼ် ကႃ = they ate. khau kin kâ 1 2

Examples.

(Showing both Suffixes used.)

မၼ် မႃ မႃ တႆ ၶင် ကဝ် မႆ man mâ mâ tai khâng kau mai 1 2 3 5 4	He came near (to) me. 1 2 3 4 5
မၼ် ကဝ် မႆ ပေႃ မႃ man kau mai pô mâ 1 3 2	He beat me 1 2 3
ပီ ၼႆ ကဝ် တပ် တိပြူ မႆ ကႃ မႃ pi nai kau tap Dìbrû mai kâ mâ 1 2 5 4 3	Last year I went to Dibrughur. 1 2 3 4 5
ကႃ လင် ၼႆ ၸဝ် သႃ ဝႃ ကႃ kâ lang nai Chau sâ wâ kâ 1 2 3 4	After this Chausa said. 1 2 3 4

Khâmtìs, like Singphos, are very fond of using the bare root of the verb for *past* as well as present time, as—

Examples.

လၢၼ် ကႝ ဢၼ် ယႂ် ၼႝ လုၵ်
phan kai an yaü nai lûk
ပႃ လႂ် ဢွ် မႃ
pâ laü au mâ

Where (did you) bring these large breeding fowls from?
(numbering: Where 1, bring 2, these 3, large 4, breeding 5, fowls 6, from 7)

ၼမ် (nam), the particle denoting *certainty* or *affirmation*, noticed at page 37 *ante*, is often tacked on to the *past tense* suffix, as—

Examples.

မႃ ၶႝ ၼႝ * ၼီ † ၵႃ ၼမ် ‡
mâ (2) khai (1) nai nî (4) kâ (3) nam

The (1) sick dog (2) has (3) recovered (4).

မႃ ငႃ ၵွ် ၵႃ တပ် § တိပြူ ¶
mâ ngâ kau kâ tâp Dîbrû
မႝ မႃ ‖ ၼမ်
mai mâ nam

Yesterday (1) I (2) went (3) to (4) Dibrughur (5, 6).

Perfect Tense.

This tense is made by suffixing ယွ် (yau), a particle denoting *completion*, to the *past* tense suffix, as—

Singular.	*Plural.*
ၵွ် ၵိၼ် ၵႃ ယွ် = I (1) have (2) eaten (3) kau (1) kin (3) kâ yau (2)	တူ ၵိၼ် ၵႃ ယွ် = we (1) have (2) eaten (3). tû (1) kin (3) kâ yau (2)
မႂ် ၵိၼ် ၵႃ ယွ် = you (1) have (2) eaten (3) maü (1) kin (3) kâ yau (2)	သူ ၵိၼ် ၵႃ ယွ် = you (1) have (2) eaten (3). sû (1) kin (3) kâ yau (2)
မၼ် ၵိၼ် ၵႃ ယွ် = he (1) has (2) eaten (3). man (1) kin (3) kâ yau (2)	ၶွ် ၵိၼ် ၵႃ ယွ် = they (1) have (2) eaten (3). khau (1) kin (3) kâ yau (2)

* *Nai* is the participial suffix particle. It is equivalent to our relative pronoun.
† *Nî* is an adjective with past tense suffix attached, *nî kâ* = literally has welled.
‡ *Yau* would do here as well as *nam*.
§ *Tâp* = town, *ndgûr*.
¶ *P* used for *b*.
‖ *Mâ* = went; *mâ* is past tense suffix.

ယွ် (yau) may be and often is used *alone*, *i.e.*, without ကၢ (kâ), as—

Examples.

ကွ် ကိၼ် ယွ်
kau kin yau
1 3 2
} I have eaten.
1 2 3

ၶေ ၼမ် ၼႆ ၶွ်* ႁိင် ကၢ ယွ်
khê nam nai khau heng kâ yau
1 3 2
} The rivers have dried up.
1 2 3

ကွ် ကိၼ် ယွ် သီ ကၢ ကွတ်
kau kin yau sî kâ kât
4 3 2 1 6 5
} Having finished eating I will go.
1 2 3 4 5 6

သိပ် ဝၼ် ထုၼ် ယွ်
sip wan thôn yau
1 2 3
} Ten days ago.
1 2 3

Future Tense.

This tense is made by *prefixing* the particle တီ (tî) to the root, as—

Singular.	*Plural.*
ကွ် တီ ကိၼ် = I will eat. kau tî kin (1 2 3) — 1 2 3	တူ တီ ကိၼ် = we will eat. tû tî kin (1 2 3) — 1 2 3
မႂ် တီ ကိၼ် = you will eat. maü tî kin (1 2 3) — 1 2 3	သူ တီ ကိၼ် = you will eat. sû tî kin (1 2 3) — 1 2 3
မၼ်း တီ ကိၼ် = he will eat. man tî kin (1 2 3) — 1 2 3	ၶွ် တီ ကိၼ် = they will eat. khau tî kin (1 2 3) — 1 2 3

တီ (tî) may be termed the *indefinite* future prefix particle. The present tense suffix ဢူ (û) is often used to express *future* time, as—

**Khê nam* = river; *nai* is the demonstrative pronoun *this*, used here for emphasis and recognition, and *khau* is the plural suffix. *Khê nam nai khau* = the rivers.

Examples.

phô kau mâ kâ cham* kau mai het† châ û — When my husband comes (he) (will) scold me.
(numbers: phô 3, kau 2, mâ 4, kâ 1, kau mai 6, châ û 5; When 1, my 2, husband 3, comes 4, scold 5, me 6)

man kau mai pô û — He (will) beat me.
(numbers: man 1, kau mai 3, pô û 2; He 1, beat 2, me 3)

(yau) the *completive* particle may be and often is used in conjunction with the future tense prefix (tî), as—

Examples.

kôn man kaw tî cham chaü‡ yau — His men also will (be) inconvenienced.
(numbers: kôn 2, man 1, kaw 3, tî 4, cham chaü yau 5; His 1, men 2, also 3, will 4, inconvenienced 5)

(nam) the particle denoting *certainty* or *affirmation* (*vide* page 37 *ante*) is also used *in conjunction* with the future tense prefix, as—

Examples.

kau kâ nü§ maü mai¶ tî het trâ nam — I will make a case against you.
(numbers: kau 1, kâ nü 5, maü mai 6, tî 2, het 3, trâ nam 4; I 1, will 2, make 3, a case 4, against 5, you 6)

or — *or*

kau maü mai¶ tî het trâ nam — I will to you case make.
(numbers: kau 1, maü 4, mai 3, tî 2, het 6, trâ nam 5; I 1, will 2, to 3, you 4, case 5, make 6)

A definite future is made by suffixing (kåt) to the root, as--

---

* *Cham* is a conditional participial particle used for the past as well as present (*vide* page 5); here *má kâ cham* means literally when having come.

† *Het chá* = make cross.

‡ *Cham chaü* is the exact equivalent to that useful Assamese word *dák*.

§ *Kâ nü* means literally above, on.

¶ *Mai* is the accusative case postposition.

Examples.

ၵွ်	ၵိၼ်း	ၵွတ်	I will eat.
kau	kin	kât	1 2 3
1	3	2	

ၵွ်	ၵႃ	ယိုၼ်	ၶႆ	တူဝ်*	ထိုၵ်†	ၵွတ်	I (am going) will go (and) shoot a bull buffalo.
kau	kâ	yü	khâi	tô	thük	kât	1 2 3 4 5 6
1	3	4	6	5		2	

Potential Mood.

Physical power or *capacity* is expressed by *adding* the word ပိၼ်း = (pen) *able* to the root, as—

Examples.

ၵွ်	လိၼ်း	ပိၼ်း‡	I can run.
kau	len	pen	1 2 3

မႂ်	ၶွ်	ဢႃ	ၼႆ	ပႃ§	ပိၼ်း	ဢူ¶	ၵေႃ‖	Can you carry this rice?
maü	khau	â	nai	pâ	pen	û	kê	1 2 3 4 5
2	5		4	3		1		

ပိၼ်း (pen) is more restricted in its meaning than its English equivalent *can*; as *to know, have knowledge of, possess information, instruction, &c.*, is expressed by the root verb ၶၢင် = châng, as—

Examples.

ၵွ်	မေႃ	ၶမ်	ၶၢင်**	ဢူ	I can sing.
kau	mô	khâm	châng	û	1 2 3
1		3	2		

မႂ်	ၶမ်	တႆး	ၶၢင်	ဢူ	ၵေႃ‖	Do you know Khâmti language?
maü	khâm	Tai	châng	û	kê	1 2 3 4 5
2	5	4	3			

Conditional Mood.

Conditional sentences are constructed by means of participles. The *conditional* participial suffix is ၵႃ ယေႃ (kâ yê), as—

---

* *Tô* is a numeral particle applied to animals.
† *Thük*, gender suffix, used for males.
‡ *Pen* would be more correct with the present tense suffix *û*, but it is often used as above.
§ *Pâ* means to carry on the back.
¶ *Û* = present tense suffix.
‖ *Kê* is an interrogative particle.
** *Châng* means to know, &c.

Examples.

ၵဝ် ၵိၼ် ၵႃ ယေ
kau[2] kin[3] kâ[1] yê — If[1] I[2] eat[3] (or had eaten).

လၵ်ႉ ၶႃ မႆ* ပေႃ ၵႃ ယေ
lak khâ mai[3] pô[2] kâ[1] yê
ႁႆႈ ဢူ†
hai û[4] — If[1] (you) beat[2] the child[3] (it) will cry[4].

ၵဝ် သိူဝ် မႆ* ႁၼ် ၵႃ ယေ
kau[2] sü mai[4] han[3] kâ[1] yê
တီႈ ပႆ
tî[5] pai[6] — If[1] I[2] see[3] a tiger[4] (I) will[5] flee[6].

ၵႃ ၸမ် (kâ cham) is also used as a *conditional* participial suffix, and is as such interchangable with ၵႃ ယေ (kâ yê), as—

Examples.

ၽူၼ် မႃ ထူၵ်ႇ ၵႃ ၸမ်
phôn[2] mâ[3] thôk[4] kâ[1] cham — If[1] rain[2] not[3] falling[4].

ၵဝ် ၵႃ ၼိူဝ် ငူ မႆ§ ယဵပ်ႇ
kau[2] kâ[4] nü ngû[5] mai[4] yep[3]
ၵႃ ၸမ်
kâ cham.[1] — If[1] I[2] step[3] upon[4] the snake[5].

The Khâmtî language likewise possesses a conjunction, namely,— သင် (sang) *or* သင် ဝႃ (sang) wâ, meaning *in that case, granting, allowing* or *supposing that*, which is often used in conjunction with ၵႃ ယေ (kâ yê) and ၵႃ ၸမ် (kâ cham), as—

---

* *Mai* = accusative case postposition.

† *Û* present tense suffix used to express past tense.

§ *Mai* here belongs to *ka nü* = above ; *ka nü mai* = upon.

Examples.

ယင် ဝႃ* ၽုၼ် မႃ တုၵ် ၵႃ ၸမ်
sang wâ phôn mâ tôk kâ cham
1 2 4 3 3

တီ လိုတ် လုင် ယဝ်
tî lüt lông yau
5 7 6

Supposing (it had not rained) rain had not fallen (it) would (have been) very hot.
(1 over "rained"; 2 rain, 3 had, 4 not; 6 very, 7 hot)

NOTE.— ယဝ် yau, the particle denoting *completion*, joined to တီ (tî) future tense suffix, forms the preterite of will, namely, would. လုတ် (lüt), an adjective meaning hot, is used here as an intransitive verb meaning *to grow hot*.

သင် ဝႃ* သွင် ၶႃ† မႃ ပၢႆ ၶိုၼ်
sång wâ sång khâ ma pai khün
1 2 3 4 5

တုၼ် မၢႆ ၵႃ ၸမ်‡ ၶၢႆ ႁေ တီ
tôn mai kâ cham khâi hê tî
7 6 9 8 10

ဢဝ် တၢႆ ယဝ်
au tai yau
11

If they both had not fled (and) climbed into (the) tree (the) wild buffaloes would have killed (them).
(1 If, 2 they both, 3 had, 4 not fled; 5 climbed, 6 into; 7 tree, 8 wild; 9 buffaloes, 10 would have; 11 killed)

IMPERATIVE MOOD.

The imperative suffix proper is တႃ (tâ). It is only used for the second person singular and plural.

ၵိၼ် တႃ (kin tâ) = eat.

ပၢႆ ၵိၼ် ၵွတ် (pai kin kåt) = let us eat.

မၼ် ႁႂ် ၵိၼ် ၵွတ်
man haü kin kåt
2 1 3
= let him eat.
(1 let, 2 him, 3 eat)

---

* Sometimes spelt ဝႃ (*wâ*).

† For explanation of *sång khâ*, see page 17 *ante*.

‡ *Kâ cham* belongs to the root verb ပၢႆ (*pai*) to flee; ပၢႆ ၵႃ ၸမ် had not fled.

Examples.

(Illustrating how used.)

ကုၼ် ႁင် တႃ kôn hâng tâ 2 1	Call (the) man. 1 2
မႂ် ဝႂ် တႃ mai wai tâ 2 1	Put (it) here. 1 2
ပႂ် ၵႃ ယိုဝ်း ၼိုဝ်* ၵႃတ် pai kâ yü nü kăt 1 2 3 4 3	Let (us) go shoot deer. 1 2 3 4

The first person singular and plural of the imperative are made by the suffix မႃ (mâ) with or without the imperative suffix proper, as—

ၵဝ် မႂ် ႁႂ်ႈ မႃ တႃ *or* ၵဝ် မႂ် ႁႂ်ႈ မႃ kau mai haü mâ tâ kau mai haü mâ 3 2 1	Give to me. 1 2 3

ႁႂ်ႈ (haü) = *permit, allow give,* is used as an auxiliary *causal* imperative, indicating authority, as—

ပႃ ယိင် ဢႃ ၼႂ် ႁိူၼ်း မၼ်း မႂ် pâ ying â nai hün man mai 3 2 6 5 4 သူင် ႁႂ်ႈ တႃ sông haü tâ 1	Escort this woman to her house. 1 2 3 4 5 6

The *prohibitive* particle is ပီ (pî) *prefixed* to the root verb, as—

Examples.

ပီ ပႂ် တႃ pî pai tâ 1 2	Don't run away. 1 2
မႃ မႂ်† ပီ ပေႃ တႃ mâ mai pî pô tâ 3 1 2	Don't beat the dog. 1 2 3

* *Nü* really means flesh.

† *Mai*, accusative case postposition.

ၼႂ် ၽၢႆ ပီ ႁဵတ်* ၸဵဝ် တႃႇ
maü phâi pî het cheô tâ
2 3 1 3 4
Don't you walk fast.
1 2 3 4

INFINITIVE MOOD.

ၼႂ် မႃ ႁဵတ် သင်
maü mâ het sang
2 3 1
Why (have) you come?
1 2 3

မႃ ယိုဝ် ၼိုဝ်
mâ yü nü
1 2 3
(I have) come to shoot deer.
1 2 3

The mere root of the verb is used for the infinitive, as—

Examples.

မၼ်း ႁဵတ် ဢႃ မူ ၼ် ပဵၼ်
•man het â mû n' pen
1 3 4 2
He is unable to do the work.
1 2 3 4

ၵဝ် ၶႃ† ယိုဝ် တေႃ ဝႃ လႆ ပိုဝ်
kau khâ yü tô wâ lai pü
1 2 3 4 5
ထိုၼ်း ၼႃ သီ မႃ ႁၼ်း ၵႃ
thün nâ sî mâ han kâ
6 8 7 9 10
I wished to shoot (it) but owing to jungle being thick (I) could not see / not saw (it).
1 2 3 4 5 6 7 8 9 10

ၼႂ် မႃ လမ် ၵႃ ၵေႃ‡
maü mâ lem kâ kê
2 3 4 5 1
(Have) you come to see the dance?
1 2 3 4 5

ၵဝ် ၵႃ သိုဝ် ၶဝ် ၼမ်§
kau kâ sü khau nam
1 2 3 4
I am going to buy dhan.
1 2 3 4

Sometimes the *casual* prefix ႁႂ် (haü) is used in conjunction with the future tense suffix ၵွတ်ႈ (kåt), to imply a command, is used to form the infinitive, as—

---

* *Het* means to make. *Ch* is always used instead of တ (*t*) in spelling it, *vide* page 4 *ante*; *het cheô* = rapid motion.

† Here the barė root of the verb *khâ* = desire, wish, &c., is used for the past tense.

‡ *Kê* is an interrogative particle.

§ *Nam* the particle denoting asertion. Here *nam* is subordinate to *kâ* (go).

NOTE.—Example 1 is not a good one, as we can say in English: "He cannot do the work."

Examples.

ꩫိတ် မႝ ဝႝ တႃ ꩭူႝ ꩭိင် ကႅတ်
net mai wai tâ haü heng kât
3 2 1 4 5 4

} Put it in the sun to dry.
Put (it) in the sun (and) let (it) dry.
1 2 3 4 5

The infinitive of purpose is ꩭင် (hang) = *for*, as—

Examples.

(Illustrating how used.)

တီ ဢႃ ꩫႝ ꩭင် ဝႝ မူ
tî â nai hang wai mû
2 1 3 4

} This place is to keep pigs (in).
1 2 3 4

ဝꩫ် ꩫႝ ꩭင် ကိꩫ် ꩫမ်
wân nai hang kin nam
2 1 3 4 5

} This cup is for drinking water.
1 2 3 4 5

Sometimes ပိ (pî) is used instead of ꩭင် (hang), as—

မꩫ် ကႃ ပိ ꩭꩫ် သႃ ꩭပ် *
man kâ pî han sâ heb
1 2 3 4

} He is going to see (the) "saheb."
1 2 3 4

မူႝ ကႃ ပိ လမ် သိုဝ် ကေ †
maü kâ pî lem sü kê
2 3 4 5 1

} Have you been to see the tiger?
1 2 3 4 5

Another example with ပိ (pî) used instead of *hang.*

ဝꩫ် ꩫိုင် ‡ ကွꩫ် ကႃ ပိ ယိုဝ် ꩫိုဝ် §
wan lüng kau kâ pî yü nü
2 1 6 3 4 5

သီ တင် တေႃ ‡ ꩫိုင် ꩫႝ ကႃ
sî kâng tô lüng nai kâ
3

} One day going (out) to shoot deer I got a samber.
1 2 3 4 5 6 7 8 9

Participles.

မိုဝ် ကိꩫ် ꩫႝ (mü kin nai) adverbial.

ကိꩫ် သီ (kin sî) perfect participle, indefinite.

ကိꩫ်ꩫႝ (kin nai) past passive and verbal noun.

---

* There is no *b* in Khâmtî, so *p* is used.

† *Kê* is the interrogative particle.

‡ *Tô* is a numeral expletive; ꩫိုင် is an abbreviation for *lüng* = one.

§ This *sî* (past participial suffix) belongs to *kâ*, root verb go.

ꩡိꩫ် ကႃ ယေ (kin kâ yê)
ꩡိꩫ် ကႃ ꩡမ် (kin kâ cham) } Conditional, present, and past.

Examples.

(Illustrating how used.)

မိုဝ် မꩫ် လုၵ် ꩭိုဝ် ဝိꩫ်* ꩫႝ ꩡိꩫ်
mü man lûk hü wen nai tin
မꩫ် ꩭၵ် ကႃ
man hâk kâ

He while jumping from the boat broke his leg.
In Khamti—His leg broke.

မိုဝ် ꩡိ† ꩡိုꩫ် ꩫႝ ကွꩫ် ငူ ꩬွꩫ် ꩡိုဝ်‡
mü tî thün nai kau ngû sảng tô
ꩭꩫ် ကႃ
han kâ

While cutting the jungle I saw two snakes.

ꩡွꩫ်ꩡိ ꩬိုဝ် မႝ** ꩭꩫ် ꩬိ ꩱွꩫ် ꩱႃ
Chaungi sü mai han sî au phâ
ꩭေႃ ꩬိုဝ် မႝ†† မꩫ် ကႃ ꩡေႃ ꩫႝ ꩱူꩡေႃ
hô sü mai mak kâ tô nai û kaw
ꩬိုဝ် မႃ ꩡႝ ꩬိ မꩫ် မႝ ကꩫ် ကႃ
sü mâ tai sî man mai kâp kâ

Chaungi seeing the tiger cut it (the tiger) over the head with a "dao," but tiger not dying bit him.

မိုဝ် မꩫ် မႃ ꩫႝ‡‡ ကွꩫ် ကႃ ကွꩫ်
mü man mâ nai kau kâ kåt

I will go when he comes.

---

* *Wen nai* is a verbal noun, root verb *wen* with participial suffix *nai*.

† *Tî nai* is also a verbal noun; root *tî* = cut.

‡ *Tô* is a numeral expletive used with animals.

** *Mai* = accusative case postposition.

†† *Mai* = locative case——*hô sü mai* = on the head of tiger.

‡‡ *Mâ nai* is a verbal noun; *mâ* = root verb come, and *nai* participial suffix.

ဝၼ် ၵျ်* ၵုၼ် ၵေႃ ၵျ်* ဢွၵ် ယိ လတ်
wan lüng kôn kô lüng au sî lat
2 1 3 7 8

ၵႃႉ လေဝ် ထိုၼ်း မၼ်း တင်† ၽူင် ၸၢင်
kâ lê thün man tang phûng châng
4 5 6 9 10 12

ႁွပ်‡ ၵၼ်း မိူဝ် ၼႆႇ မၼ်း ပႆႇ ၶိုၼ်
hop kan mü nai man pai khün
10 13 14 15 16

တွၼ် မႆႇ ၵႃႉ။ ၽူင် ၸၢင် ၵေႃႉ ႁၼ်
tôn mai kâ. phûng châng kaw han
18 13 19 20 21 22

မၼ်း ယိ ပႆႇ ၵႃႉ။ မၼ်း လုၵ်ႉ တွၼ်
man sî pai kâ. man lûk tôn
23 22 24 25 27 28

မႆႇ လူင် ယိ ၶမ်ႈ ၵႃႉ။
mai lông sî châm kâ
27 26 29

One day a man went
1 2 3 4
to stroll (in the)
5
jungle with a
6 7
gun. He met a
8 9 10
herd (of) ele-
11
phants.
12
Then he ran away
13 14 15
(and) climbed into
16 17
(a) tree. The herd
18 19
of elephants too
20 21
on seeing him
22 23
fled. He descend-
24 25 26
ing from tree
27 28
tracked (them).
29

The last sentence (on this page) shows how peculiarly verbal suffixes are often placed with reference to the verb they belong to. For instance: first the past tense suffix '*kâ*' of the verb *pai,* to run away, is put at the end of the sentence; *han* "*mü nai man* '*pai*' *khün tôn mai kâ,*" then the participial suffix *si* of the verb '*han*' is put after "*man phûng châng kaw* '*han*' *man si.*" This shifting of the verbal tense suffixes is a noticeable feature of the language, and is practised for the sake of euphony. It will also be noticed how often bare roots of verbs are used and nouns without case postpositions, '*kâ lê thün,*' for instance=went for a stroll in the jungle: '*kâ,*' bare root

* ၵျ် abbreviation for *â lüng* = one, *vide* page 15 and 53 *ante.*

† *Tang* = with; *tang phûng châng* = with a herd of elephants.

‡ *Kan* is a reciprocal particle.

of verb go, '*li*,' bare root of verb to stroll, are used, and the noun '*thün*' alone to express *in* the jungle. Again, bare root of the verb '*hŏp*,' to meet, is used for the past tense.

ပိ ကႝ ၵႃမၼ်* တင် သင် ဝႃ ႁူဝ် ၼမ်
pî kai khâman Tangsang wâ hô nam
ထူ ရိ မႝ ႁုၼ် ဢုတ် ဢႃ လိုင် ယင် ဢူ
Thû rî mai hün ût â lüng yâng û
သင် ဝႃ ၸွ ပႃ လိုင် ၶႃ လႅမ် ကႃ ယေ
sang wâ chau pâ lüng khâ lem kâ yê
(*or* ကႃ ၸမ်) ကႃ လႅမ် တႃ။
(kâ cham) kâ lem tâ

Last year Tangsang Mishmi said, at the head of the Thuri river there is a brick house, if your honour desire seeing (it) go (and) see.

သင် တမ်ငႃ† ၶွ‡ ကႃ ၶႃ ပႃ§ ကႃ
sang tamngâ khau kâ khâ pâ kâ
ၸမ် ပႃ တိ ၼႝ လုင်
cham pâ tî nai lông

Supposing Dums went fishing, fish would get many.

ကႃယေ (kâ yê) and ကႃ ၸမ် (kâ cham) are conditional *past* participle suffixes, but they are used to express *present* time *also*, as—

Examples.

ကွ သိုဝ် ႁၼ် ကႃ ယေ (*or* ကႃ ၸမ်)
kau sü han kâ yê kâ cham

If I see (or had seen) a tiger.

The participle in ၼႝ (nai) is used as a verbal noun, as—

Examples.

မႂ် တိမ် (*or* တႅမ်) ၼႝ ၼိုဝ် ၼီ
maü tem nai n' nî

Your writing (is) not good.

---

* *Khâmtis* call Mishmis "Khâman."
† *Khâmtis* call Dums "Tamngâ."
‡ *Khau* is simply the plural suffix particle.
§ *Khâ pâ*, literally search for fish = fish.

မၼ်း ၶႃႈ ၼႆႉ ၵႃႈ ယင်
man khâ nai kâ sang
2 3 1

What (is) he wanting?
1 2 3

Relation of Cause and Effect.

Cause is expressed by using the word လႆႈ ပိူဝ်ႈ (lai pü) equivalent to our English word *because, for the reason that,* as—

Examples.

လႆႈ ပိူဝ်ႈ ၵဝ် ၵေႃႈ ၼႆႉ* ၵဝ် ၵိုၼ်း မႆႉ မႆႉ ၶိုၼ် ၵႃႈ
lai pü kau kô nai kau tôn mâi mai khün kâ
5 6 7 1 4 3 2

I climbed into the tree because I (was afraid) fearing.
1 2 3 4 5 6 7

လႆႈ ပိူဝ်ႈ လုၵ်ႈ ဢွၼ်ႇ တွင်ႇ မႆႈ* ၼႆႉ ႁႆႈ ဢူႉ
lai pü lûk ån tång mai nai hai û
4 1 5 3 2

The child is crying because (it is) hungering.
1 2 3 4 5

လႆႈ ပိူဝ်ႈ ၵႆႇ ယႂ်ႇ ၼႆႉ* ၵဝ် သွင် တူဝ်† မႆႉ‡
lai pü kai yaü nai kaü sång tô mai
6 4 7 1 3

ၵြႃႇ ဢဝ် ၵႃႈ
trâ aú kâ
5 2

I took two fowls for the rupee because they are large.
1 2 3 4 5 6 7

လႆႈ ပိူဝ်ႈ ၽူၼ် တူၵ်း ၼႆႉ§ မၼ်း တိ မႃး မႃႇ
lai pü phôn tôk nai man tî mâ mà
1 2 3 4 5 6 7

Because rain falling he will not come.
1 2 3 4 5 6 7

---

* *Kő nai* and *tang mai nai* are verbal nouns; *yaü* (in the third sentence) is an adjective, meaning large, and has the participial suffix *nai* attached directly to it, *yaü nai* meaning being large.

† *Tő* is a numeral expletive.

‡ *Mai* accusative case postposition, *kai sång tő mai* = two fowls.

§ *Tők nai* is a verbal noun, or rather *phőn tők nai* is.

Effect is expressed by the word လႝ ပိုၼ် ၼႝ (lai pü nai) *or* လႝ လင် ၼႝ (lai lang nai) either with or without the participial suffix ယိ (sî) (used also as an adverbial particle), as—

Examples.

ၵဝ် ၵုဝ် ယိ လႝ ပိုၼ် ၼႝ ၵဝ် တုၼ် မႝ မႝ ၶိုၼ် ၵႃ
kau kô sî lai pü nai kau tôn mai mai khün kâ
(2, 3, 4, 7, 6, 7)
— I feared, therefore I climbed into the tree.
(1, 2, 3, 5, 6, 7)

လႝ ပိုၼ် ၼႝ ယိ ၵဝ် ၵႃ*
lai pu nai si kau kâ
(1, 2, 3)
— On that account I went.
(1, 2, 3)

ၽုၼ် တုၵ် ၵႃ ၸမ် ၶဝ် ႁဵတ်† ဢႃ မူ မႃ ပိၼ် လႝ လင် ၼႝ ၶဝ် မႃ ထုၵ်‡ ၸႂ်
phôn tôk ka cham khau het âmû mâ pen lai lang nai khau mâ thôk chaü
(2, 3, 4, 6, 7, 5, 8, 9, 10, 11)
— If rain falling they are unable to do (any) work, therefore they don't like (it).
(1, 2, 3, 4, 5, 6, 7, 8, 9, 10, 11)

ၵဝ် တုဝ် ဢၢၼ် မႝ§ ပေႃ ၵႃ လႝ ပိုၼ် ၼႝ ယိ ႁႝ ဢူ
kau tô ån mai pô kâ lai pü nai sî hai û
(1, 3, 2, 4, 6, 5)
— I beat the child, therefore (it) is crying.
(1, 2, 3, 4, 5, 6)

The following illustrations will show the construction used in Khâmtî after verbs of *asking*, *entreating*, *commanding*, *seeing*, *hearing*, and *feeling*.

---

* *Kâ* (go) bare root of verb used for past time, *vide* page 41 *ante*.

† *Het* means make, do; *het âmû* = do work.

‡ ထုၵ် means literally to hit, mark, &c., ထုၵ်ၸႂ် = please mind (ၸႂ်) = (chaü) mind.

§ *Mai* accusative case postposition.

Examples.

မၼ် ၵွ် မႝ* ထံ မၼ် မႝ ႁႂ် ၸီ ႁႂ်†
man kau mai thâm man mai haü chî haü
1 3 6 4

He asked me to show (it) to him.
1 2 3 4 5 6

မၼ် မႝ ထံ တႃ မူ မၼ် တီ ၶႝ ၵႝ‡
man mai thâm tá mû man tî khai kai
2 1 7 6 3 5

Ask him to sell his pig.
In Khâmtí—
Ask him will (he) sell his pig.
1 2 3 4 5 6

ၵွ် ၶွ် မႝ တီ ႁႂ် ၵႃ § ၵေ¶
kau khau mai tí haü kâ kê ?
2 4 1 3 5

Shall I ask them to dance.
In Khâmtí—
Shall I command them to dance.
1 2 3 4 5

ၵွ် ၵႃ ၵၢတ်‖ ၼႝ ယၢၼ် ဢႃ ၶၢင်
kau kâ kăt nai yǎn â khâng
1 2 4 3

I begged him to let me go.
In Khâmtí—
I am going {order solicited permission do.
1 2 3 4

မၼ် ၵွ် မႝ ႁႂ် ဢႃ ၶၢင် မႃ** ႁႂ် ၼၢင်
man kau mai haü â khâng mâ haü nang
1 3

He bade me sit down.
1 2 3 4

မၼ် မႝ ဢႃ ၶၢင် ႁႂ် တႃ†† ႁႂ် ႁႂ်‡‡ ႁိဝ် ၸိပ် ႁွႝ§§
man mai â khâng haü ta haü haü hü sip hôy
2 1 3 5 4

Order him to supply ten boats.
1 2 3 4 5

---

* *Mai* = accusative case postposition.
† *Haü chí haü* is a compound causal verb (Assamese *dekwai dibole*) *haü chí* = (cause) to show and second *haü* = give.
‡ *Kai* is a particle of probability.
§ *Haü ká* = cause, command, to dance.
¶ *Kê* = interrogative particle.
‖ *Kăt* = definite future tense suffix; *kâ kăt nai* = Assamese *jâm bôlí*.
** *Mâ* belongs to *haü*; *haü â khâng mâ* = literally gave order. Verbal tense suffixes are often separated from the root in this way.
†† *A khâng haü tâ* = give order.
‡‡ *Haü haü* = command to supply.
§§ *Hôy* is a numeral expletive.

မုဝ် မၼ် ပေႃ မႂ် မႝ ၼႝ * ၵဝ် ႁၼ် ဢူ
mü man pô maü mai nai kau han û
1 2 3 4 3 5 7 6

I saw him strike you.
In Khâmti—
When he striking you
1 2 3 4
I am seeing.
5 6 7

မုဝ် ၼုဝ် လုမ် ၼႝ မႂ် ႁၼ်ၵႃ ၵေႝ †
mü nü lôm nai maü han kâ kê
1 2 3 4 5

Did you see the deer fall?
In Khâmti—
When deer falling you
1 2 3 4
saw?
5

မၼ် မႝ ဝႃ ၼႝ ၵဝ် ၼႝ ႁိၼ်ၵႃ
man mai wâ nai kau nai hin kâ
3 4 1 2

I heard him saying (it).
1 2 3 4

မႂ် ၽႃ ၼင် ၼႝ ႁိၼ် ဢူ ၵေႝ †
maü phâ nang nai hin û kê
4 3 1

Do you hear the
1 2 3
thunder?
4

ၵဝ် လႃ ၶႃ ႁႝ ၼႝ ဢိုဝ် ‡ ၼႝ ႁိၼ်
kau lâ khâ hai nai n' nai hin
1 4 5 2 3

I did not hear the
1 2 3
child crying.
4 5

ၵဝ် ဢိင် သၼ် ႁူ ဢူ
kau ing san hû û
1 3 2

I felt the earthquake.
1 2 3

တိၼ် မႂ် မႝ § မၼ် ၵိတ်ၼႝ ‖ ႁူ ဢူ ၵေႝ †
tin maü mai man kit nai hû û kê
6 4 3 2 1

(Did you) feel him
1 2
touching your leg?
3 4 5

12.—Passive Voice.

The Khâmtî verb has no distinct passive form. Some verbs are used in a passive sense without any change of form.

---

* This *nai* belongs to *pô* = root of verb (to) beat; *pô nai* = striking.

† *Kê* is the interrogative particle.

‡ This is the diphthong noticed at page 33 *ante*, used here as a negative particle.

§ *Mai* is the locative case postposition.

‖ *Kit nai* is a verbal noun, root *kit*, with *nai* participial suffix attached.

13.—*Causative Verbs.*

Some verbs acquire a causative form when the particle ဢွၵ် (au) (denoting the agent) is prefixed to them, as—

Examples.

တုဝ် ဢွၼ် မႆ* ဢွၵ် ဢၢပ် ၼမ်† တႃ tô ân mai [2] au âp nam tâ [1]	Bathe [1] the child [2].
သႆ ဢွၵ် ၶတ် တႃ sai [2] au khat tâ [1]	Break [1] the string [2].
ၼမ် ဢွၵ် တုမ် တႃ nam au tôm tâ [1]	Boil [1] the water [2].
မႃ မႆ* ဢွၵ် တႆ တႃ mâ mai au tai tá	Kill [1] the dog [2].
ၽႃ ၼႆ ဢွၵ် လပ် မဵပ်‡ တႃ phâ [3] nai [2] au lâp mep tâ [1]	Hide [1] this [2] cloth [3].

Sometimes the causative imperative verb ႁႂ် (haü), indicating *authority*, is used to form a casual verb, as—

Examples.

မၼ်း မႆ¶ ငုဝ် ႁႂ် သဵဝ် တႃ။§ man mai [2] ngô [4] haü [1] sîau tâ [3]	Make [1] (command) him [2] catch [3] the cow [4].

14.—*Compound*

Compound verbs are formed by (*a*) compounding one verbal root with another; (*b*) combining a noun or an adjective with a verb; (*c*) combining a participle with a verb; (*d*) combining a noun or adjective with the auxiliary verb ယင် (yang) and the verb ပဵၼ် (pen) = become. When thus formed the compound verb is conjugated as a simple one, as—

---

* *Mai* = accusative case postposition.

† *Âp nam* = bathe; *tâ* imperative suffix.

‡ *Lâp mep* = hide, secrete.

¶ *Mai* is the accusative case postposition.

§ *Tâ* (imperative suffix) belongs, of course, to the root verb *haü*.

(a) **Examples.**

ပွၵ် မႃ (pȧk mâ) = return, come back (mâ = come).
ဢဝ် ပွၵ် (au pȧk) = take back (au = take).
ၶိုၼ် ႁႂ် (khün haü) = give back (khün = again, haü = give).
ၶိုၼ် ဢဝ် မႃ (khün au mâ) = bring back (au mâ = bring.)
ႁဵတ် ပဵၼ် (het pen) = able to do (het = do, pen = able).
ဝႃ ပဵၼ် (wâ pen) = able to speak (wâ = speak).
ၶႃ ၵိၼ် (khâ kin) = desire to eat (khâ = desire, kin = eat),
&c., &c., &c.

(b) **Examples.**

ၽွႆ ယႃ ထွႆ (phôy yâ thôy) = weed (phôy yâ = weed).
ႁဵတ် ဢႃမူ (het âmû) = work (het = do, âmû = work).
တၼ် တၼ် (tân kan) = converse (tân = speak, kan reciprocal particle).
ႁိမ် ဢဝ် (him au) = seize by force.
လိူတ် တုၵ် (lüt tôk) = (bleed, lüt = blood, tôk = fall).

(c) **Examples.**

ၵႃ ယီ ထံ = (kâ sî thâm) go and ask (kâ = go, thâm = ask).
ယိပ် ယီ ဝႆ = (sĭ au sî wai) seize and keep (sĭ au = seize, wai = place).
ၵိပ် ယီ ၼႆ = (kep sî nai) find accidentally (nai = get, obtain).
ၶႃ ယီ ၼႆ = (khă sî nai) find by searching (khâ = search, nai = obtain).
ႁွႆ ယီ ဝႆ = (hoi sî wai) hang up (hoi = suspend, wai = put, place).
&c., &c., &c.

(d) **Examples.**

ပဵၼ် ထဝ် = (pen thau) become old (pen = become, thau = old).
ပဵၼ် မႃ = (pen mâ) become a fool (pen = become, mâ = fool).
ပဵၼ် ၶႆ = (pen khai) become ill (pen = become, khai = ill),
&c., &c., &c.

Verbal tense suffixes may be put *directly* to adjectives, as—

ကတ် (kat) *or* ၼွ် (nau) = cold.
ကတ် ဢူ = (kat û) ၼွ် ဢူ = (nau û) is cold.
ကတ် ကႃ = (kat kâ) ၼွ် ကႃ = (nau kâ) become cold.
or ယွ် *or* yau ယွ် *or* yau.
တီ ကတ် = (tî kat) တီ ၼွ် = (tî nau) will be cold.
&c., &c., &c.

ထွ် = (*thau*) *old*.
ထွ် ဢူ = (thau û) is old.
ထွ် ကႃ *or* ထွ် ယွ် = (thau kâ *or* yau) become old.
တီ ထွ် = (tî thau) will be old.

ၸိၼ် = (*sen*) *pretty*.
ၸိၼ် ဢူ = (sen û) is pretty.
ၸိၼ် ယွ် = (sen yau) become pretty.
တီ ၸိၼ် = (tî sen) will be pretty.
&c., &c., &c., and numerous others.

15.—*Interrogative form of Verb.*

The interrogative particle is ကေ် (kê). It is used with all the tenses, and may be put directly to adjectives and adverbs, as—

Examples.

ဢႃ ၼႆ ကုၼ် ကေ်
â nai(2) kôn(3) kê(1) — Is(1) this(2) a man(3)?

ဢႃ ၼႆ ငူ ကေ်
â nai(2) ngû(3) kê(1) — Is(1) this(2) a snake(3)?

ၽင် ၼမ် ၵၼ် ဢူ ကေ်
phang(3) nam(2) kân û(4) kê(1) — Is(1) the river(2) bank(3) breaking(4)?

သီ လတ် ယတ် ကေ်
sî lat(2) sat(3) kê(1) — Is(1) the gun(2) loaded(3)?

မႃ ပိတ် ကေႃ mâ pit kê	Does the horse kick?
သိူဝ် မႆ* မႂ် ယိူဝ် ကႃ† ကေႃ sü mai maü yü ka kê	Did you shoot the tiger?
ၼမ် လွင် ကႃ† ကေႃ nam lång ka kê	Has the river risen?
ၶဝ် သူ တင် မိုင် ပတ် ယဝ်‡ ကႃ ကေႃ khau sû tang müng pat yau kâ kê	Have you cut all your paddy?
မႂ် ပီ ကဝ် မႆ¶ ႁၼ် ကႃ ကေႃ maü pî kau mai han kâ kê	Have you seen my elder brother?
မႂ် ၵႆ ဢႃ ၼႆ§ ၶဝ် တီ သိူဝ် ကေႃ maü kai â nai khau tî sü kê	Will you buy these fowls?
မၼ် မႃ ၼႆ တီ မႃ ကေႃ man mâ nai tî mâ kê	Will he come today?

Negative interrogatives are made by using the interrogative particle ကေႃ (kê) in conjunction with the negative particle မႃ (mâ), as—

Examples.

ၶဝ် မႆ မႃ ယင် ကေႃ khau mai mâ yang kê	Are they not here?
ဢႃ ၼၼ် ငူ မႃ ၸူ ကေႃ â nan ngû mâ chaü kê	Is not that a snake?

* *Mai* = accusative case postposition.

† *Ka* = past tense (verbal) suffix.

‡ *Yau* = (verbal) suffix denoting completion.

¶ *Mai* = accusative tense postposition.

§ *Khau* = plural suffix ; *â nai khau* = these.

မွ် မၼ်း မႂ် ၼင် ၼႂ် မႃ ဝႃ ၵေႃး maü man mai nang nai má wâ kê	Did you not tell him so?
မွ် ငိုၼ်း မႃ ဢၼ်း ၵေႃး maü ngün mâ an kê	Have you not counted the rupees?
သီလတ်မွ် ၵွ် မႂ် တီမႃၶီၵေႃး sî lat maü kau mai tî mâ chî kê	Will (you) not show me your gun?
သင် ၾုၼ်း တုၵ်း ၵႃ ယေႃး မွ် sang phôn tôk kâ yê maü တီ မႃ ယမ်း ၵေႃး tî mâ yam kê	Supposing rain falling (if it rains) will you not get wet?

Interrogative alternatives are made by using the interrogative ၵေႃး (kê), or the particle ဢႃ (la), as—

Examples.

ဢႃ ၼၼ်း ငူဝ် တူဝ် * မေ လႃ â nan ngô tô mê lâ တူဝ် * ထိုၵ် tô thük	Is that a cow or a bullock? *In Khâmtî—* Is that gôrû female or male?
မွ် သမ်း ပေႃ † ၵေႃး ထႂ် maü Sampho kê Tai	Are you (a) Singpho (or a) Khâmtî?

If the question is a *doubtful* one the suffix particle ၵႂ် (kai), equivalent to that useful Assamese particle *bá*, is substituted for ၵေႃး (kê) *or* ဢႃ (lâ), as—

Examples.

ဢႃ ၼႂ် ၶမ်း ၵႂ် a nai kham kai	Is this gold (doubtful)?

* *Tô* is numeral expletive used with animals.

† Khâmtis call Singphos 'Samphos.'

ၸုၼ် တီ တုၵ်* ၵႆ
phôn[2] tî tôk[1] kai } Will[1] it rain[2] ?

ꩬူ ၼႆ† တီ ၸူ ၵႆ တီ ꩡုမ် ၵႆ
sau nai[2] tî[1] phû[3] kai tî chôm[4] kai } Will[1] the post[2] float[3] or sink ?

Interrogative particles are *never* used if there is a word in the sentence which *implies* interrogation, as—

Examples.

မၼ် မႃ လႆ ၵႃ ၵႃ
man mâ laü kâ kâ } When did he go ?

ၼင် ၼႆ‡ ၸႆ ဝႃ မႃ
nang[3] nai phaü[1] wâ mâ[2] } Who[1] said[2] so[3] ?

ဢႃ ၼႆ မူ ၸႆ
â nai[3] mû[2] phaü[1] } Whose[1] pig[2] (is) this[3] ?

မႆ ၼိူဝ် ၶႃ လႆ ႁၼ် ၵႃ
maü[4] nü[2] khâ laü[1] han[5] kâ[3] } How many[1] deer[2] did[3] you[4] see[5] ?

မႆ မၼ် မႆ ႁဵတ်သင် ဝႃ ၵႃ
maü[3] man mai[5] het sang[1] wâ[4] kâ[2] } What[1] did[2] you[3] tell[4] him[5] ?

16.—*Negative form of Verbs.*

Khâmtîs use two particles *prefixed* to the root of the verb for expressing negation, namely, ဢိုၼ် (*ün*) and မႃ (mâ). The first, ဢိုၼ် (*ün*), is used in sentences expressing *direct* negation. In *conditional* negative sentences, however, မႃ (mâ) *only* is used, and မႃ (mâ), *not* ဢိုၼ် (*ün*), is *alone* used as the *negative interrogative particle.*

---

* *Tôk* means to fall; *phôn tôk* = to rain.

† *Nai* is the demonstrative pronoun used for emphasis and recognition.

‡ *Nang* = like; *nai* = this.

Examples.

Shan		English
မၼ် ဢိုဝ် ၶေႃ man n' khô 1 2 3	}	She (is) not laughing. 1 2
မၼ် တႆ * လဝ် ဢိုဝ် ၸႂ် man tai lau n' chaü 1 3 2	}	He (is) not drunk. 1 2 3
ၵဝ် ဢိုဝ် ႁဵတ် kau n' het 1 2 3	}	I (did) not do (it). 1 2 3
ၵဝ် ၽႃ မႂ် ဢိုဝ် ႁၼ် kau phâ maü n' han 1 5 4 2 3	}	I have not seen your cloth. 1 3 4 5
ၵဝ် ဢိုဝ် ၵႃ kau n' kâ 1 2 3	}	I will not (or I did not) go. 1 2 2 3
မၼ် ၵဝ် မႆ † တၢင် ဢိုဝ် ၸီ man kau mai tâng n' chî 1 4 5 2 3	}	He will not show me (or does not show me) the road. 1 2 3 4 5
ၵဝ် ၵႃ ဢိုဝ် ပဵၼ်း kau kâ n' pen 1 4 3 2	}	I can not go. 1 2 3 4
သင် မႂ် မႃ ၵႃ ၵႃ ယေး sang maü mâ kâ kâ yê 1 2 4 5 3	}	If you had not gone. 1 2 3 4 5
မႂ် မႃ ၵိၼ် ၵႃ ၸမ် တီ တႆး maü mâ kin kâ cham tî tai 1 2 3 4 5	}	*If you do not eat you will die.* You not eating if will die. 1 2 3 4 5

The negative particles may be *prefixed directly* to adjectives, as—

Examples.

Shan		English
ၵဝ် ဢိုဝ် ၶႆး kau n' khai 1 2 3	}	I (am) not ill. 1 2 3

---

* တႆ = die လဝႃ = *mâd* (liquor to eat) = drunk.

† *Mai*, accusative case postposition.

ယိုဝ် ၸဵၼ်	n'[1] sen[2]	not[1] pretty[2].
ယိုဝ် ပေႃ	n'[1] pô[2]	not[1] sufficient[2].
ယိုဝ် ၵႂ်	n'[1] kaü[2]	not[1] near[2].
ယိုဝ် ထဝ်	n'[1] thau[2]	not[1] old[2].

17.—ADVERBS.

These may be classified as follows:—

Of Time.

မႃ ၼႆ (mâ nai)=today.

မႃ ႁုၵ်း (mâ hôk)=morrow.

မႃ ႁိုဝ် (mâ hü)=day after tomorrow.

မႃ ငႃ (mâ ngâ)=yesterday.

မႃသုၼ် (mâ sûn)=day before yesterday.

ၵူ မိုဝ် (kû mü)=daily.

ၵၢင် လႂ် (kâng laü)=early morning.

ငႆ (ngai)=now.

ၵၢင် ၶိုၼ် မႆ * (kâng khün mai)=at night.

မႃ ၸမ် (mâcham)=soon, presently.

မႃ လႂ် † (mâlaü, mâlaü)=sometimes.

or ယေဝ် ပၢၼ် † (yê pânpân)=sometimes.

မိုဝ် ၼၼ် (mü nan)=formerly, in by-gone times.

ၶိုၼ် ၼႃ ၵဝ် ပၢၼ် လိုင် (khün nâ kau pân lüng)=once more.

ဢွၼ် တင် (ân tâng)=first.

ၵႃ ၼႃ (kâ nâ)=before.

ၵႃ လင် (kâ lâng)=afterwards, behind.

ဝႆ လင် (wailang)=

ပီ ၼႆ (pî nai)=this year.

ပီ ၼႃ (pî nâ)=next year.

ပီ ၵႆ (pî kai)=last year.

ၶိုၼ် ၼင် ၵဝ် (khün nang kau)=again.

or ၶိုၼ် ၼႃ ၵဝ် (khün nâ kau)=again.

တုၵ် ၸဵမ် ငႆ (tôk chem ngai)=yet.

---

* *Mai* is the locative case postposition.

† The doubling of the final mark (ˆ) denotes that the word must be repeated.

Of Time—concluded.

မႃ လႆ ၵေႃ ဢိုဝ် ၸႆ mâ laü kaw n' chaü } =never.

သင် ၵေႃ (sang kô)=at first newly, for first time.

Made by using ၼင် (nang) = like, resembling, *vide* examples post } =nearly almost.

No word = always. ထုၼ် ယႂ် (thôn yau) = ago, past.

Of Place.

မႆ (mai)=here.

မၼ် (man)=there.

ပုၼ် (pûn) = there, some distance off.

ၵႃ ၼႃ မႆ (kâ nâ mai) *or* ၶင် ၼႃ မႆ (khâng nâ mai) } = in front, presence of.

ႁုမ် ၵၼ် (hôm kan)=together.

ၵႃ ၼိူဝ် * (kâ nu)=above.

ၵႃ တႂ် * (kâ tau)=below.

ထႆ ၶင် (tai khâng *or* ထႆ tai } = near, adjacent to.

တီ တင် မိူင် မႆ tî tâng müng mai places all in } =everywhere.

လုၵ် မၼ် (lûk man)=thence.

ၵႃ ၼွၵ် မႆ (kâ nâk mai) = outside.

ၵႃ ၼႂ် မႆ (kâ naü mai) *or* ၼႂ် မႆ (naü mai) } =inside.

Of Quality.

လေ် (lê lê)=quite.

In conjunction with ယႂ် (yau) =entirely.

ၼင် ငႆ *or* (nang ngai) ၼင် ၼႆ (nang nai) } in this manner.

ၼင် ၼၼ် (nang naǹ)=in that manner.

မႃ ၼီ ၸီ (ma nî sî)=badly.

ၼီ ၸီ (nî sî)=well.

ၼႆ (nai)=alone.

ဢိုဝ် ထင် (n' thâng)=probably.

တီ တေ ၸီ (tî tê sî) *or* မၼ် † ၸီ (mân mân sî) } = certainly.

---

* Used with postposition *mai*.

† The doubling of the mark (ႇ) shows that the word must be repeated.

Of Quality—concluded.

ထ' ပိုဝ် ၼ' ယိ (lai pü nai sî) = therefore (on account of this or that).

ၶၼ် * ယိ (khan khan sî = quickly).

ယိ ၼ' ယေဝ် (sî nai yê) = then in that case.

or ၼ' ကႃ ယေဝ် (nai kâ yê) = then in that case.

လုင် (lông) = very.

ကႃ ႁိင် (kâ hêng) *or* ဢွၵ် ႁိင် (au hêng).

ၶုၼ် ၼႃ ၵွၵ် (khun na kau) = more.

ကႃ ႁိင် လုင် (kâ heng lông) = much.

Made by using ကႃ လႅ in conjunction with a participle (*past*) and ၵေႃ *vide* examples post. = as much as, as many as.

Sometimes ကႃ (ka) = is used.

ၽုင် ၼ' *or* (phûng nai). ၶ' လိုင် (khai lung) = this much or many.

ၽုင် ၼၼ် *or* (phûng nan). ၶၼ် လိုင် (khan lüng) = that much or many.

ၶၼ် (khan) = about, approximately.

ၽေဢဝ် (phê au) = too, more than enough.

ၵမ် ၽွင် (kam phång) = some

ဢႃ လိုင် ဢႃ လိုင် { (a lüng) (a lüng) } = some ; literally one one.

Some is also made by prefixing the particle ယေဝ် (yê) to certain other particles, for instance: numeral particles and nouns *vide* example post.

ၵေႃ (kaw) = also (and).

Interrogative.

ႁိလ်ၸင် (hetsang) = why ?

မ' (mai) *or* ၼႃ မ' (na mai) = where ?

မႃ လႅ (ma laü) = when ?

လုၵ် ၼႃ မ' (lûk na mai) = whence.

ႁိ လိုဝ် (hî lü) = how, generally used in conjunction with ယိ (sî), ႁိၼိုဝ် hî nü is also used instead of hî lü.

ၶႃ လႅ (khâ laü) = how many, much.

---

* Doubling of the mark (*) shows that the word must be repeated

Examples.

(Illustrating how used.)

[Khamti script]
ma nai het tâ — Do (it) _today._
Word order: 2 1 — 1 2

[Khamti script]
mâ hôk phôn tî tôk — It will *rain tomorrow.* *In Khâmti*— Rain will fall _tomorrow._
Word order: 4 1 2 3 — 1 2 3 4

[Khamti script]
mâ ngâ kau nü tô lüng* yü kâ — _Yesterday_ I shot a deer.
Word order: 1 2 5 4 3 — 1 2 3 4 5

[Khamti script]
mâ sûn kau kai såṅg tô sü kà — _The day before yester-day_ I bought two fowls.
Word order: 1 2 5 4 3 — 1 2 3 4 5

[Khamti script]
tû kü mü tam khau û — We husk paddy _daily._
Word order: 1 4 2 3 — 1 2 3 4

[Khamti script]
nam chê _khün nâ_ _kau_ khai _kü mü_ _au mâ tâ_ — Bring milk and eggs _daily._
Word order: 2 3 4 4 1 — 1 2 3 4 5

[Khamti script]
kang laü† chaü mâ tâ (chaü chaü.) — Come _at dawn._
Word order: — 1 2

[Khamti script]
kâng khün mai pî‡ _mâ tâ_ — Don't come _at night._
Word order: 4 3 1 2 — 1 2 3 4

[Khamti script]
kau ngai kâ n' pen — I cannot go _now._
Word order: 1 5 4 3 2 — 1 2 3 4 5

[Khamti script]
kau mai ngai haü mâ — Give it to me _now._
Word order: 3 2 4 1 — 1 2 3 4

---

* [Khamti abbreviation sign] abbreviation for *lüng* = one, *vide* page 17 *ante.*

† Doubling of the mark ( ) denotes that the word is to be repeated.

‡ Locative case postposition.

မၼ်း မႃ ၸမ် တီ မႃ man mâ cham tî mâ 1 4 2 3	He will come presently. 1 2 3 4
မၼ်း ၵဝ် မႂ် ယေ ပၼ်း ၼၼ်း ဢူ man kau mai yê { pân pân } nan û 1 3 4 2	He scolds me sometimes. 1 2 3 4
မိုဝ် ၼၼ်း ၶႃ တူ ယင် ဢူ mü nan khâ tû yang û 1 4 2 3	Formerly we had slaves. 1 2 3 4
ၶုၼ် ၼႃ ၵဝ် ပၼ်း လိုင် ဝႃ တႃ khün nâ kau pân lüng wà tâ 3 2 1	Say (it) once more. 1 2 3
ၵဝ် ၵႃ ၼႃ ၽူၼ်း တူၵ် ၼႂ် * မၼ်း kau kâ nâ phôn tôk nai man 1 5 6 7 4 မႂ် ထိုင် ၵႃ mai thüng kâ 3 2	I arrived at the village 1 2 3 4 before rain fell. 6
မၼ်း ဢၼ်း တင် ယိုဝ် ၵႃ man ån tâng yü kâ 1 3 2	He fired first. 1 2 3
မိုဝ် ၵဝ် ဢၼ်း တင် မႃ ၼႂ် † မၼ်း mü kau ån tâng mâ nai man 1 2 3 4 5 မႂ် ယင် ဢူ ‡ mai yang û 7 6	When I first came he was 1 2 3 4 5 6 here. 7
ၵႃ လင် မႂ်ႈ မိုဝ် ၼႂ် † ၵဝ် ၼိုဝ် kâ lang maü mü nai kau nü 1 2 3 4 7 သင် တူဝ် ¶ ႁၼ်း ၵႃ sång tô han kâ 6 5	After you left I saw two 1 2 3 4 5 6 deer. 7

---

* *Phôn tôk nai* is a verbal noun = raining or rain falling.

† *Mâ nai* = coming; *mü nai* = leaving; and *yü nai* = firing, verbal nouns.

‡ *Û* the present tense suffix is here used to express past time, *vide* page 87 *ante*.

¶ *Tô* is a numeral particle used with animals.

wai lang[1] kau[2] yü nai*[3] nü[4] pai[5] kâ	After[1] I[2] fired[3] the deer[4] ran away[5].
kau[1] pî[4] nai[3] mai mâ thüng†[2] kâ	I[1] arrived[2] here[3] this year[4].
pî nâ[1] kau[2] hü[4] hôy‡ lüng¶[5] tî sü[3] nam‖	Next year[1] I[2] shall[3] buy[4] a[5] boat[6].
pî kai§[1] A[2] bors Miris[5] sî kô**[4] au tai kâ[3]	Last year[1] the Abors[2] killed[3] four[4] Miris[5].
tôk chem ngai[3] nü[1] n' pai[2] tai[4]	The deer[1] is not[2] yet[3] dead[4].
Tai[1] mâ laü kaw[2] †† n' lâk[3]	Khâmtîs[1] never[2] steal[3].
kau[1] man mai[4] kâ nâ[5] †† mâ laü kaw[2] n' han[3]	I[1] never[2] saw[3] him[4] before[5].

* *Ma nai* = coming; *mu nai* = leaving; and *yu nai* = firing, verbal nouns.

† *Mâ thüng* is a compound verb; *mâ* = come, *thüng* = arrive.

‡ *Hôy* is a numeral particle.

¶ is an abbreviation for *lüng* = one.

‖ *Nam* is an assertive particle.

§ *P* is used because the Khâmtî alphabet has no *b*.

** *Kô* is a numeral expletive used with human beings.

†† *Má laü kaw* = when, even, which, with the negative particle *ün* = never.

Shan	English
မႃ ၼႆ ၽႃ သင် ကေႃ ၼိတ်* ဢူ mâ[4] nai phâ[1] sang kaw[3] net[2] û	The[1] sun shone[2] at first[3] today.[4]
သီ လတ် ၼႆ ဢၼ် သင် ကေႃ သိုဝ် sî[4] lat nai[1] an sang kaw[2] sü[3]	This[1] (is) a newly[2] bought[3] gun.[4]
ၼင်† တီ တႆ nang[1] tî tai[2]	Nearly[1] dead.[2]
လႆ ပိုဝ် ၶုၼ် တင် မုၼ် ၼႆ ၵဝ် lai[1] pü khôn tâng[2] mûn[4] nai[3] kau[5] ၼင် တီ လုမ် nang[6] tî lôm	Owing to[1] (the) road[2] being[3] slippery[4] I[5] nearly[6] fell.[7]
သိပ် ပီ ထုၼ် ယဝ် sip[1] pî[2] thôn[3] yau	Ten[1] years[2] ago.[3]
မႃ မႆ တႃ‡ *or* မႆ မႆ¶ မႃ တႃ mâ[1] mai tâ[2] mai mai[2] mâ[3] tâ	Come[1] here.[2]
မၼ် မႆ¶ ဝႆ တႃ man mai wai tâ	Put (it) *there.*
ၵႃ ၼႃ *or* ၶင် ၼႃ ၵဝ် မႆ¶ သဝ် တႃ kâ nâ khâng[3] nâ[3] kau[4] mai[2] sau tâ[1]	Stand[1] in[2] front[3] of me.[4]
ၵုၼ် ဢၼ် ၵႃ ၵႃ ၼႃ မႆ¶ ၼႆ‖ ၽဝ် kôn[2] an[3] kâ[4] kâ[6] nâ[5] mai[4] nai phaü[1]	Who[1] (is) the man[2] who[3] (is) going[4] in[5] front.[6]

* *Phâ net* = sunshine, *phâ net û* = is sunny. This sentence means it was sunny during the first part of the day.

† *Nang* means like, resembling ; *tî* is the future tense suffix ; *nang tî tai* = like will die.

‡ *Tâ* (imperative suffix) belongs to *mâ*.

¶ *Mai* locative case postposition.

‖ *Nai* belongs to *kâ* = go ; *kâ nai* = going.

hâng khü (1) hôm kan (2) het* (2) â mû nam† (2) — We two (1) worked (2) together (3).

khâi nai‡ khau (1) hôm kan (3) û¶ nam† (2) — The buffaloes (1) were (2) together (3).

eng (3) nin (2) kâ (4) nü (4) 'chầng' (5) mai§ (4) wai tâ (5) — Put (1) the earth (2) (en) vessel (3) on (4) the 'chầng.' (5)

tai (3) khang (5) phai (4) mai§ (4) pî (1) kâ (2) tâ — Don't (1) go (2) near (3) (to) the (4) fire (5).

mü hü‖ (1) yê (3) nam ti** tang müng mai (4) yang (2) û — (In the) rainy season (1) there is (3) water (2) everywhere (4).

nü (1) tai (3) lêlê (2) yau — The deer (1) (is) quite (2) dead (3).

het (1) nang (2) ngai (3) tâ†† or â nai nâ kan (2) het tâ (1) — Do (1) (it) like (2) this (3).

---

* *Het* (spelt heek) means to do ; *het â mû* = do work.

† *Nam* is an affirmative particle.

‡ *Nai* is the demonstrative pronoun used here for emphasis and recognition. *Khai khau* (without *nai*) might mean their buffaloes.

¶ *Û* means stay, remain ; *hôm kan û* = remain together.

§ *Mai* is the locative case postposition.

‖ *Mü hü* means summer ; *yê* is the participial suffix.

** *Ti* = place ; *tang müng* = all, *mai* = in, *ti tang müng mai* = in all places, everywhere.

†† *Tâ* (imperative suffix) belongs to *het*.

ၽႃ ဢႃ ၼႆ ႁႂ်ႈ မႃ ၼီ သီ ယပ် ၵႃ။
phâ â nai maü mâ nî sî yap kâ
5 4 1 6 3 2

You have sewn this cloth badly.
1 2 3 4 5 6

သုၼ်* ၼီ သီ ၶုၼ် တႃ။
sûn nî nî sî khôn tâ
2 3 1

Mix the lime well.
1 2 3

ၵဝ် ၼႆ ၵႃ ၵေႃ ဢူ။
kau nai kâ kô û
1 5 4 3 2

I am afraid to go alone.
1 2 3 4

မၼ်း ၼႆ မႃ ၵႃ။
man nai mâ kâ
1 3 2

He came alone.
1 2 3

မႃ ၼႆ ၽုၼ် တီ တုၵ်း ၼ်ထိင် ထင်။
mâ nai phôn tî tôk n' thâng
5 1. 2 4 3

Rain will probably fall today.
1 2 3 4 5

မၼ်း တီ တေ သီ တီ မႃ။
man tî tê sî tî mâ
1 3 2 4

He will certainly come.
1 2 3 4

ၽႃ ဢႃ ၼႆ ဢွၼ် ဢူ လႆ ပိုၼ် ၼႆ သီ
phâ â nai ǎn û lai pü nai sî
2 1 4 3 5

ၵဝ် ငိုၼ်† သွင် တြႃ ၼ် ႁႂ်ႈ။
kau ngün sâng trâ n' haü
5 3 9 7 8

This cloth is small, therefore, I will not give two rupees.
1 2 3 4 5 6 7 8 9 10

ၶၼ်‡ သီ မႃ တႃ။
khan khan sî mâ tâ
2 1

Come quickly.
1 2

မၼ်း ၶႆ လူင် ဢူ။
man khai lông û
1 4 3 2

He is very ill.
1 2 3 4

တင် ၵႃ ႁဵင် မုၼ် ၼမ်။
tâng kâ hêng mûn nam
1 2 3

The road (is) very slippery.
1 3

* The doubling of the *i o* denotes that the word is to be repeated.

† *Ngün* = silver; *tra* = rupee; *ngün tra*=a rupee.

‡ The doubling of the final mark (ꩻ) denotes that the word is to be repeated.

ဢွ် ႁိုင် *or* ၵႃ ႁိုင် လိုတ် ဢူ။ au hêng kâ hêng lüt û 2 2 3 1	It is very hot. 1 2 3
ၵွ် မႂ် ၵုၼ် ၶိုၼ် ၼႃ ၵွ် လႂ် မႃ။ kau mai kôn khün nâ kau laü mâ 2 4 3 1	Give me more men. 1 2 3 4
ၶွ် သၼ် ၶႃ လႂ် ၶႃ ၼႂ် * သီ ဢူ khau sân khâ laü khâ nai sî û 1 2 3 ၵေႃ ဢွ် တႃ။ kaw au tâ 4 5	Take as much rice as you wish. Rice how much 1 2 requiring even take. 3 4 5
ၽၼ် † ၶွ် မၼ် ၶႂ် လိုင် ယင် ဢူ။ phan khau man khai lŭng yang û 2 3 1 4 5	His seed paddy this much is. 1 2 3 4 5 He possesses this much seed paddy.
မၢၼ် မႂ် ၵုၼ် ၶၼ် သွင် ပၵ် ယင် ဢူ။ mân mai kôn khan sâng pâk yâng û 7 6 5 2 3 4 1	There are about two hundred men in the village. 1 2 3 4 5 6 7
ၽုင် ၼႂ် မႂ် ၶႂ် ၶၼ် သမ် သိပ် phûng nai mai khâi khan sâm sip 7 6 5 4 2 3 ယင် ဢူ။ yang û 1	There are about thirty buffaloes in this herd. 1 2 3 4 5 6 7
ႁိုဝ် ဢႃ ၼႂ် ‡ ယွ် ၽိဝ်။ hü â nai yau phiau 2 1 4 3	This boat is too long. 1 2 3 4

* *Khâ nai* is a verbal noun; *sî û kaw* belongs to *khâ laü*; *khâ laü si û kaw* =how much, being are even, *i.e.*, as much as.

† *Phan* is equivalent to the Assamese *hâs* = seed grain, or animals kept specially for breeding.

‡ ိဝ် is the second diphthong mentioned at page 2 *ante*. The present tense suffix ၶ should be attached to it, but *phiau* is often used alone.

တပ် ဒြိပ္ဃူ ကႆ ၸိဝ် ဢူ ၵဝ် ၼ် ကႃ။
tâp Dibrû kai phiau û kau n' kâ
2 1 5 4 3 6 7 8

Dibrughur is too far, I will not go.
1 2 3 4 5 6 7 8

မူ ကံ ၸွင် ပီ ဢူ ကံ ၸွင် ယံ ဢူ။
mû kam phăng pî û kam phăng yăm û
2 1 4 3 5 7 6

Some pigs are fat some are lean.
1 2 3 4 5 6 7

This sentence may likwise be construed by using ဢႃ လုင်* ဢႃ လုင်* (â lüng â lüng) = one, one = some, *or* ယေ † တုဝ် ‡ (yê tô tô) = some, as—

မူ ဢႃ လုင်* ဢႃ လုင်* ပီ ဢူ
mû â lüng â lüng pî û
2 1 4
ဢႃ လုင်* ဢႃ လုင်* ယံ ဢူ။
â lüng â lüng yăm û
1 7 6

Some pigs are fat some are thin.
1 2 3 4 1 6 7

မူ ယေ တုဝ် ‡ ပီ ဢူ ယေ တုဝ် ‡ ယံ ဢူ။
mû yê tô tô pî û yê tô tô yăm û
2 1 4 5 7 6

Some pigs are fat some are thin.
1 2 3 4 5 6 7

ၵဝ် ၶႆ ႁေ¶ တုဝ်* လုင် ၼိုဝ်
kau khâi hê tô lüng nü
1 5 3 8
သွင်¶ တုဝ် ကေႃ ယိုဝ် ကႃ။
săng tô kaw yü kâ
7 6 2

I shot a wild buffalo, also two deer.
1 2 3 4 5 6 7 8

မႂ် မၼ် မႆ ႁိတ် သင် ပေႃ ကႃ။
maü man mai het sang pô kâ
3 5 1 4 2

Why did you strike him?
1 2 3 4 5

မႂ် ကႃ § မႆ (*or* ၼႃ မႆ) § မႃ။
maü kâ mai (nâ mai) mâ
1 2 3 3 4

Where have you been?
In Khâmti—
You go where come?
1 2 3 4

---

* လုင် is an abbreviation for *lüng* = one.

† The doubling of the mark (ᐟ) denotes the repetition of the word.

‡ *Yê kô kô*=some men, *kô* being a numeral particle used with human beings. *Yê tî tî* = some places; *tî* = place, spot.

¶ *Tô* is a numeral expletive used with animals.

§ *Kâ mâ* is a compound verb; *kâ* = go, *mâ* = come. It will be observed that the bare root is used for past time.

နူ ၼႃ မႂ် ဝႂ် ၵႃ။ } Where have you put (it)?
maü na mai wai kâ — 1 2 3 4
3 1 4 2

နူ မၼ် မႂ် * မႃ လူ ႁၼ် ၵႃ။ } When did you see him?
maü <u>man mai</u> mâ laü han kâ — 1 2 3 4 5
3 5 1 4 2

ၵွ် ႁိ လိုဝ် ယိ တိ ႁိတ် } How shall I do it?
kau <u>hî lü sî</u> tî het — 1 2 3 4
3 1 2 4

The adverbial suffix is ယိ (sî), as—

ၶၼ် ယိ † (khan khan sî) *or* ၸဵဝ် ယိ (çheô sî) = quickly.

ၼိ ယိ (nî nî sî) = well, &c., &c.

A few of the adverbs are repeated for the sake of emphasis, as ၶၼ် † (khan khan) = quickly, လွႆ † (loi loi) = slowly, &c., &c., &c.

ဢွ် (au) = with, instrument.

တင် (tang) = with, along with, by way of.

ႁင် (hang) = for, for the purpose of.

ပုၼ် (pôn) = past, beyond.

တႂ် ၶင် မႂ် ‡ (tai khang mai) = adjacent to.

ၵႃ ၼူ မႂ် ‡ (ka nü mai) = within, inside.

ၵႃ ၼွၵ် မႂ် ‡ (kâ nâk mai) = without, outside.

မႃ ယင် ¶ (mâ yang) = without, otherwise than with.

ၵႃ ၼိုဝ် မႂ် * (kâ nü mai) = upon, at the top of, also up stream.

ၵႃ တူ မႂ် * (ka taü mai) = down, below.

လုၵ် (lûk) = from.

ၶိုင် ၵင် မႂ် * (khüng kâng mai) = in the middle.

ဝင် ၵင် မႂ် * (wâng kâng mai) = between.

ၵႃ (kâ) = until.

---

* *Mai* is the accusative case postposition.

† The doubling of the marks ႈ, ႉ, and ႊ denote that the word is to be repeated.

‡ *Mai* is the locative case postposition.

¶ *Yang* is the substantive verb with the negative verbal prefix attached.

The English prepositions *to, unto, in, into, on,* and *at* are made by using the postposition မ' (mai).

Examples.

(Illustrating how Prepositions are used.)

တ' ၶင် မႃ မ' ပီ ကႃ တႃ။ tai khâng[3] mâ[4] mai pî[1] kâ[2] tâ	Don't[1] go[2] near[3] the horse.[4]
ႏူ ကတ် ကႃ ယေ တ' ၶင် ၽ' မ' maü[2] kat[3] kâ[1] yê tai khâng[5] phai[7] mâi[6] ၼင် တႃ။ nang[4] tâ	If[1] you[2] are cold[3] sit[4] near[5] to[6] the fire.[7]
ၼူ ကႃ ၼူ ႁူ မ' ယင် ဢူ။ nü[1] kâ naü[3] hû[4] mai yang[2] û	The mouse[1] is[2] inside[3] the hole.[4]
ကႃ ႁွၵ် ႁိူၼ် မ' လိုတ် လိုမ် ဢူ။ * kâ hâk[1] hün[2] mai lüt[4] lüm û[3]	Outside[1] the house[2] it is[3] warmer.[4]
ႁွၵ် † မႃ ယင် ယေ ကၢဝ် ကႃ ၼ'ပိၼ်။ håk mâ[5] yang[4] yê kau[1] ka[3] n' pen[2]	I[1] cannot[2] go[3] without[4] a spear.[5]
ကႃ ၼိုဝ် ၸင် မ' ၶီ တႃ။ kâ nü[2] châng[3] mai khî[1] tâ	Mount[1] upon[2] the elephant.[3]
ကႃ ၼိုဝ် ၼွႆ မ' မွႆ ယင် ဢူ။ kâ[6] nü noi[4] mai môy[3] yang[1] û	There is[1] snow[2] on[3] the hill.[4]
ကၢဝ် ငူ မ' ဢၢဝ် ႁိၼ် ဢၢဝ် တ' ကႃ။ kau[1] ngû mai[3] au[4] hin[5] au tai kâ[2]	I[1] killed[2] the snake[3] with[4] a stone.[5]

---

* *Û* (present tense suffix) belongs to *lüt* (hot) ; *lüm* is a comparative suffix.

† *Hăk ma yang yê* = spear not possessing.

ၼူ တင် ကွ် တပ် တြိုပ်ူ မႆ တီ
maü tang kau tâp Dibrû mai tî
2 4 5 8 7 6 1
ကႃ ကေ်။*
kâ kê
3

Will you go with me to Dibrughur.
1 2 3 4 5 6 7 8

ဢႃ ၼႆ ႁင် ၼူ။
â nai hang maü
1 2 3

This is for you.
1 2 3

ငိုၼ် ၼႆ ႁင် သိုဝ် ကႆ။
ngün nai hang sü kai
2 1 3 4 5

This money is for purchasing fowls.
1 2 3 4 5

မိုဝ် ၼႆ ကွ် လပ် မိပ် သီ† ဢူ ကႃ
mü nai kau lâp mep sî û kâ
1 2 4 3
လႆ ပိုဝ် ၼႆ ၶႆ ႁေ ကွ် မႆ မႃ ႁၼ် သီ
lai pü nai khâi hê kau mai mâ han sî
5 7 6 10 8 9
လိၼ် ပွၼ် ကႃ။‡
len pôn ka
11 12

Then I remained hiding, therefore the wild buffalo not seeing me ran past.
1 2 3 4 5 6 7 8 9 13 11 12

ၶိုင် ကင် ႁိုဝ် မႆ ၼင် တႃ
khüng kâng hü mai nang tâ
3 4 2 1

Sit in the middle of the boat.
1 2 3 4

ဝင် ကင် ၼမ် သွင် ၶေ¶ မႆ ထိုၼ်
wông kâng nam sâng khê mai thün
3 5 4 5 2
ယင် ဢူ
yang û
1

There is jungle between the two rivers.
1 2 3 4 5

From the above examples it will be seen that prepositions *precede* their nouns.

---

* *Kê* is in the interrogative particle.
† *Lâp mep sî* = having hidden ; *û kâ* = remained.
‡ This *ka*, past tense suffix, belongs to the root verb *len*=run.
¶ *Nam khê* or *khê* ; *nam* = a river.

19—*Conjunctions.*

ကော (kaw) = and, also (copulative).

လႆ ပိုၼ် ၼႆ (lai pü nai) = therefore.

သင် (sang) = if (conditional).

လႆ ပိုၼ် ၼႆ (lai pü nai) = because.

Made by using ကႆ *kai*, a particle of probability, *vide* illustrative sentences post. } = either, or

တော ၼႆ ဢူ ကော } *or* (tô nai û kaw) } = but.
တော ဝါ } (tô wâ)

Made by using the past participle သီ in conjunction with ကော (kaw) even, *vide* examples post. } = although.

Made by a participle and a negative particle, *vide* examples post. } = unless, if not.

ၼင် (nang) = as, like.

Examples.

(*Illustrating how used.*)

မႂ် ကော * ကဝ် ကော မၼ်း ကော တီ တါ } You and I and he will go.
maü kaw kau kaw man kaw tî kâ

[1 3 2 5 4 6 7] — You [1] and [2] I [3] and [4] he [5] will [6] go [7].

ကော (kaw) connects *words* only. In *sentences* where in English the conjunction *and* would be used, Khâmtîs use a participle, as—

Examples.

ကတ် မႆ † ကါ သီ ကႆ တူဝ် ၵႆႈ သိုဝ် တါ } Go to the 'hat' and buy a fowl.
kat mai kà sî kai tô lüng sü tà

[3 2 1 6 5 4] — Go [1] to the [2] 'hat' and [3] buy [4] a [5] fowl [6].

---

* *Khâmtis* say I and, you and, he and!

† *Ka sî*=having gone, past participle.

တုဝ် ဢွၼ်မႝ* ၼမ် မႝ† ဢွ် ၵႃ သီ
tô ân mai nam mai au kâ sî
1 2 3 4
ၼမ် ဢွ်‡ ဢၢပ် တႃ
nam au âp tâ
5

Take the child to the river and bathe it.
Child river to taking bathe (it).
1 2 3 4 5

When put *after* a noun or pronoun ၵေႃ (kaw) means, *also*, as—

Examples.

ၵဝ် ၼိုဝ် ၵေႃ ယိုဝ် ၵႃ။
kau nü kaw yü kâ
1 3 4 2

I shot (a) deer also.
1 2 3 4

ၵဝ် ၵေႃ ဢူ မၼ် ၼမ်။
kau kaw û man nam
1 2 3 4

I also was there.
1 2 3 4

The following sentence will illustrate how *either*, *or*, are made in Khâmtî :—

ၵဝ် ၵႝ¶ မႂ် ၵႝ¶ ၽိတ်
kau kai mau kai phet
1 2 3 2 4

I or you (are) false.
1 2 3 4

This sentence can be construed as follows: likewise,—

မႂ် မႃ ၸႂ်† ၵဝ် ၽိတ်
maü mâ chaü kau phet
1 2 3 4 5

You not are I false.
1 2 3 4 5

or as follows :—

မႂ် မႃ ၸႂ်§ ယေ ၵဝ် ၽိတ်
maü mâ chaü yê kau phet
1 2 3 4 5

You not being I false.
1 2 3 4 5

မႃ ၵဝ် ၼင် မႃ မႂ် ၼိုဝ် ၼမ်
mâ kau nang mâ maü n' nam
1 2 3 4 5 6 7

My dog is not as black as yours.
Dog my like dog yours not black.
1 2 3 4 5 6 7

---

* *Mai*=accusative case suffix.

† *Mai*=locative case postposition.

‡ *Au*=casual prefix particle.

¶ *Kai* is a particle of vague probability like the Assamese *bá*.

§ *Chaü* is the substantive verb. In the last sentence it has the participial *yê* suffixed; *mâ chaü yê*=not being.

SYNTAX.

Having enumerated a few leading rules I will follow the plan adopted in my Miri and Singpho Outline Grammars, namely, give an additional number of illustrative sentences arranged in groups and numbered with reference to the sentences bearing the same numbers in the accidence, as I feel sure that these sentences will, with their explanatory notes, do more to give any future student an insight into the structure of the language than any syntactical *rules* I may be able to formulate with my present comparatively limited knowledge of the language.

General Rules.

(*a*) The adjective follows the noun it qualifies.

(*b*) Numerals sometimes precede, at others follow, the nouns they qualify. When a numeral particle is used they invariably *follow* the noun they qualify.

(*c*) Demonstrative pronouns are generally placed immediately *after* the nouns they qualify, except in relative clauses when they may *either* be put at the *beginning* or at the *end* of the sentence, as—

Examples.

ၵုၼ်	ဢၼ်	ဢွ်	တႝ	ငဝ်*	ၼႝ	ဢႃ	ၼႝ
kôn	an	au	tai	ngô	nai	â	nai
1	2		3	4	3		5

This is the man who killed the cow.
Man (1) who (2) killing (3) cow (4) this (5).

or

ဢႃ	ၼႝ	ၵုၼ်	ဢၼ်	ဢွ်	တႝ	ငဝ်*	ၼႝ
â	nai	kôn	an	au	tai	ngô	nai
	1	2	3		4	5	4

ၸွႝ ဢူ
chaü û
6

This (1) man (2) who (3) killing (4) cow (5) is (6).

(*d*) Relativo clauses stand *before* antecedent clauses.

(*e*) Interrogative pronouns rarely ever stand *first* in a sentence.

(*f*) Adverbs are *generally* placed *after* a verb.

* *Nai* belongs to the transitive root verb *au tai* = kill; *au tai nai* is a verbal noun.

ကႃ ၶၼ်* တႃ။

kâ {khan khan} tâ — Go quickly.
(kâ 1, khan 2, tâ 1; Go 1, quickly 2)

This sentence would, however, be equally correct; thus—

ၶၼ်* ကႃ တႃ။ *or* ၶၼ်* သီ ကႃ တႃ။

khan khan kâ tâ khan khan si kâ tâ — Go quickly.
(khan khan 2, kâ 1; Go 1, quickly 2)

(*a*) Adverbs of time are *generally* placed *before* the verb, as—

ၵွင် ငႝ တီ ကႃ

kau ngai tî kâ — Now I will go.
(kau 2, ngai 1, tî 3, kâ 4; Now 1, I 2, will 3, go 4)

မႃ ၼႝ လိုတ် ဢူ

mâ nai lüt û — Today (it) is hot.
(mâ nai 1, lüt 3, û 2; Today 1, is 2, hot 3)

(*b*) Adverbs are often placed *after* adjectives to *intensify* their meaning, as—

ၵုၼ် ထွင် လုင်

kôn thau lông — (A) very old man.
(kôn 3, thau 3, lông 1; very 1, old 2, man 3)

(*g*) Prepositions *precede* their nouns, as ကႃ ၼႂ် ႁိူၼ် = inside the house.

(*h*) The order of words in a predicative sentence are (1) subject, (2) direct object, (3) indirect object, and (4) verb.

2. In an interrogative sentence the order is (1) subject, (2) indirect object, (3) direct object, and (4) verb.

Khâmtîs are fond of flattery; hence when a man addresses a superior in writing numerous words (the meaning of which is obscure) head his epistle. The three words most often met with are ၸွ ပႃ လိုင် = *chau pa lüng*, somewhat, though not quite, equivalent to the Bengali "hozur" (your honour);

* The doubling of the mark (ᵔ) denotes that the word is to be repeated.

ဢေႃ ဝႃ တႃ = *aw wá tá*, the meaning of which I cannot get, even approximately, and ꩡွ် ꩣေꩬ် ꩡူ = *chau kê chú*, somewhat, though not quite, resembling the Bengali "dharmabotar."

တိ ၶႃ tî khâ, the meaning of which I cannot get, is also invariably used by a man when addressing a superior. It is tacked on to the end of every answer given, thus; if I address a Khâmtî as follow: "Are you well," he would reply:

ꩫိ တိ ၶႃ ဢူ "Nî tî khâ û, (I) am well," the û being the present tense suffix, and belonging to nî. Again, supposing a Khâmtî wished to ask me the question: "Shall I come tomorrow?" He would say,—

ꩣွ် မႃ ႁွꩬ် တိ မႃ တိ ၶႃ ꩣေꩬ်
kau mâ hôk tî mâ tî khâ kê
2 4 1 3

} Shall I come tomorrow?
1 2 3 4

"*Kê*" is simply the interrogative particle.

A favourite method of greeting a superior in writing is as follows:—

ꩫမ် ဝꩫ် ၶမ် ꩫိ ꩣွ် ꩡွ်
nam wân khâm nî kau chau
2 1 4 3 5

ꩫီ လွ်* မႃ တိ မႂ် ꩡွ် သႃ
ngî lau mâ tî maü chau sâ
6 7 8

ႁိꩬ် လုင် မႂ် ꩫမ်
heb lông mai nam.
10 9

Literally rendered:
Sweet water good words of
1 2 3 4
chaungi sent to you 'bara'
5 6 7 8 9
sahib
10

Freely rendered:
Chaungi greets your honour with expressions of respect.

A few examples showing how *ti khá, chau kê chú*, &c., are used.

ꩡွ် ꩣေꩬ် ꩡူ ꩣွ် ၶႃ ꩫိုꩫ်† မွတ်‡
chau kê chû kau khâ ngün môt
1 2 3 4 5

တိ ၶႃ ယွ်
tî khâ yau
5

Honoured Sir! Your slave's rupees are finished.
1 2 3 4 5
(Said to me by my teacher who had received money for bazaar expenses).

* *Lau* means tell, inform, and *ma* come; but *lau má* here means despatched, sent.

† *Kau khâ ngün* = literally "I slave's money;" *trá kau khá* = literally "I slave's complaint."

‡ *Môt yau* (the suffix *yau* is put at end of sentence) = done, finished.

ၸွ် ကေဝ် ၸူး တြႃ* ကွ် ၶႃ ၸမ်‡
chau kê chû tra kau khâ cham
3 1 2
ဢႃ ၼႆ‖
â nai
4

Honoured Sir! Your[1] slave's[2] complaint[3] is this.[4]

ၸွ် ကေဝ် ၸူး ကွ် ၶႃ ၶႃ ၵႃ ႁိူၼ်
chau kê chû kau kha khâ kâ hün
1 2 3 4 5 6
တီ ၶႃ ဢူ ¶ တႆ ၵေႃ ကွ် ၼႆ § လႆ ၵွတ်း
tî kha û tai kô kau nai lai kåt
10 9 8 7
သၢင် ဝႃ ၸွ် ပႃ လိူင် ပွႆ ၵႃ ၸမ် ‖ ကွ်
sang wâ chau pâ lüng poi kâ cham kau
11 12 13 14
ၶႃ မိူဝ် ပိၼ် တီ ၶႃ ဢူ ကွ် ၶႃ ႁိူၼ် မႆ
khâ mü pen tî kha û kau khâ hün mai
15 17 16 18 19 23 22
ႁႃ ဝၼ်း ဢူ သီ ပၢၵ် မႃ ၵွတ်း
hâ wan û sî påk ma kåt
24 25 21 20 27 26

Honoured Sir! I[1] slave[2] desire[3] to[4] go[5] home.[6] I will[7] change[8] my[9] companion.[10] If[11] your honour send[12] (me) I[13] slave[14] can[15] return (home)[16] I[17] slave[18] having[19] remained[20] at home[21] five[22] days[23] will[24] return.[25][26][27]

---

* *Kau khâ ngün* = literally "I slave's money;" *trâ kau khâ* = literally "I slave's complaint."

‡ *Cham* is a participial particle, denoting an hypothesis.

¶ *Û* (present tense suffix) belongs to *kha* = desire, wish; *kau kha* = I slave; *kha* = desire; *ka* = to go; *hüm* = home (*hün* = literally house).

§ *Nai* is a demonstrative pronoun, used here for emphasis and recognition; it belongs here to *tai kô* = companion.

‖ *Poi kâ cham* = sending; conditional participle.

NOUNS.

1.—Gender.

မူ ကွ် လုက် သီ တူဝ် ယင် ဢူ သွင် mû kau lûk sî tô yang û sâng 2 1 5 4 3 6 တူဝ် * မူ ထိုက် သွင် တူဝ် * မူ မေ tô mû thük sâng tô mû mê 7 8 9	My pig has four young (ones), two male (and) two female. 1 2 3 4 5 6 7 8 9
မန် ငူဝ် † ထႝ ၼႝ သွင် ပင် ယင် ဢူ man ngô thaî naî sang pang yang û 1 6 5 3 4 2	He has two pair of ploughing bullocks. 1 2 3 4 5 6
ကွ် မေ ၵႃ မန် ကုၼ် ‡ ၽၼ် kau mê khâ man kôn phan 1 2 3 2	I (am) a poor Mishme woman. 1 2 3 4
ကွ် ၼင် ¶ သွ် သွင် ကုဝ် ၼင် ¶ ၸႝ ကုဝ် kau nâng sau sâng tô nâng chai kô 1 4 3 6 လိုင် ‖ ယင် ဢူ lüng yang û 5 2	I have two sisters (and) one brother. 1 2 3 4 5 6
ယႃ ထွ် ၼႝ § ၶုဝ် ပွင် ဢူ yâ thau nai khô pâng û 1 3 5 4	The old woman has goitre. *In Khâmti* the old woman's neck is swollen. 1 2 3 3 5
ကွ် ၵႃ ပယိင် သွင် ကုဝ် ၵႃ သိုဝ် ဢူ** kau khâ paying sâng kô khâ sü û 1 6 5 4 2 3	I want to purchase two female slaves. 1 2 3 4 5 6

---

* *Tô* is a numeral expletive used with animals.

† *Ngô* means a quadruped of the bovine genus. The word *thai* (plough) shows here its gender.

‡ *Kôn phan* means poor person.

¶ *Nâng sau*=younger sister ; *nâng chai*, younger brother.

‖ Abbreviated form of *lüng* =one.

§ *Nai* is the demonstrative pronoun used here for recognition.

** This *û* (present tense suffix) belongs to *khâ sü*, the bare root of the verb buy, is used for the infinitive, *vide* page 49 *ante*.

ႁႂ် ၼိုဝ် တူဝ် ထိုၵ် ၵေႃ* တူဝ် မေ ၵေႃ* ယိုဝ် ၵႃ maü[2] nü[7] tô[4] thük kê[5] tô mê[6] kê yü kâ[3]	Did[1] you[2] shoot[3] a male[4] or[5] female[6] deer[7]?
ၵဝ် ၵႃ ယိုဝ် ၶႆ တူဝ် ထိုၵ် ၼမ်† kau[1] kâ[2] yü[3] khâi[5] tô thük[4] nam	I[1] (am go (ing)[2] (to) shoot[3] (a) bull[4] buffalo[5].
ၵဝ် ၼႆ လိင် တူဝ် မေ ဢဝ် မႃ kaû[2] mai ling[4] tô mè[3] au mâ[1]	Bring[1] me[2] a female[3] monkey[4].
ငူဝ် တူဝ် မေ တိၼ် ႁၢၼ် ၵေႃ ngô tô mê[1] tin han[2] kê	(Is) the cow[1] lame[2]?

2.—*Number.*

တူဝ် ဢွၼ် ၼႆ ၶဝ် လဵၼ် ဢူ tô ån nai khau[1] len[3] û[2]	The children[1] are[2] playing[3].

3.—*Case.*

တူဝ် ဢွၼ် ႁႆ ဢူ tô ån[1] hai[3] û[2]	The child[1] is[2] crying[3].
ငူဝ် ႁႂ် သိုဝ် ၵပ် ၵႃ ngô[5] maü[4] sü[1] kâp[3] kâ[2]	The tiger[1] has[2] bitten[3] your[4] cow[5].
ၵူၼ် ၼႆ ပၢတ် ၶဝ် ဢူ kôn[2] nai[1] pat[4] khau[5] û[3]	The[1] man[2] is[3] cutting[4] paddy[5].
ၵူၼ် ၵူဝ် လိုင် ၼမ် ၼႆ တုၵ် ၵႃ kôn[2] kô[1] lüng nam[6] mai[5] tôk[4] kâ[3]	A[1] man[2] has[3] fallen into[4] the river[6].
တိၼ် ငူဝ် တူဝ် မေ ႁၢၵ် ၵႃ tin[2] ngô tô mê[1] hâk[3] kâ	The cow's[1] leg[2] is broken[3].
ဢႃ ၼႆ ႁူၼ် မႃ ၵေႃ* â nai[1] khôn[3] mâ[2] kê	Is this[1] horse[2] hair[3]?

* *Kè* is the interrogative particle.
† *Nam* is a particle of assertion.

ၵိဝ် မုၼ် ၽႝ လုင် ဢူ	kheo môn phai lông û 2 1 5 4 3	Otter's teeth are very sharp. 1 2 3 4 5
လုက် ငူဝ် တူဝ် မေ ၾိုက် ၵွ် တႝ ၵႃ	lûk ngô tô mê phük kau tai kâ 4 3 2 1 5	My white cow calf (is dead) died. 1 2 3 4 5
မႃ ၼႝ * ႁၢင် တႃ	mâ mai hång tâ 2 1	Call (the) dog. 1 2
မႂ် သိုဝ် ၼႝ * ႁၼ် ၵႃ ၵေ †	maü sü mai han kâ kê 2 4 3 1	Have you seen the tiger? 1 3 4 4
မႂ် ၼိုဝ် ၼႝ * ထုက် ၵႃ ၵေ †	maü nü mai thôk kâ kê 2 4 3 1	Did you hit the deer? 1 2 3 4
ၶွ် သၼ် လိုဝ် ၼႝ ‡ ၵႝ ၼႝ ၶွ် ၼႝ ¶ ႁႂ် တႃ	khau sân lü nai kaî nai khau mai haü tâ 4 3 2 1	Give the fowls the surplus rice. 1 2 4 3
လုက် တူဝ် ဢၼ် ၼႝ ‖ မိတ် ဢွ် တႃ	lûk tô ân mai mit au tâ 3 4 2 1	Take the knife from the child. 1 2 3 4
လုက် သႃႁဝ် ၼႝ ၵေ§ မႂ် ယမ် ၼႝ ၵႃ	lûk saheb mai kê maü yâm nai kâ 5 6 5 2 4 3 1	Did you get the powder from the sahib? 1 2 3 4 5 6
မႂ် ၵင် မႂ် လုက် ၼႝ ၼႝ ††	maü kång maü lûk mai nai 2 5 4 6 1 3	Where (do) you get your poison from 1 2 3 4 5 6
မႂ် ဝႃ ၵႃ တပ် တိပြူ ၼႝ	maü wâ kâ tâp Dibrû mai 1 2 3 6 5 4	You must go to Dibrughur. 1 2 3 4 5 6

---

* *Mai* is the accusative case postposition.
† *Kê* is the interrogative particle.'
‡ *Lü nai* is a verbal noun meaning remaining.
¶ *Kai nai khau*=fowls ; *mai*=to give to the fowls.
‖ This *mai* belongs to *lûk mai*, meaning from.
§ *Ke* is the interrogative particle. If it was put at the end of this sentence, *lük saheb mai maû yâm nai kâ* would mean ' have you received the powder, either promised or owed, from the sahib.
†† *Nai*=bare root of verb to obtain, used for present case.

မိုဝ် ကွ် ခ် ကၢ ယင် ကေၢ ဆိုဝ် ယင် mü kau mai <u>kâ sang kaw</u> n' yang 3 2 1 4 5	I have nothing in my hand. In my hand nothing exists. 1 2 3 4 5
ၼိတ် ခ် ဝ် တၢ net mai wai tâ 3 2 1	Put (it) in (the) sun. 1 2 3
ၸၢ ခ် ႁူ ယင် ဢူ phâ mai hû yang û 4 3 2 1	There is a hole in the cloth. 1 2 3 4
ကၢ ၼိူဝ် တုၼ် ခ် ဢၢ ၼၼ် ခ် ၼုၵ် kâ nü tôn mai â nan mai nôk 4 6 5 3 3 တူဝ် လိုင် ယင် ဢူ tô lüng yang û 1-a 1	There is a* bird on the top of that tree. 1 1-a 2 3 4 5 6
ႁူ ဢၢ ၼ် ခ် ငူ ယင် ဢူ ၵေ် † hû â nai mai ngû yang û kê 5 4 3 2 1	Is the snake in this hole? 1 2 3 4 6

4.—*Adjectives.*

ႁိူဝ် မႂ် hû maû 2 1	A new boat. 1 2
ၸၢ တုၼ် phâ tün 2 1	A torn cloth. 1 2
မႃ ၼမ် mâ nam 2 1	A black dog. 1 2
ၼမ် လိုၵ် nam lük 2 1	Deep water. 1 2
ခ် ၼ် ‡ ယွ် ဢူ mai nai yau û 2 1 4 3	The bamboo is long. 1 2 3 4
တုၼ် ခ် ၼ် သုင် ဢူ <u>tôn mai</u> nai sûng û 2 1 4 3	The tree is high. 1 2 3 4

* I have put *1-a* here because the sentence is wrongly numbered. *Tô lüng* is here equivalent to our *a* (a one) certain one.

† *Kê* is the interrogative particle.

‡ *Nai*=demonstrative pronoun used here for emphasis and recognition.

Comparison.

ႁိူဝ် ဢႃ ၼႆ ၶိုၼ် ယႂ် hü â nai khen yaü 2 1 3 4	This boat (is larger) more large. 1 2 3 4
ၽႃ ဢၼ် ၶိုၼ် မၢင် ၼႆ ၵဝ် မႆ * ၸီ တႃ phâ an khen mâng nai kau mai chî tâ 3 4 5 6 7 2 1	Show me (a thinner cloth) cloth which more thin being. 1 2 3 4 5 6
ၶဝ် သၢၼ် ဢၼ် ၶိုၼ် ၶဝ် ၼႆ ၶဝ် မႆ khau sân an khen khau nai khau mai 3 4 5 6 7 2 ဢဝ် မႃ တႃ au mâ tâ 1	Bring me (whiter rice) rice which more white being. 1 2 3 4 5 6 7
လုၵ် ဢွၼ် ဢႃ ၼၼ် မႆ † လုၵ် ဢွၼ် lûk ân â nan mai lûk ân 1 2 3 4 ဢႃ ၼႆ ၶိုၼ် သုင် â nai khen sûng 5 6 7	This child is taller than that; child that from child this more tall. 1 2 3 4 5 6 7
ၶဝ် သၢၼ် ဢႃလႂ် ၶိုၼ် ၼီ လိူမ် ‡ တင်မိုင် khau sân âlaü khen nî lüm tângmüng. 1 2 3 4 5 6	Which is the best rice of all? Rice which more good than all. 1 2 3 4 5 6
ငူဝ် ၵဝ် ဢၼ် ၶိုၼ် ၼီ လိူမ် တင် မိုင် ngô kau an khen nî lüm tang müng 2 1 3 4 5 6 7 ၵဝ် ၶႆ ၵႃ kau khai kâ 8 10 9	I have sold my best cow. My cow which more good than all I have sold. 1 2 3 4 5 6 7 8 9 10

* *Mai*=dative case postposition.
† *Mai*=accusative case postposition.
‡ *Lüm* would be more correct with the participial suffix *si*.

5.—*Numeral Adjectives.*

ကုၼ် ဢၼ် ၵႂ် တင် ႁုၵ် ကုဝ် * ကတ် မႂ် kôn an kau tâng hôk kô kat mai 3 4 5 6 2 8 7 ႁၼ် ကႃ han kâ 1	(I) saw six persons whom I know at the 'hat.' 1 2 3 4 5 6 7 8
မႂ်ႇ ပီ ၼႂ် မၼ် တူ မႂ် ကုၼ် သိပ် သၢမ် ကုဝ် * maü pî nai mân tû mai kôn sip sâm kô 1 3 2 9 8 7 5 4 တႂ် ကႃ ယဝ်ႉ † ႁုၵ် ကုဝ် * ပႃ ၸႂ် ၸိတ် ကုဝ် * tai kâ yau hôk kô pa chaî chet kô 6 10 11 12 ပႃ ယိင်း လုၵ် ဢၼ် ၽႃ ႁၼ် ‡ ၼႃ ပိတ် ကုဝ် * pâ ying lûk ân phwa han na pet kô 13 15 16 14 ႁႃ ကုဝ် ပႃၸႂ် သၢမ် ကုဝ် ပႃ ယိင်း hâ kô pâchai sâm kô pâ ying 17 18 19 20	During this year thirteen people died in our village, six males (and) seven females. Eight children (were) born, five males (and) three females. 1 2 3 4 5 6 7 8 9 10 11 12 13 14 15 16 17 18 19 20
ကုၼ် သွင် ကုဝ် ႁိုဝ် မႂ် ႁႂ်¶ ကႃ တႃ kôn sâng kô hü mai haü kâ tâ 3 2 6 5 1 4 ၶိုၼ် ၼႃ ၵႂ် ကုၼ် သီ ကုဝ် တင် ၸၢင် khün nâ kau kôn sî kô tang châng 7 10 9 11 12 ပွႆ ႁႂ်¶ တႃ poi haü ta 8	Let two men go in the boat (and) send four men with (the) elephants. 1 2 3 4 5 6 7 8 9 10 11 12

* *Kô* is a numeral expletive used with human beings.
† *Yau* is a vebal particle denoting completion of au act.
‡ *Han*=see ; *na*=a face ; *phwa han na* means came into life.
¶ *Haü*=give, is used as a causative imperative, *vide* page 48 *ante*.

ႁၢင် ၶိုဝ် ၵၢင် သၢင် တူဝ် ၶႆ ႁေ
hang khü kâng sâng tô khâi hê
1 4 3 7 6
တူဝ် * လုင် † ၼႆ ၵႃ
tô lüng nai kâ
5 2

We (two) got two sambur (and) a wild buffalo.
1 2 3 4 5 6 7

မၢင်ငႃ ၵၢင် ၶိုၼ် မႆ ‡ သိုဝ် တူ * လုင် †
mângâ kâng khün mai sü tô lüng
1 2 4 3
မၢၼ် မႆ ၶဝ် သီငူဝ် သၢင်တူဝ် * ၵပ်ၵႃ
mân mai khau sî ngô sâng tô kâp kâ
6 5 9 8 7

Last night a tiger entering the village bit two cattle.
1 2 3 4 5 6 7 8 9

ၵဝ် ၶႃ ၼႆ ၶႆ သီႁွႆ ၼႆ
kau kha nai khai sî hôy nai
1 3 5 4 2

I only require (requiring) four eggs.
1 2 3 4 5

ႁၵ်လဵမ် ¶ ၼႆ ၼ်သိမ် သိမ်
hâk lem nai n' sem
2 1 3 4

The spear is not sharp.
1 2 3 4

မၢၼ်ဢႃ ၼႆ မႆ သီလတ်သီလဝ် ‖ ယၢင် ဢူ
mân â nai mai sî lat sî lau yang û
6 5 4 3 2 1

There are four guns in this village.
1 2 3 4 5 6

Pronouns.

6.—Personal Pronouns.

ၵဝ် တႃ မူတ်
kau tâ mot
1 2

I (am) blind.
1 2

မႂ် မၢၼ် မႆ ႁၢင် တႃ
maü man mai hâng tâ
1 3 2

You call him.
1 2 3

မၢၼ် မၢၼ် မႆ ယၢင် ဢူ
mân man mai yang û
1 4 3 2

He is in the village.
1 2 3 4

---

* *Tô* is a numeral expletive used with animals.

† လုင် is an abbreviation for *lüng*.

‡ *Mai* is postposition, meaning in or during (the night)

¶ *Lem* is a numeral expletive used in enumerating spears, &c.

‖ *Lau* is a numeral particle used with guns.

Khamti (romanized, with word order)	English
kau mai (2) haü mâ (1)	Give (1) (it) to me (2).
tû (1) mâ (4) hôk tî (2) mâ (3)	We (1) will (2) come (3) tomorrow (4).
khau (1) khâ pâ (2) *	They (1) fish (2).
tû (1) Tai (2) kem (3) khâ (4) nam †	We (1) Khâmtîs (2) keep (3) slaves (4).

The following sentences are given to illustrate the remarks made at page 24 *ante* :—

Khamti (romanized, with word order)	English
maü chau (2) kau mai (4) bång (3) kâ (1) kê ‡	Did (1) you (2) call (3) me (4) (an inferior speaking) ?
mân chau (1) ân (3) ngün (4) û (2) ¶	He (1) is (2) counting (3) the money (4).
pai (1) hâ (2) kâ (3) yü (4) nü (5) kåt ‖	Let (1) *us* (2) go (3) shoot (4) deer (5).
hang khü (1) hôm kan (4) kham (2) nam (3) kâ §	We two (1) crossed (2) the river (3) together (4).
sång khü (1) mâ (2) het (3) trâ (4) kê ‡	Have you both (1) come (2) to make (3) a complaint (4).
sång khâ (1) kau mai (3) pau mâ (2)	They both (1) abuse (2) me (3).

* *Khâ pâ* = *literally* search fish.
† *Nam* is a particle of assertion.
‡ *Kê* is interrogative.
¶ *Û* belongs to *ân* = count ; *ân û* = is counting.
‖ *Kåt* belongs to *kâ* = go ; *kâ kåt* = will go.
§ *Kâ* belongs to *kham* = cross ; *kham kâ* = crossed.

khau hau sûk mâ û	Our paddy is (ripening) coming ripe.
thûng Tai tû cham nang nai n' chaü	This is not our Khâmtî custom. Our Khâmtî custom is not this wise.

8.—Relative Pronouns.

nü mü an û noi mai cham tî peng mai û ma pen	Animals that live in the hills cannot live in the plains.
lim an kau yü nü nai â nai chaü û	This is the arrow which I shot the deer with.
hü an châm nai ngai yê han û	The boat which sunk (can) now (be seen) see.
kôn an maü han nai kau nam chaü û *or*	I am the man whom you saw.
kôn lâk sî lat kau nai maü nam	You are the man who stole my gun. Man gun my stealing you.

* *Cham* is a conditional particle.

† *Yü nai* and *cham nai* are past participles passive.

‡ *Yê* is an adverbial participial suffix.

¶ *Han nai* is a past participle passive.

‖ *Nam* is an assertive particle.

§ *Nai* belongs to *lâk*, root verb to steal; *lâk nai* is a verbal noun. This separating o verbal particles, for sake of euphony, is a noticeable feature in the language.

7.—*Interrogative Pronouns.*

သႃ လတ်* ၵွ် ၽႂ် လၵ် ၵႃ။ sâ lat kau phaü lâk kâ ? 4 3 1 2	Who stole my gun ? 1 2 3 4
သွပ် မႂ် မႆ ၵႃ သင် ယင် ဢူ။ sôp maü mai ka sang yâng û ? 5 4 3 1 2	What is in your mouth ? 1 2 3 4 5
ပႃ ယိင် ဢႃ လႂ် မေ မႂ်။ pâ ying â laü mê maü ? 2 1 4 3	Which woman (is) your wife ? 1 2 3 4
ၽႃ ဢႃ လႂ် ၶႅၼ် ၼီ တင် မိုင်။ phâ â laü khen nî tâng müng ? 2 1 3 4	Which cloth (is) best of all ? 1 2 3 4

9.—*Demonstrative Pronouns.*

မႃ ဢႃ ၼႆ <ins>တႃ မတ်</ins>။ mâ â nai <ins>ta måt</ins> 2 1 3	This dog (is) blind. 1 2 3
ဢႃ ၼႆ ႁိုၼ် မႂ် ၵေ။† â nai hün maü kê ? 1 3 2	(Is) this your house. 1 2 3
ၶွ် သၼ် ဢႃ ၼႆ ၶွ် သၼ် ဢႃ khau sân â nai khau sân â 2 1 7 ၼၼ် <ins>ၼႃ ၵၼ်</ins> ၸိုင် ၶႂ်။ nan <ins>nâ kan</ins> n' chaü 6 5 4 3	This rice is not like that rice. 1 2 3 4 5 6 7
<ins>တုၼ် မႆ</ins> ဢႃ ၼၼ် တႆ ၵႃ။ <ins>tôn mai</ins> â nan tai kâ 2 1 3	That tree died (it is dead). 1 2 3
ၵုၼ် ဢႃ ၼၼ် ၼွင် ၸႆ မႂ် ၵေ။† kön â nan nâng chai maü kê ? 2 1 4 3	(Is) that man your brother ? 1 2 3 4
<ins>ဢႃ ၼႆ ၶွ်</ins>‡ မူ မႂ် ၵေ။† <ins>a nai khau</ins> mû maü kê ? 1 2 3	(Are) those pigs yours ? 1 2 3

---

* *Sâ lat* and *sî lat* are the same. It is sometimes spelt one way, sometimes the other.

† *Kê* is the interrogative particle.

‡ *Khau* is the plural suffix used with these pronouns, *vide* page 31 *ante*.

11, 12, 13, 14, 15, 16—Verbs.

မႃ မႆ မတ် ယင် ဢူ။
mâ mai mat yang û
4 3 2 1

There are fleas on the dog.
1 2 3 4
(The dog has fleas.)

မိရိ ဢူ ႁိမ် ၼမ် မႆ။
Miri û him nam mai
1 2 5 4 3

Miris live on the river bank.
1 2 3 4 5

သိုဝ် ၼမ်။ *
sü nam
2 1

It is a tiger.
1 2

ၵေႃ ၵူၼ် ထေႃ ၼမ်။ *
kau kôn thau nam
1 4 3 2

I am an old man.
1 2 3 4

လိုတ် ဢူ။
lüt û
2 1

It is hot.
1 2

မၼ် မေႃ ၶမ် ဢူ။
mân mô kham û
1 3 2

She is singing.
1 2 3

ၽူၼ် တုၵ် ဢူ
phôn tôk û
1 2 3

(It is raining) rain falling is.
1 2

ၵေႃ ႁိုဝ် ဢႃ လိုင် ၶႃ ၼႆ† ဢူ။
kau hü â lüng kha nai û
1 2 3 4 5

(I want a boat) I boat one wanting am.
1 2 3 4 5

ၵေႃ မႃ ငႃ‡ ၶႆ ၼမ်။
kau mângâ khai nam
1 3 2

I (was) ill yesterday.
1 2 3

ၵေႃ ငူ တူဝ်¶ လိုင် ႁၼ် ၵႃ။
kau ngû tô lüng han kâ
1 4 3 2

I saw a snake.
1 2 3 4

ၵူၼ် ၼႆ ၶေႃ|| ပႆ ယေႃ။ §
kôn nai khau pai yau
1 2

The men ran away.
1 2

---

* *Nam* is an assertive.

† *Kha nai* is a verbal noun.

‡ *Mângâ* show past time is meant, hence no verb required. *Nam* is an assertive particle.

¶ *Tô* is a numeral expletive used with animals.

|| *Nai khau* is the plural suffix.

§ *Yau* is the perfect tense suffix.

ကွ် ၼမ် မႂ်* ဢွ် ပေ ၶမ် ကႃ။ kau nam mai au pe khâm kâ 1 3 4 5 2	I crossed the river on (by means of) a raft. 1 2 3 4 5
ပီ ကႂ် ကွ် ကႃ ငိုဝ် ႁႂ်ႈ ယွ်။† pî kai kau kâ ngô haü yau 1 2 3 5 4 6	I paid for the cow last year Last year I cow price gave. 1 2 3 4 5 6
ကွ် ၸၢင် ဢမ်ႇ ႁၼ် ကႃ။ kau chảng n' han ka 8 5 3 4 2	I did not see the elephant. 1 2 3 4 5
ကွ် သီ လၢတ် ၼႂ်‡ ဢမ်ႇ လၵ်။ kau sî lat nai n' lâk 1 4 2 3	I (did) not steal the gun. 1 2 3 4
မၼ်း မႃ ငႃ ကႃ ယွ် man ma ngâ kâ yau 1 3 2	He went yesterday. 1 2 3
ငိုၼ်း ၼႂ်‡ ကွ် မၼ်း မႂ် ႁႂ်ႈ ယွ်။ ngün naî kau man mai haü yau 5 4 1 3 2	I gave him the money. 1 2 3 4 5
ၵႂၢႆး မႂ် ၶႂ်* တီ ပႂ်။ maü mai khâi tî pai 4 1 2	The buffalo will horn you. 1 2 3 4
ကွ် သီ လၢတ် ကွ် တီ ၸီ။ kau sî lat kau tî chî 1 5 4 2 3	I will show (you) my gun. 1 2 3 4 5
မႃ ၼႂ် ၽူၼ် တူၵ် လၢင် ၼမ် တီ mâ nai phôn tôk lång nam tî 1 3 4 2 5 6 လွင် လူ ယွ်¶ lång lông yau 7 8	Today much rain fell (hence) the rivers will † rise greatly. 1 2 3 4 5 6 7 8
ကွ် တုၼ် မႂ် ၶိုၼ် ပဵၼ် ဢူ။ kau tôn mai khün pen û 8 4 3 2	I can climb a tree. 1 2 3 4
ကွ် ယိုဝ် သီ လၢတ် ပဵၼ် ဢူ။ kau yü sî lat pen û 1 3 4 2	I can fire a gun. 1 2 3 4

* *Mai* is the accusative suffix.
† *Yau* is the perfect tense suffix.
‡ *Nai* is the demonstrative pronoun used here for emphasis and recognition.
¶ *Yau* is a completive particle and is used here as such.

လိုတ် လုင် သၢင် * ၵုၼ် ၼွႆ မႃ ဢူ
lüt lông sang kôn noi mâ û
1 2 3 5 4 6 7

တီ ပိင် မႆ ၸမ် † တီ တႆ ယၢဝ်။
tî peng mai cham tî tai yau
9 8 11 10

(The) heat (is) great. Supposing that hill men came to reside in the plains (they) would die.
1 3 3 4 5 6 7 8 9 10 11

ၵၢဝ် ၵုၼ် ႁုပ် ၵႃ ယေ မႂ် မႆ
kau kôn hôp kâ yê maü mai
2 4 3 1 7

ပွႆ ႁႂ် မႃ ‡ ၵၢတ်။
poi haü ma kåt
6 5

If I meet a man (I) will send (him) to you.
1 2 3 4 5 6 7

မႂ် ယၢဝ် ၵႃ ယေ ႁိုဝ် လုမ် ဢူ။
maü sau kâ yê hü lôm û
2 3 1 4 6

If you stand up (the) boat (will) capsize.
1 2 3 4 5

တေႃ ဢၢၼ် မႆ ¶ ယုၵ် တႃ။
tô ån mai yôk ta
2 1

Lift up the child.
1

ႁိုဝ် ဝၢၵ် တႃ။
hü wâk ta
2 1

Paddle the boat.
1 2

My Khâmtî teacher running out of liquor (which I supplied him with periodically) wrote to me for more, and the following is a copy of his note:—

ၸၢဝ် ၵေ ၸူ။ လဝ် ႁိုဝ် မုတ် တီ ၶႃ ‖ ယၢဝ်။ ၸၢဝ် ပႃ လိုင် ႁၢၵ် ဢူ
Chau kê chû lau hü môt tî kha yau chau pâ lüng hâk û
1 2 3 3 4 5

ၸမ် ႁႂ် မႃ တႃ။ § ၵၢဝ် ၶႃ သီ သႃ ပွႆ ႁႂ် ** မႃ ယၢဝ်
cham haü mâ tâ kau khâ sî sâ poi haü mâ yau
7 8 9 10 11 13 12

* *Sang* is a particle denoting an hypothesis.
† *Cham*, the conditional participle, belongs to *sang*.
‡ *Poi haü mâ* is a compound causal verb meaning cause to come.
¶ *Mai* is the accusative case suffix.
‖ *Yau* belongs to *môt môt*; *yau* means 'done,' 'finished;' Assamese *dûkhâlê*.
§ *Haü mâ tâ* = give, imperative second person.
** *Haü mâ* is a compound verb; *haü*= give, *mâ*=come; *poi* is to send, *sâ poi haü mâ yau* means 'have sent.'

Translation of Above.

Incarnation of justice[1] liquor[2] done.[3] Your honour[4] kind[5] is[6] if[7] give.[8] I,[9] slave,[10] bottle[11] have[12] sent.[13]

ၸဝ်ႈ = chau is a *respectful* mode of address; *always* had recourse to by any one addressing a superior. It is somewhat equivalent to our Sir or Mr., and has already been noticed at page 24 *ante*.

ပီ ၼႆ မိူင် ၼမ် လင်ၼႆ* ၶေႃ pî[5] nai[4] mü[1] nam[2] lângnai[3] khô[8] မၢၼ် တူ ႁၵ်း ၵႃ mân[7] tû[6] hâk[9] kâ	When[1] the rivers[2] (rose) rising[3] this[4] year[5] our[6] village[7] bridge[8] broke.[9]
မိူင် မၢၼ် ၵဝ် မႆ ပေႃ* ၼႆ ပႃ mü[1] mân[2] kau[4] mai pô[3] nai Pâ- လင် ဢူ ႁၼ် ၵႃ lang[5] û han[6] kâ	(Palangû saw him strike me). When[1] he[2] struck[3] me[4] Palangû[5] saw.[6]
သွင် ၶႃ ႁူမ် ၵႃ သီ ၵၢင် Sâng khâ[1] hôm[2] kâ[3] sî kâng[6] သွင် တူဝ်† ၼႆ ၵႃ sâng[5] tô nai[4] kâ	(They both went together and got two sambur). They two[1] together[2] going[3] got[4] two[5] sambur.[6]
ၶႆ ၵႃ ၸမ်‡ ဢႃ ပဵတ် khai kâ cham[1] â pet[3] ယင် ဢူ yang[2] û	It is wrong to sell (it). Selling[1] (it) is[2] wrong.[3]

---

* *Lângnai* and *pônai* are verbal nouns.

† *Tô* is a numeral expletive.

‡ *Kâ cham* is a conditional participial suffix. In the last sentence *au mâ sí* = having brought; *khai ka cham* = sold supposing.

သၢင် ၼၢင် မီ ၼႆ ဢဝ် မႃး သီ* sang nang mî nai <u>au mâ</u> sì 1 5 4 3 2 ၶၢႆ ၵႃႈ ၸမ်* ငိုၼ်း ၼႆ ဢူႈ <u>khai kâ cham</u> ngün nai û 6 7 8	Supposing he had brought in the bear's skin he would have *got money by selling it.* Supposing having brought bear's skin by selling money get. (Supposing 1, having 2, brought 3, bear's 4, skin 5, selling 6, money 7, get 8)
မႂ်ႉ တူဝ်ဢၼ်ႇ ႁဵတ်းသၢင် ဢဝ် ႁႆႈ maü <u>tô ån</u> <u>het sang</u> au hai 2 4 1 3 5	Why (are) you making the child cry. (Why 1, you 2, making 3, child 4, cry 5)
ငူဝ်း ၼႆ † ႁႂ်ႈ လဵင် တႃႈ ngô nai haü lêng tâ 2 1 3	Have the cow tied up. Let the cow be tied up. (Let 1, cow 2, tied 3)
ၸဝ်ႈ ပႃ လိူင်း မၼ်း မႆ chau pâ lüng man mai 1 3 ႁႂ်ႈ† ႁိင်း သီ ထၢမ် တီ ၶႃ haü hăng sì thâm tî khâ 2 4 2 5 တႃႈ‡ tâ	Let your honour call and question him. Your honour having had him called question (him). (Your honour 1, having 2, had him 3, called 4, question 5)
မႂ်ႉ ၼွင်ႉ ယၢင်ႇ ဢူႈ ၵေႃႈ¶ maü nâng yâng ü kê ?	Have you a brother ?
ပၢင် ဢႃ ၼႆ မႆ ၼိူဝ် ဢူႈ ၵေႃႈ¶ pâng â nai mai nü û kê ? 5 4 3 1 2	Are there deer on this 'chapri ?' Do deer remain on this 'chapri ?' (deer 1, remain 2, this 3, chapri 5)
မႂ်ႉ ႁိူဝ်း ဢဝ် မႃး ၵႃႈ ၵေႃႈ¶ maü hü au mâ kâ kê ? 2 4 3 1	Have you brought the boat ? (Have 1, you 2, brought 3)

---

* *Ka cham* is a conditional participial suffix. In the last sentence *au mâ sì* = having brought ; *khai ka cham* = sold supposing.

† *Haü* is a causal imperative suffix.

‡ တႃႈ *Tâ* belongs to *thâm thâm tâ*, meaning ask (imperative).

¶ *Kê* is the interrogative particle.

ဒွ̂ တင် ခ' ဟက် ပက် ကျ khau tâng mai khâk pâk kâ 2 6 5 4 3 1 ကေ် * kê ?	Have they ('panjied' the road) fixed 'panjies' on the road ? (Have 1, they 2, fixed 3, 'panjies' 4, on 5, the road 6)
ချ ကပ် ထူ† ကေ် * mâ kâp û kê ? 2 3 1	Will the dog bite ? (Will 1, the dog 2, bite 3)
or	*or*
ချ တိ ကပ် က' ‡ mâ tî kap kai ? 2 1 3	Will the dog bite ? (Will 1, the dog 2, bite 3)
နွဲ ယိုဝ် ယိ လတ် ပိၼ် ထူ ကေ်* maü yü sî lat pen û kê ? 2 3 4 1	Can you fire a gun ? (Can 1, you 2, fire 3, a gun 4)
ခၼ် ချ ကျ ယေ် တိ ႁႂ္ ယွ̂ man mâ kâ yê tî haü sau 2 3 1 4 6 5 ကေ် ‡ kê ?	If he comes shall (I) make (him) wait ? (If 1, he 2, comes 3, shall (I) 4, make 5, (him) wait 6)
ၼိုဝ် တိပ် ယိ ကွ̂ တိ ပၼ် ကေ် * nü tap sî kau tî pan kê ? 2 1 5 4 6	Having <u>cut up</u> the deer shall I distribute (it) ? (Having 1, cut up 2, the deer 3, shall 4, I 5, distribute (it) 6)
ကွ̂ နွဲ ခ' ငိုၼ် ယိပ် တြျ kau <u>maü mai</u> ngün sip trâ 2 4 7 5 6 ႁႂ္ တျ ၸံ ‖ နွဲ က' တိ haü <u>kâ cham</u> maü kai tî 3 1 9 11 8 ယိုဝ် ႁႂ္ ကေ် * sü haü kê ? 10	If I give you ten rupees (silver) will you purchase (me) fowls ? (If 1, I 2, give 3, you 4, ten 5, rupees 6, (silver) 7, will 8, you 9, purchase 10, (me) fowls 11)

---

* *Kê* is the interrogative particle.

† *Û* is the present tense suffix, used here to express the future.

‡ *Kai* is a particle of vague probability.

‖ *Kâ cham* is a *conditional* participial suffix.

ၵုၼ် တင် ဢၼ် ၵႃ မိုင်
khôn tâng an kâ müng
2 3 4 6
ႁူၵ် ၵွင် ၼႂ်* ၼင်† တင် တိၼ်
Hû kâng nai nang tâng ten
5 9 11
ၵြႃ ၼႃ† ၵၼ် ဢိုၼ်‡ ၸႂ်
krâ nâ kan n' chaü
10 9 8 7

The road which (goes) going
1 2 3 4
(to) Hukong country is not
5 6 7 8
like the Bengal high road.
9 10 11

မၼ် ႁဵတ်¶ ၼႃ ငႆ သီ ပေႃ သီ
man het nâ ngai sî pô sî
2 5 4 3
ဢူ‖ ၵႃ ၸမ် ၵဝ် ၶႃ တင်
ü kâ cham kau khâ tang
1 6 7 11
မၼ် ဢူ ဢိုၼ်‡ ပိၼ်
man ü n' pen
12 10 9 8

(Woman complaining *against her husband.*)

If he continues beating (me)
1 2 3 4
thus, I slave cannot
5 6 7 8 9
remain with him.
10 11 12

ၸင် ၵႃ ပႃ လႅဝ် ၵေႃ မၼ် မႃ‡
châng kâ pâ laü kaw man mâ
6 7 5 3 1 2
ႁၼ်
han
4

He (did not even see *in what direction* (the) elephant went
1 2 3 4 5 6 7

မႃ ငႃ ပုၼ် ပိုၼ် ၵဝ် မႂ် ၶႂ်
mâ ngâ pûn pün kau mai khai
2 1 3 5 4
သိင် ၸေ တင် မေ မႂ် ႁၵ်
Seng chê tang mê maü hâk
6 9 11 10
ၵၼ် ၼမ် တေႃ ၼႂ် ဢူ ၵႃ
kan nam tô nai û kâ
8 7 12 0
ၵဝ် မႃ ယုမ်
kau mâ yûm.
13 14 15

From before people informed
1 2 3 4
me, 'Sengchî is intriguing
5 6 7 8
with your wife, but I (did)
9 10 11 12 13
not believe (it).
14 15

---

* This *nai* belongs to *kâ*. *Kâ nai* is a verbal noun.
† *Nang* and *nakan* both mean *like*.
‡ *N'* (ဢိုၼ်) and *mâ* (မႃ) are negative particles.
¶ *Het* means to do ; *het nâ gai sî* = doing thus.
‖ *Pô sî û* ; *sî û* is the present tense definite suffix.

kau(1) khau(5) n'(2)* pai(3) kin(4)	I(1) (have) not(2) yet(3) eaten(4) (my) rice.(5)
kau(1)† tâp(7) Dibrü mai(6) păk(5) lüng kaw(3) n'(2)* pai kâ(4)	I(1) (have) not(2) even(3) been(4) once(5) to(6) Dibrughur.(7)

17.—*Adverbs.*

maü(3) lûk(1) mâ(2) laü khai(5) sî(4) û?‡	Since(1) when(2) have you(3) been(4) ill?(5)
kâ(3) nâ yü(5) sü(4) kau(1) û(¶) mân(2) nam¶	I(1) was there(2) before(3) the tiger(4) was shot.(5)
kâ(3) nâ kau(4) mai khâ(2) mai â lüng‖ pâk(1) tâ haü(5) hôm(6)§	Place a branch(1) in(2) front of(3) me(4) for(5) shade.(6)

---

* *N' pai* means not yet.

† *Tâp* = town.

‡ *Khai sî û* means still ill; *sî û* is the present tense definite, and is used to express a present act or event which is not yet completed.

¶ *Û* is a root verb meaning to be; *û nam* = was there; *nam* is an assertive particle.

‖ *Â lüng* = one; is an abbreviation for *one* = lüng.

§ *Haü* = give; *haü hôm* = give shade.

ႁွ် တိ* ႁုံ ကၢၼ် ကၢ့ ကေ်†
hau tî hôm kan kâ kê ?
2 1 4 3
Shall we go together ?
1 2 3 4

ႁိုဝ် သွင် ဢၢၼ်‡ ႁုံ ကၢၼ် ၽုၵ်
hü sâng ân hôm kân phûk
3 2 4 1
တႃ
tâ
Tie the two boats together.
1 2 3 4

မိုဝ် ႁိုဝ် ၼႂ် တၢၵ် ၵု¶တိ မႂ်
mü hü mai tâk kû tî mai
2 1 4 5
ယၢင် ဢူ
yang û
3
In the rains there are leeches everywhere.
1 2 3 4 5

မႂ်ႈ ၼႂ် ၼပ် သိင် မႂ်‖ ကႃ ကေႃ
maü nai nap sing mai kâ kô
1 4 6 5 3 2
ကေ်†
kê ?
2
(Are) you afraid to go alone in the dark ?
1 2 3 4 5 6

ၵွ် မႃ ႁုၵ် တပ် တိပြူ မႂ် ကႃ
kau mâ hôk tâp Dibrû mai kâ
1 7 6 5 4 3
ၼိုဝ် ထၢင်
n' thâng
2
I (will) probably go to Dibrughur tomorrow.
1 2 3 4 5 6 7

မုၼ် ၼၢင်§ ပႃ ၼႃကၢၼ်§ လွႆ
môn nang pâ nâkan loi
1 3 4 3 2
Otters swim like fish.
1 2 3 4

---

* This *tî* (future tense prefix) belongs to *kâ*. Khâmtis are very fond of separating tense suffixes or prefixes from the root in this way.

† *Kê* is the interrogative particle.

‡ *An* is a numeral particle, *vide* page 18 *ante*.

¶ *Kû* = each ; *tî* = place ; *mai* = in ; *kû tî mai* = in each place, everywhere.

‖ *Mai* = locative case postposition.

§ *Nang* and *nâkan* both mean like ; they are usually used together in this way.

ၵွ် မႂ် ၶွ် ယၢၼ် ၵွႆ ၵွင် **kau mai khau sân koi kång** 2 4 3 ႁႂ် မႃ **haü mâ** 1	**Give me much rice.** 1 2 3 4
ၵွ် ၼိုဝ် တူ လိူင်* ၼႆ ႁၢၼ် ၵႃ **kau nü tô lüng nai han kâ** 1 4 3 5 2	**I saw one deer only.** 1 2 3 4 5
သွ် † လဵမ် ၼႆ ယႂ် ၽဵဝ် ဢူ **sau lem nai yaü phiau û** 2 1 5 4 3	**The post is too large.** 1 2 3 4 5
မႂ် ၽႃ ၵွ် မႃ ၼီ သီ‡ ယၢပ် **maü phâ kau mâ nî sî yâp** 1 5 4 6 3 ၵႃ **kâ** 2	**You have sewn my cloth** 1 2 3 4 5 **badly.** 6
ၼီ ၵေႃ မႃ ၸႂ် မႃ ၼီ ၵေႃ **nî kaw mâ chaü mâ nî kaw** 1 2 4 3 5 6 ၼိုင် ၸႂ် **n' chaü** 8 7	**(It is neither good nor bad.** **Good also is not bad also is** 1 2 3 4 5 6 7 **not).** 8
ၵႃ မႃ ၼပ် သိင် ၵွ် တီ ဢူ **kâ mâ nap sing kau tî û** 1 2 3 4 5 6	**I will stay until it is dark** **(until not dark I will stay).** 1 2 3 4 5 6
တွၵ် ၸဵမ်¶ ငႆ လဵင် ဢူ **tôk chem ngai lêng û** 2 3 1	**(It) is still light.** 1 2 3
ၵႆ‖ ၼႆ တွၵ် ၸဵမ်¶ ငႆ ငၢမ် ဢူ **kai nai tôk chem ngai ngåm û** 2 1 4 5 3	**The fowl is still sitting.** 1 2 3 4 5

* *Tô* is numeral expletive. လိူင် is an abbreviated form of *lüng* = one.

† *Lem* is a numeral expletive.

‡ *Sî*, the participial suffix, is likewise used as an adverbial suffix.

¶ *Chem* may be spelt both ways, namely, ၸိမ် and ၸဵမ်; the latter is preferred.

‖ *Nai* is the demonstrative pronoun, used here like our *the* for emphasis and recognition.

ၼႂ် ၽိတ် ၼႝ မႃ ၸႂ် မၼ်း
maü phet nai mâ chaü man
1 2 4 3 5
ၽိတ်
phet
6

Either your or he are lying
In Khamti—
You lying are not he lying.
1 2 3 4 5 6

ၼႂ် ႁိတ်* သင် ႁိတ်ႉ ၵႃ
maü het sang het kâ
3 1 4 2

Why did you do it?
1 2 3 4

မၼ်း ႁိ လိုဝ် သိ ႁိတ်ႉ ၵႃ
man hî lü sî het kâ
3 1 4 2

How did he do it?
1 2 3 4

ၶဝ် မႃ လႂ် ႁိတ်ႉ ၵႃ
khau mâ laü het kâ
3 1 4 2

When did they do it?
1 2 3 4

မၼ်း မႃ လႂ် ႁိတ်ႉ ၵႃ ၵႝ †
man mâ laü het kâ kai
5 4 6
ၵဝ် ၼိုဝ် တင်
kau n' lång
1 2 3

I don't know when he did it.
1 2 3 4 5 6

မၼ်း ႁိတ်ႉ သင် ႁိတ်ႉ ၵႃ ၵႝ ‡
man het sang het kâ kai
5 4 6
ၵဝ် ၼိုဝ် တင်
kau n' tång
1 2 3

I don't know why he did it.
1 2 3 4 5 6

မၼ်း ႁိ လိုဝ် သိ ႁိတ်ႉ ၵႃ ၵႝ †
man hi lü sî het kâ kai
5 4 6
ၵဝ် ၼိုဝ် တင်
kau n' tång
1 2 3

I don't know how he did it.
1 2 3 4 5 6

ၼႂ် ၼႃ မႝ ႁိတ်ႉ ၵႃ
maü nâ mai het kâ?
3 1 4

Where did you do it?
1

ၼႂ် တိ ႁိတ်ႉ ၼႃ မႝ
maü tî het nâ mai?
3 2 4 1

Where will you do it?
1 2 3 4

* *Het* is spelt *hech*, though occasionally *het*.
† *Kai* is a particle of vague probability, used interrogatively.

man mai* het kâ† kai kau n' tång	I don't know where he did it.
man tî het mai* kai kau n' tång	I don't know where he will do it.

19.—Conjunctions.

maü mâ kin kâ yê‡ tî tai	You will die unless you eat. You not eating if will die.
laî pü khau sân maü mâ nî¶ naî kau n' sü	I will not buy your rice because (it is) bad being.
kau thau sî û kaw kheo kau n' mâng||	Although I am old my teeth (are) not broken.
maü hü mâ au ma lai pü nai si chau sahib khâ châ	You (did) not bring the boat, therefore the sahib (is) angry.

* This should be *nâ mai*.
† *Kai* is a particle of vague probability, used interrogatively.
‡ *Kâ yê* is a conditional participial suffix.
¶ *Mâ nî* = not good, bad; *nai* is the participial suffix.
\|\| *Măng* only applies to the breaking of das, axes, and teeth!

Miscellaneous Phrases.

လုက် တပ် * သေယႃ ဒိ ယႃ † မဲ lûk tâp Sa dî yâ mai 5 6 5 မိုင် ခံ ဒိ ခႃ လွဲ ကဲ ‡ müng Khâmtî khâ laü kaî 4 3 1 2	How far (is the) Khâmtî 1 2 3 country from Sadiya ? 4 5 6
လွႆ ¶ ကႃ ကႃ ယေ နိုၼ် လိုင် loi loi kâ kâ yê nün lüng 1 2 3 5 4 ဝႃ ကႃ။ wâ kâ 6 7	Going slowly it takes a month. Slowly going if 1 2 one month must go. 4 5
ခၼ် ¶ ကႃ ကႃ ယေ ခၼ် khan khan kâ kâ yê khan 1 2 3 4 သေႃ ဝၼ် ဝႃ ကႃ sau wan wâ kâ 5 6 7 8	Going fast it takes about 20 days. Fast going if about 20 1 2 3 4 5 days must go. 6 7 8
တႆ ၼမ် ¶ တပ် သေယႃ ဒိ ယႃ Tai nam nam tâp Sa dî ya 1 2 5 4 မဲ မႃ ဢူ ကေ mai mâ û ke ? 3 6	Do many Khâmtîs visit Sadiya ? Khâmtîs many to 1 2 3 Sadiya town come. 4 5 6
ၸွႆ ဢူ။ ကူ ပီ ၼမ် ‖ မႃ ဢူ chaü û kû pî nam nam mâ û 1 4 5 2 3	Yes ! Numbers come in 1 2 3 (yearly) each year. 4 5
ခေႃ မႃ ႁဵတ်·ကႃ သင် khau mâ het kâ sang ? 1 2 3 4	Why do they come in ? They come (to) do what ? 1 2 3 4
ခေႃ ၽႃ ဢေႃ မႃ ႁင် ၶဲ khau phâ au mâ hang khai 1 3 2 4 5 ၽႃ ကေႃ မဲ ကေႃ သိုဝ် ဢူ phâ kaw mai kaw sü û 7 8 9 6	They bring (in) 'das' for 1 2 3 4 sale and purchase cloths 5 6 7 and cotton. 8 9

---

* *Tâp* means town.

† *Mai* belongs to *lûk* ; *lûk mai* = from.

‡ *Kai* is a particle of vague probability, used interrogatively.

¶ The doubling of these words is made by repeating the mark over the letter, *vide* page 17 of Grammar.

‖ Doubling of the mark (°) means word is to be repeated, *vide* page 17 of Grammar.

Tai nai* khau kûng wân 1 3 2 tô nai û kaw kû pî 4 5 6 mâ nî† nam 7	The Khâmtîs sow cotton, but each year it is bad. 1 2 3 4 5 6 7
khau lûk Sing‡phô mai sü¶ 1 3 4 2 nai û tô nai û kaw 5 khan nak‖ 6 7	They obtain (it) from the Singphos, but the price (is) dear. 1 2 3 4 5 6 7
khau tek lûk mai nai 2 4 5 1 3	Where (do) they get (their) iron from? 1 2 3 4 5
müng khau pâ chau mai nai§ 5 4 3 2 1 khau lûk nin mai khût au** 6 8 9 7	(It is) found in their own country. They dig (it) from the ground. 1 2 3 4 5 6 7 8 9
müng Khâm tî mai†† chü 7 6 3 chau phâ lông kau mai 5 4 2 lau mâ 1	Tell me the names of the big chiefs of the Khâmtî country. 1 2 3 4 5 6 7

* *Nai* is the demonstrative pronoun, used for emphasis and recognition. *Khau* is the plural suffix.

† *Mâ nî* = not good, bad.

‡ Khâmtîs call Singphos 'Samphô.'

¶ *Sü nai* is a compound verb; *sü* = purchase and *nai* = get; *sü nai* = obtain by purchase.

‖ *Nak* means heavy.

§ *Nai* = got, obtained.

** *Khût au* is a compound verb; *khût* = dig; *au* = take.

†† *Mai* = locative case postposition.

ၸွ် ၽႃ ၶၼ် ၽၼ် Chau phâ Khân phan လုၵ်ႉ ၶုၼ် ၸွ် ၽႃ ၸွ် ႁိုင် lûk khûn Chau phâ Chau hüng ၽၼ် မၢၼ် ၸေ သွင် * ၶႃ phan Mân chê sâng * khâ ယႆ လိုမ် † တီ တင် မိူင်း။ yaü lüm † tî tang müng	Chaupha Khân, of the Lûk khûn clan, (and) Chauphâ Chauhüng, of the Mânchî clan, are the biggest of all.
ၸွ် ၽႃ ဢၼ် ၵေႃ ၼမ် ‡ Chau phâ ân kaw nam nam ယင် ဢူ။ yang û	There are many small chiefs also.
ၶဝ် ၵႃ ႁဵင် ၼၢၼ် ၵၢၼ် ၵေ။ ¶ khau kâ hêng nan kan kê ?	Do they quarrel much ?
ၸႂ် ဢူ။ လႆ ပိုဝ် ၵူၼ် ၼ်ၶႃ ‖ chaü û lai pü kôn n' khâ လင် ၼိၼ်း။ lang nin.	Yes ! On account of men and land.

---

* *Sâng khâ*, they two, *vide* page 24 of Grammar.

† *Lüm* is a particle used to express comparison somewhat like our *than*.

‡ The doubling of the mark (°) denotes that the word is to be repeated.

¶ *Kê* is the interrogative particle.

‖ *N'khâ* means these two, *vide* page 24 of Grammar.

ၸွ် ၾႃ * ဢၼ် ၵႃ ၼႃ ၶႆ Chau phâ an kâ nâ khai 2 4 3 သွင် ၵွၼ် ၼႆ တပ် သျႃ တီ ယႃ sâng kô nai tâp Sâ di yâ 1 7 မႆ မႃ ဢူ ၵေး mai mâ û kê 6 5	Have the two chiefs mentioned before been to Sadiya? 1 2 3 4 5 6 7
ဢိုၼ် မႃ။ တွၼ် ၼႆ ဢူ ၵေႃ n' mâ tô nai û kaw 1 2 လုၵ် မၼ် ၶွ် ပီ ၼွင် lûk man khau pi näng 4 3 6 မၼ် ၶွ် မႃ ဢူ။ man khau mâ û 5 7	No! But their sons and their relations come. 1 2 3 4 5 6
တႆ ၵေႃ † တႃ မႃ မႃ ၸွႆ ၵေး Tai Kô tâ mâ mâ chaü kê 3 4 2 1	Khâmtîs are Buddhists are they not? Are not Khâmtîs Buddhists? 1 2 3 4
ၸွႆ ဢူ Chaü û 1	(They) are. 1
ၵူ မၼ် မႆ ၸွင် ယင် ဢူ kû mân maî chăng yâng û 4 5 3 2 1 ၵေး။ kê?	Is there a temple in each village? 1 2 3 4 5
ယင် ဢူ။ yâng û 1	There is. 1
တႆ ယိုၼ် ၼိုၼ် ‡ ဢူ ၵေး။ Tai yü nü û kê 1 2	Do Khâmtîs shoot? 1 2

* *An kânâ khai sâng kô nai* is a relative clause = the two chiefs spoken of before.

† Khâmtis call Guatama *Kôtâmâ*.

‡ *Nü* means literally flesh ; *yü nü* = shoot flesh, *i.e.*, 'shikar.'

ယိုဝ် ယူ။ ယေ် * ကုဝ် ယေ် ကုဝ် yü û yê kô yê kô 1 2 ၸမ်† ၸၢင် ကေႃ ၶႆ ႁေ cham châng kaw khâi hê 5 6 8 ကေႃ ၼမ် ၼမ် ယိုဝ် ၼမ်‡ kaw nam nam yü nam 4 3	(They) shoot. Some shoot 1 2 3 many elephants and wild 4 5 6 7 buffaloes. 8
ၶဝ်¶ ၶႃ ယင် ယူ ၵေႃး‖ khau khâ yang û kê ? 2 3 1	Have they slaves ? 1 2 3
ယင် ယူ။ yang û 1	(They) have. 1
ၶႃ ၼႆ§ ၶဝ် တင် ၸဝ် khâ nai khau tang chau 1 3 မၢၼ် ၶဝ် ႁုမ် ယူ ၵေႃး** man khau hôm û kê ? 5 4 2	Do the slaves live with 1 2 3 their masters ? 4 5
ယေ် ကုဝ် ယေ် ကုဝ် ႁုမ် ယူ ယူ†† yê kô yê kô hôm û û 1 3 2 ယေ် ကုဝ် ယေ် ကုဝ် တီ ၶျႃ ယူ။†† yê kô yê kô tî khyâ û 4 6 5	Some reside together, some 1 2 3 4 reside apart. 5 6
ၶဝ် ၶႃ ၶဝ် လုၵ် ၼႃ မႆ khau khâ khau lûk nâ mai 2 5 4 6 1 သိုဝ်။ sü ? 3	Where (do) they purchase 1 2 3 their slaves from ? 4 5 6

* For meaning of *yê kô yê kô* see page 97, *ante*.
† *Cham* is a particle of supposition.
‡ *Nam* is an assertive particle.
¶ *Khau* = their ; *khâ* = slaves ; *yâng û* = exist.
‖ *Kê* is the interrogative particle.
§ *Nai* is the demonstrative pronoun, used here for emphasis and recognition *Khan* is the plural suffix.
** *Hôm* = together ; *û* = live, remain.
†† *Û* is the present tense suffix.

ကံ ၸွင် လုက် သိင် ၸေႃ မႝ * kam phâng[2] lûk[3] Sing phô[4] mai သိုဝ်။ ကံ ၸွင် လုက် ၶႃ sü[1] kam phâng[5] lûk[6] khâ မၢၼ် မႝ သိုဝ်။ * man[7] mai sü[8]	(They) purchase[1] some[2] from[3] the Singphos[4] and some[5] from[6] the Mishmis[7] (purchase)[8].
ၽိင် ၶၼ် ၶႃ ၸမ် ၶႃ လႅဝ်။ † pêng[3] khan[2] khâ[4] cham[1] khâ laü	What[1] (is the price[2]) rate[3] (for) slaves[4].
သင် ၶႃ ပႃ မွၵ် ပႃ သွၵ် ၵႃ sang[1] khâ[2] pâ[3] mau pâ[4] sau kâ[5] ၸမ် ‡ ပၵ် သီ သိပ်။ cham pâk[6] si sip[7]	If[1] slave[2] (is a) young man[3] or young woman[4], the price[5] (is) one hundred[6] and forty[7].
ၵူၼ် ထွၵ် ၸမ် ပိတ် သိပ် ပၵ် kôn thau[2] cham[1] pet sip[3] pâk[5] လိူင် တူဝ် ဢွၼ် ၸမ် ႁႃ သိပ် lüng[4] tô ân[2] cham[1] hâ sip[2] ႁူၵ် သိပ်။ hôk sip[4].	If[1] (an) old[2] man eighty[3] (rupees or) one[4] hundred[5]. If[1] a child[2], fifty[3] (or) sixty[4].
ၵူၼ် မိူင် ¶ ၶမ်း တီ ၼႝ ၶွၵ် kôn müng Khâm tî nai khau[1] ၶႃ ၶွၵ် ၼင် ဢႃပွတ် ၼႃ khâ[4] khau[3] nang[7] Abors nâ ၵၼ် တပ် ‖ သေႃ တီ ယႃ kan[7] tâp Sa di ya[6] မႝ ဢွၵ် မႃ ဢူ ၵေ § mai[5] au mâ[2] û kê	Do the Khâmtis[1] bring[2] their[3] slaves[4] into[5] Sadiya[6] like[7] the Abors[8]?

* *Mai* belongs to *lûk lûk mai* = from.

† *Khâ laü* means how many.

‡ *Cham* is a conditional participial suffix; it belongs here to *kâ* = price.

¶ *Kôn* = men; *müng Khâmti* = of Khamti country; *nai Khamthay kôn müng Khâmti nai khau* = Khâmtis.

‖ *Tâp* means town.

§ *Kê* is the interrogative particle.

ယေ် ၵုဝ် ယေ် ၵုဝ် ဢွ် မႃ ဢူ။ yê kô yê kô au mâ û 1 2 တေႃ ဝႃ ၶႃ ပႃ ယိင် ၸမ် tô wâ khâ pâ ying cham 3 6 7 4 ထိုဝ် ဢွ် မႃ။ n' au mâ 5	Some bring (them), but (they) don't bring in slave women. 1 2 3 4 5 6
တႝ ၼႝ* ၶွ် လုၵ်း ႁိုဝ် ဢၼ် Tai nai khau lûk hü an 1 4 3 ၼီ† ယင် ဢူ ၵေႃ။ nî yâng û kê ? 2	Do the Khâmtîs possess good boatmen ? 1 2 3 4
ယင် ဢူ။ တႝ ဢၼ် ဢူ တႝ ၶင် yâng û Tai an û tai khâng 1 3 4 5 6 တပ် ‡ သေႃ ဒီ ယႃ မႝ tâp Sadiyâ mai 7 ၼမ်° ¶ ထိုဝ်‖ ႁိုဝ် ၸင် ဢူ။ nam nam thô hü châng û 2 9 10 8	Possess. Many Khâmtîs who reside near (to) Sadiya know how to work boats. 1 2 3 4 5 6 7 8 9 10
ၵုၼ် မိုင် ၶမ် တီ ဢၼ် ဢူ kôn müng Khâm tî an û 2 8 7 3 4 ႁိမ် ၼမ် ၼႝ § ၶွ် ၵေႃ ၼင် him nam nai khau kaw nang 6 5 1 12 ၵုၼ် မႝ ၼႃၵၼ် ထိုဝ် ‖ ႁိုဝ် kôn mai nâkan thô hü 14 15 13 10 11 ၸင် ဢူ châng û 9	Also the Khâmtîs, who live on the river banks in the Khâmtî country, know how to work a boat the same as the men here. 1 2 3 4 5 6 7 8 9 10 11 12 13 14 15

---

* *Nai* is the demonstrative pronoun used with the plural suffix *khau* for emphasis and recognition. *Tai nai hkau* = the Khâmtis.

† *An ní* who (are) good.

‡ *Tâp* simply means a town.

¶ Doubling the mark (°) denotes that the word is to be repeated.

‖ *Thó* means a pole ; *hô hü* to pole boat.

§ This *mai khau* belongs to *kôn* (first word in sentence) = the men (Khâmtîs).

kôn[1] mūng[4] Khâm[3] tî *nai khau* * hü[6] phan[5] û kê?	Do the men[1] residing in the[2] Khâmtî[3] country[4] cut[5] boats?[6]
phan[1] û *tô*[2] *wâ* hang[4] khai[5] n'[3] chaü[3] † hang[7] khau[8] pâ[9] chau sûng[10] nai[6] nam ‡	(They) cut[1] but[2] not[3] for[4] sale,[5] only[6] for[7] their[9] own use.[10]
Tai[4] pâ[7] lâk au[5] siau[6] nai ¶ mai[3] het[2] nang[1] hü?	What[1] (like) is[2] done to[3] a Khâmtî[4] who[5] is caught[6] stealing?[7]
man mai[1] maü[3] lông[2] *khün nâ*[4] *kau*[5] kâ ngün[6] an maü nai ma[7] haü nai saü khü[9] wai.[8]	He[1] is heavily[2] fined,[3] and[4] until[5] the fine[6] is paid[7] he is placed[8] in the stocks.[9]
sû[1] yâ[5] sû[3] pâ[4] chau pûk[2] mâ[7] chaü[6] kê?	You[1] plant[2] your[3] own[4] tobacco[5] do[6] you not?[7]

* *Nai khau* is the plural suffix.

† *Chaü* is the substantive verb here in its negative form. *Hang khai n' chaü* = not for sale or selling.

‡ *Nam* is an assertive particle.

¶ *Nai* belongs to *siau* (seize); *siau nai* meaning seized. It is the past participle passive. *Tai pâlâk*=a Khâmtî thief; *au*=who; *siau nai* (has been) seized

ပုၵ် ဢူး တူ ဢုံ ၶိုၼ် ၼႃ ၵွ
pûk û tû ôm khün nâ kau
1 2 3 4
လုတ် ၼံး*
lût nam
5

(We) plant (it). We chew and smoke (it).
1 2 3 4 5

ၸွ မုၼ်† ၼႆ ၶွ ႁိုဝ် ၼိုဝ်
chau môn nai khau hü nü
2 1
သီ ၼႆ ၵိၼ်း
sî nai kin
3 4

How (do your) priests obtain food?
1 2 3 4

ၵူ မိုဝ် ၸၢင် မႆ ၶွ သုၵ်
kû mü chäng mai khau sûk
5 7 6 4
ၵုၼ် မၼ် ႁႂ် ဢူး
kôn man haü û
1 2 3

The (villagers) men of the village give cooked rice daily to the temple.
1 2 3 4 5 6 7

Complaint No. 1.

Incarnation of justice! Your slave's complaint is this: About ten days ago Sengchê came to my house and induced my wife to leave her home with him. People told me before that Sengchê was intriguing with my wife, but I did not believe them. Now, however, he has gone off with her.

He has also stolen and carried off all my property to the value of about fifty rupees, namely, one necklace, worth about fifteen rupees, and a pair of silver bracelets, worth about rupees thirty-five.

It is desirable that your honour send for and question him about your slave's complaint.

---

* *Nam* is a particle of assertion.

† *Chau môn* = priest; *chau môn nai khau* = priests. The *nai* is the demonstrative pronoun, used for emphasis and recognition. *Chau môn khau* alone might mean their priest.

chau kê chû trâ kau khâ*
1 4 2 3
cham â nai mâ nai khan sip
5 6 7 8
wan thôn yau Seng chê hün
9 10 11 16
kau mai mâ sî me kau mai†
15 14 13 12 18 17
lau sî au pai kâ
19 20 21
mâ ngâ pûn pün kau mai khai
23 22 24 26 25
Seng chê tang mê maü
27 29 31 30
hâk kan nam‡ tô nai û kaw
28 32
kau mâ yûm tô wâ ngai
33 34 35 37 36

Incarnation of justice My!
1 2
slave's complaint this:
3 4 5
Today, about ten days past,
6 7 8 9 10
Sengchê having come to
11 12 13 14
my house, my wife deceiv-
15 16 17 18 19
ing, made (her) run away
20 21
(with him).
From before people informed
22 23 24 25
me Sengchê is intriguing
26 27 28
with your wife, but I (did)
29 30 31 32 33
not believe (it). Now,
34 35 36 37

* *Cham* is a conditional participial particle, but is used like its Assamese equivalent *hólé*, to express other ideas likewise. Sometimes it is purely explanatory; as, {trâ kau khâ cham â nai} = my slave's complaint is this. Sometimes it is used somewhat like our English *but*; as, {nam Tengâ mai cham pâ chang mâ û} but porpoises do not remain in the Tenga pani. Sometimes *cham* is an emphatic particle pure and simple; as, {â mû kau cham mü nan pûn yau yau} my work (it) was finished previously. In the following sentence:— {kau cham kâ mâ mü cham mâ kâ} I went but you didn't. (*Cham* appears to be a euphonic or ornamental particle.

† *Mai* is the accusative case postposition and belongs to *mê*.
‡ *Nam* is an assertive particle.

man au kâ kâ khüng kau
38 40 39 43 42
kaw khan ngün hâ sip lâk
41 44 46 45 48
sî au kâ yau poi thiau[*] lüng
47 50 49 52 51
khan sip hâ trâ wen ngün
53 54 55 58 57
kû lüng khan sâm sip hâ trâ
56 59 60 61
chau pâ lüng man mai haü[†]
64 68
hâng sî trâ kau khâ nai
66 65 72 70 71 69
thâm[‡] haü mâ cham nî tî khâ
67 63
û
62

however, he has taken (her) (and) likewise my things (worth) about fifty rupees having stolen (he) has taken away: one necklace (worth) about fifteen rupees (and) a pair of silver bracelets (worth) about thirty-five rupees. (It) is desirable (that) your honour having called question him (about) this my slave's case.

Complaint No. 2.

The gist of my (Pokham) statement is recited to your honour. Yesterday evening I, slave, determining to return home and having placed all my goods in the shop of Nantô went to stroll in the "hat."

Subsequently, however, Phulâ came and stole my *eria* cloth, and while he was stealing it my companion was present, for after the theft my companion came and told me that Phulâ had stolen my *eria* cloth. Therefore I have come to complain to your honour.

---

* *Thiau* is a numeral expletive; [symbol] is an abbreviation for *lüng* = one.

† *Haü hâng* is a compound causal verb; *haü* = give, cause; *hâng* = call. *Si* is the participial suffix; *man mai haü hâng si* = having caused or commanded him to appear (*haü* is used as an imperative causal).

‡ *Thâm haü* is a compound verb meaning to interrogate.

aw wâ tâ â-kyawng kham
2 5
kau Pô khâm mâ laü chau pâ
3 4 6 8
lüng mai tî khâ nam mâ ngâ
7 9
pang khâm kau khâ mü kåt
10 11 12 14
nai sî khüng kau tang müng
13 19 18 17
wai chî Nan tô mai sî kau
16 22 21 20 15 23
khâ kâ lê kat kâ kâ
24 25 26 27
lang nai Phû lâ mâ sî phâ
28 29 30 31 36
sam sû kau lâk au kâ
35 34 32 33
mü lâk nai tai kô kau han
37 38 40 39
kâ kâ lang nai tai kô kau
41 42 44 43
mâsî kaumai lau mâ phâ sam
45 47 46 53
sû maü Phu lâ lâk au yau
52 51 48 50 49

The gist of my, Pokham, statement is recited to your honour. Last evening I, slave, intending to return home, having placed all my traps in Nanto's shop I, slave, went to stroll (in the) 'hat.' After this Phûlâ coming stole and took away my *eria* cloth. While stealing my companion saw (him) (for), afterwards my companion coming told me, Phulâ has stolen your *eria* cloth. Therefore

3 2 4 5 6 7 8 9 10 11 12 13 14 15 16 17 18 19 20 21 22 23 24 25 26 27 28 29 30 31 32 33 34 35 36 37 38 39 40 41 42 43 44 45 46 47 48 49 50 51 52 53 54

* *Mâ lau* is a compound verb (*mâ* = come, *lau* = tell) meaning inform, &c.

† *Mü* is a root verb meaning to return home; *mü kåt* = will return; *nai si* = home.

‡ *Wai* the past participial suffix *si* (belonging to *wai*) is put in after *mai*.

¶ This *kâ* belongs to *kâ* root verb meaning go.

‖ *Yau* is a verbal particle denoting completion. *Lâk au* is a compound verb meaning (with *yau* suffixed) stolen and walked off with.

[illegible]
lai pü nai si kau khâ mâ
[illegible]
het trâ chau pâ lüng mai ti
[illegible]
khâ nam.

I, slave, (have) come to complain to your honour.

Complaint No. 3.

Aw watâ ! The gist of my, Dhatû Dum, statement I recite to your honour. Yesterday Puaram Dum caught fish in waters which I have leased (from Government). On my asking him why he fished in my waters, he replied : ' I did not fish in your water, I fished in the Tengâ pânì.' I, however, saw a porpoise in his boat ; but porpoises do not exist in the Tengâ pânì, therefore I, slave, think he fished in my waters and I consequently request your honour to make enquiries into this my, slave, complaint.

[illegible]
Aw wâ tâ â kyawng
[illegible]
khâm kau Dhâ tû tam ngâ
[illegible]
mâ lau chau pâ lüng mai ti
[illegible]
khâ nam. Mâ nga Pû â ram
[illegible]
tam ngâ kâ naü nam au kau
[illegible]
sü mai* khâ† pâ kau man
[illegible]
mai wâ kâ maü het sang nam

Aw watâ ! The gist of my Dhâtû Dum's statement (I) recite to *your honour.* Yesterday Puaram Dum fished inside the waters which I bought. I said to him why (do) you fish in my waters ? Then he said I (did) not search fish in

* This *mai* (locative case postposition) belongs to *kâ naü* ; *ka naü mai* = inside.
† *Khâ* = search ; *pâ* = fish.

kau mai khâ pâ mü nai man
18 17 16 20 21

wâ kau nam maü mai pâ n'
22 23 29 28 27 26 24

khâ kau khâ pâ nam Tengâ
25 30 31 34 33

mai nam* kau hü man mai
32 35 41 40 39

lem kâ pâ chang yang
36 37 38

tô wâ nam Tengâ mai cham†
42 48 47 46

pâ chang mâ û lai pü nai sí
43 44 45 49

kau khâ kha laü man khâ pâ
50 51 52 53 54

nam kau mai chaü û‡
57 56 55

lai pü nai sì trâ kau khâ
58 65 63 64

nai chau pâ lüng pyet haü tì
62 59 61 60

khâ nam*

your water. I fished in
28 29 30 31 32

the Tengâ pânî. I saw a
33 34 35 36

porpoise is in his boat, but
37 38 39 40 41 42

porpoises don't live in the
43 44 45 46

Tengâ pânî, therefore, I,
47 48 49 50

slave, presume he fished
51 52 53 54

in my water; consequently
55 56 57 58

(I pray) *your honour* to
59

make enquiries (into) thîs
60 61 62

my, slave, case.
63 64 65

Complaint No. 4.

Chausang said: on Saturday, the 15th day of the third moon, time noon, Sengmet came to my house and asked for liquor. Then I said, if you drink liquor you will quarrel with

---

* *Nam* is a particle of assertion.
† *Cham* is an hypothetical particle.
‡ *Chaü û* is used here as a verb of assertion; he *certainly* fished in my water.

people, I will not give you liquor. If I do so you will fight with people. Then Sengmet said, how many times have I been drunk (from liquor)? Tell me how many times you have seen me (drunk), and speaking thus, he struck me two blows with a stick. One blow hit me on the left hand and one blow hit me on the loin.

Therefore I, slave, have come to complain to your honour.

ၵျွ် ေသွင် ဝါ ၼိုၼ် ေသံ * ၼႆ
Chau sång wâ nün sâm nai
1 2 8 7
ႁါ ဝၼ် ဝၼ် ၸါ ေၼ ဢါ ၶိင်
hâ wan wan châ nê â khing
5 6 4 3 9
ကင် ဝၼ် တိင် ယိင် ေမတ် ႁိုၼ်
kâng wan teng Seng met hün
10 11 15
ကွ် မႆ မါ သီ ယွၼ် † လွ် ႁိုဝ်။
kau mai mâ sî yån lau hü
14 13 12 16 17
မိုဝ် ၼႆ ကွ် ဝါ ကါ မႂ် လွ် ႁိုဝ်
mü nai kau wâ kâ maü lau hü
18 19 20 22 24
ကိၼ် ကါ ေယ် ၼၼ် ပိုၼ်။ ကွ်
kin kâ yê nan pün kau
23 21 26 28
မႂ် မႆ လွ် ႁိုဝ် ၼိုဝ် ႁႂ်။ ေသင်
maü mai lau hü n' haü sang
30 29 31 32 33 34
ကွ် ႁႂ် လွ် ႁိုဝ် သီ ‡ မႂ်
kau haü lau hü sî maü
35 36 37 38
ကိၼ် ကါ ေယ် မႂ် တီ ကၼ် ပိုၼ်
kin kâ yê maü tî kan pün
39 40 41 42 43
မိုဝ် ၼႆ ယိင် ေမတ် ဝါ ကွ် ကီ
mü nai Seng met wâ kau kî
44 45 46 47 48

Chausång said (on) Saturday,
1 2 3 4
(the) fifth day (of the)
5 6
third moon, time midday,
7 8 9 10
Sengmet coming to my
11 12 13 14
house asked (me) (for)
15 16
liquor. Then I said, if you
17 18 19 20 21 22
drink liquor you (will)
23 24 25
quarrel (with) people. I
26 27 28
to you liquor will not give.
29 30 31 32 33
If I giving liquor you
34 35 36 37 38
drinking (it) you will fight
39 40 41 42
people. Then Seng met
43 44 45

* *Nai* is merely used here for emphasis.

† *Yån* is bare root of verb, used here for past time, *vide* page 41 of Grammar.

‡ This participial suffix *sî* belongs to the root verb *haü* = give; *sang kau haü lau hü sî* = if I giving you liquor.

ပၵ်ႉ ၵိၼ် * လဝ် ႁိုဝ် သီ ပဵၼ်
pâk kin lau hü sî pen
49 50 51 53
မႃ ၵႃႈ ၼႆႉ ၵီ ပၵ်ႉ ႁၢၼ် ၵႃ
mâ kâ maü kî pâk han kâ
54 52 55 56 57 58
ၵဝ် မႆႈ လဝ် မႃး ဝႃ ၼင် ငႆ†
kau mai lau mâ wâ nang ngai
59 60 61 62
သီ¶ ၵဝ် မႆႈ ဢဝ် မႆႈ လဝ် သွင်
sî kau mai au mai lau sâng
63 64 65 66
ႁွႆႈ ပေႃ မႃး ႁွႆႈ ၼိုင်‡ ထၵ်ႉ¶
hôi pô mâ hoi lüng thôk
67 68 70 69 71
မိုဝ်း ပႃ သၢႆႈ မႆႈ ႁွႆႈ ၼိုင် ထၵ်ႉ¶
mü pâ sai mai hoi lüng thôk
74 73 72 76 75
ႁၢင် ဢဵင် မႆႈ ၼႆႈ ပိုဝ် ၼႆႈ သီ ၵဝ်
hang êng mai lai pü nai sî kau
78 77 79 80
ၶႃ မႃ ႁဵတ်း တြႃ ၸဝ်ႈ ပႃ လိုင်
khâ mâ het trâ chau pâ lüng
81 82 83 84 86
မႆႈ တီ ၶႃ ၼမ်း||
mai tî khâ nam.
85

said I how many times
46 47 48 49
drinking liquor have
50 51 52
become foolish? You
53 54 55
how many times seen me
56 57 58 59
(drunk) tell (me), speaking
60 61
thus (he) me with (a) stick
62 63 64 65
two blows struck. One
66 67 68 69
blow hit (me) on left hand
70 71 72 73 74
(and) one blow on the loin.
75 76 77 78
Therefore I, slave, come
79 80 81 82
(to) make complaint to
83 84 85
your honour.
86

Complaint No. 5.

The day before yesterday two persons came to my house at night and opened a box. Then awaking I ran (to the spot) and saw their two bodies carrying off my box; but, as I did not see their faces, I do not know who the men are.

Then I stood and called out to my neighbours and acquainted them with the facts of the theft. On the following morning I went to the thana and told the officer in charge, and he went and made an investigation and arrested Chaungo and Chaunam, but on their giving the thana officer thirty rupees he let them both go. Therefore I, slave, being dissatisfied, have come to complain to your honour.

---

* *Kin* is the bare root of the verb used as a verbal noun.

† *Nang* = like ; *ngai* or *nai* = this.

‡ ၼိုင် is an abbreviated form of *lüng* = one.

¶ *Thôk* = bare root of verb used for past time, *vide* page 41 of Grammar.

|| *Nam* is a particle of assertion.

မါ သုမ် ကၢင် ၶိုၼ် မႆ ကုၼ်
Mâ sûm kâng khün mai kôn
1 3 2 5

သွင် ကုၼ် ႁိုၼ် ႁႂ် မႆ မါ သီ
sång kô hün hau mai mâ sî
4 9 8 7 4

ပုတ် * တိၵ်း မိုဝ် ၼႆ ၵႂ် တိုၼ်
pût tek mü nai kau tün
10 11 12 13 14

သီ လိၼ် ၵါး † ၵႂ် တူဝ် သွင်
sî len kâ kau tô sång
16 17 19

ၶါ မႆ ‡ ႁၼ် ၵါး ဢုံ တိၵ်
khâ mai han kâ ûm tek
20 18 21 22

သီ ¶ ပႆ ၵါး တေႃ ၼႆ ဢူ ၵေႃ
sî pai kâ tô nai û kaw
23 24

ၼါ သွင် ၶါ မါ ႁၼ် ၵါ
nâ sång khâ mâ han kâ
25 26 27 28

လႆ ပိုဝ် ၼႆ ၵႂ် ၵုၼ် မါ
lai pü nai kau kôn mâ
29 30 33 31

တွင် ၵါး မိုဝ် ၼႆ ၵႂ် သွ်ႂ သီ
tång kâ. Mü nai kau sau sî
32 34 35 36

ၵုၼ် တီ ၵိုဝ် ၼႆ ‖ ၶႂ် မႆ
kôn tî kaü nai khau mai
38 39 40 41

ႁွင် ၵါး ပွင် ၶမ် ပါလၵ်ၼႆ
hång kâ pång khâm pâ lâk nai
37 43 44

ၵေႃ ၶႆ ၵါး ၼင် § မါ ႁုၵ်
kaw khai kâ nang mâ hôk
45 42 46

The day before yesterday, at
1 2

night, two persons coming
3 4 5 6

to my house opened a box,
7 8 9 10 11

then I awaking ran (to
12 13 14 16

the spot) ; I saw bodies of
17 18 19

both carrying box and ran,
20 21 22 23

but faces of both not seen,
24 25 26 27 28

therefore I don't know
29 30 31 32

the men.
33

Then I standing called peo-
34 35 36 37 38

ple place near in (and) ac-
39 40 41

quainted (them) with par-
42

ticulars of thieves, also
43 44 45

next morning I going to
46 47 48 49

* *Pût* = open, is the bare root of the verb used here to express past time.

† *Kâ* is the past tense suffix.

‡ *Mai* is the accusative case postposition.

¶ This *si* (participial suffix) belongs to the root verb *ûm* = carry (in front of one).

‖ *Nai khau* is the plural suffix belonging to *kôn kôn nai khau* = persons ; *mai* is the accusative case postposition.

§ *Nang* is a conjunction meaning as, when, &c.

[illegible] *
kang laü kau kâ thâ nâ mai
46 47 48 50 49

[illegible]
sî chau thâ nâ mai lau kâ chau
54 53 52 51 55

[illegible]
thâ nâ kâ sî tai kâ Chau-
56 57 59

[illegible] ¶
ngô Chau nam sâng khâ mai
60 61

[illegible]
sî au kâ mü nai sâng khâ
58 62 63

[illegible] † [illegible]
haü â nip kâ nügn sâm sip
64 65 66 67

[illegible]
chau thâ nâ sâng khâ mai
69 68 71

[illegible] (*or* [illegible] ‡ [illegible])
poi kâ poi haü kâ
70 70

[illegible] ¶
lai pü nai kau khâ chaü mâ
72 73 74 76

[illegible]
tai sî mâ het trâ chau pâ
75 77 78 79 81

[illegible] ¶
lüng mai tî khâ nam
80

'thana' told to thânâ dâr.
50 51 52 53 54
Thânâ dar going investi-
55 56 57
gated (and) arrested
58
Chaungô (and) Chaunam
59 60
both of them. Then they
61 62 63
gave (a) bribe (of) rupees
64 65 66
thirty (and) thânâ dâr re-
67 68 69
leased *them both.* There-
70 71 72
fore I, slave, being dis-
73 74 75
satisfied come (to) make
76 77 78
(a) complaint to *your*
79 80
honour.
81

Sporting Tale.

One day Bordum 'gam' came and informed me that there was a herd of wild buffaloes on a chapuri, up the Dibang, accompanied by a large bull, and he continued, "if your honour desires to shoot it do so." Then I ordered my syce

---

* *Mai* is the locative case particle.

† *Kâ* belongs to the root verb *haü.*

‡ *Haü* = give is used here as a causal verb ; *poi haü ka* meaning caused them to be released or gave them their liberty.

¶ *Chaü mâ tai si* means literally mind not dying.

to bring my horse, and upon his doing so I gave Bordum my gun and said: 'let us go quickly,' and going off with him (Bordum 'gam') I shot a large, wild, bull buffalo. I hit it in the head, and it died. I have the horns of that bull still in my house.

ဝၼ် ၵျ် ပေါ တုံ* ကံ*
Wan lüng Bor dûm gam
2 1 3 4

မါ ၸီ ၵွ် မႝ လွ်။ ငွၼ် ၵၢင်
mâ sî kau mai lau ngån kang
5 7 6 13

ၼံ တိ ပၢင်* မႝ ၶႝ ႁေၵ်
nam Di bang mai khâi hê
16 15 14 12 11

ၾုင် ၵျ် ယၢင် ဢူ။ ၶႝ ထုၵ်
phüng lüng yang û khâi thük
10 9 8 20 19

လုင် ၵေႃ ဢၢ ၵျ်။ လုႁ် ဢူ။
lông kaw â lüng hôy û
18 21 17 23 22

သၢင် ဝၢ မွ်† ၸွ် ၶၢ ယိုဝ်
sang wâ maü chau khâ yü
24 25 26 27

ၵၢ ၸမ်‡ ၵၢ ယိုဝ် တၢ။ မိုဝ် ၼႝ
kâ cham kâ yü tâ mü nai
26 28 29 30

ၵွ် ၵႝ သၼ် ၵွ် မႝ မၢ
kau kai san kau mai mâ
31 34 33 32 39

ဢွ် မၢ တၢ ၼႝ ဢၢ ၶၢင်
au mâ tâ n a i â khâng
38 35 36

ႁွ် ၵၢ။ ဢႝ သၼ် ၵွ် မၢ
haü ká ai san kau mâ
37 41 40 42

ဢွ် မၢ မၢ။ ¶ မိုဝ် ၼႝ ၵွ် ၸီ
au mâ mâ mü nai kau sî
43 44 45 4

One day Bordum gam com-
1 2 3 4 5
ing informed me there is
6 7 8
a herd of wild buffaloes
9 10 11 12
on a chapuri in the Di-
13 14
bang river, a large male
15 16 17 18 19
buffalo also is accompany-
20 21 22 23
ing (them). If you wish-
24 25 26
ing to shoot (it) go (and)
27 28
shoot (it). Then I to my
29 30 31 32 33
syce this order gave, bring
34 35 36 37 38
(my) horse; my syce horse
39 40 41 42
brought. Then I giving
43 44 45 46

* The spelling of these words is peculiar because the Khâmti alphabet has not got the necessary letters.

† *Maü chau* is respectful; *vide* page 24 of Grammar.

‡ *Kâ cham* (conditional participial suffix) belongs to *khâ*, root verb, meaning wish, &c.

¶ The doubling of the vowel *â* denotes that the word is to be repeated, *au mâ* = bring; *au mâ mâ* = brought.

လတ် ၵွင် ပေႃ တုံ မႂ်
lat kau Bor dum mai
47 50 49

ႁႂ် သီ ဝႃ ၵႃ၊ ပႂ် * ႁႃ ၵႃ
haü sî wâ kâ pai kâ kâ
46 51 53 54

ၶၼ်ၶၼ် † ၵွတ် မိုၼ် ၼႂ် ၵွင်
khan khan kât mü nai kau
55 52 56 57

တင် ပေႃ တုံ ၵမ် ၵႃ သီ
tang Bor dum gam kâ sî
58 59 60 61

ၶႂ် ႁေ ၶႂ် ‡ ထိုၵ် လုင်
khâi hê khái thük lông
67 65 66 64

တေႃ လိုင် ¶ ယိုဝ် ၵႃ၊ ထေႃၵ် ၵႃ
tô lüng yü ká thôk kâ
63 62 68

ႁူဝ် မႂ် တႂ် ၵႃ၊ ၶွ ၶႂ် ၼၼ်
hô mai tai kâ khau khâi nau
70 69 71 72 74 73

ထေႃၵ် ၶိမ် ငႂ် ႁိုၼ် ၵွင် မႂ် ||
tôk chem ngai hün kau mai
76 79 78 77

ယင် ဢူ။
yang û
75

my gun to Bordum said let
47 48 49 50 51 52

us go quickly. Then I
53 54 55 56 57

with Bordum gam going
58 59 60 61

shot a large, wild, male
62 63 64 65 66

buffalo. (I) hit (it) in
67 68 69

(the) head (and) (it) died.
70 71

The horns of that buffalo
72 73 74

are still in my house.
75 76 77 78 79

Shooting Story No. 2.

One day Pâlangkhü went with Chauphâhôm to stroll in the jungles, and (they) met a wild pig. Pâlangkhü fired and hit the pig in the leg, but the pig not dying fled. They both tracked and overtook it. Chauphâhôm fired and hit it in the ribs; then the pig not having been killed charged him. Pâlangkhü fled, but Chauphâhôm failing to do so the pig ripped him. While the pig was ripping Chauphâhôm,

---

* *Pai* = come, *hâ* = we, *kâ* = go, *khau khau* = quickly; *kât* = will; but *pai hâ kâ khau khau kât* means let us go quickly.

† The doubling of the final mark (ᨿ) denotes the repetition of the word. Khâmtis often add several, but the word is only to be repeated *over*.

‡ *Khái thük* = male buffalo.

¶ *Tó* is a numeral expletive, and ႁိုင် an abbreviation for *lüng* = one.

|| *Mai* is the locative case postposition.

Pàlangkhü fired from a distance, and hitting the pig in the head killed it, but soon afterwards Chauphâhôm likewise died.

ဝၼ် ၵျ ပႃလင် ၶိုၼ် တင်	Wan lüng Palang khü tang	2 1 3 7	One day Pàlangkhü went to	1 2 3 4
ၸဝ် လႃ ႁွမ် ကႃ * လေ ထိုၼ်။	Chau phâ hôm kâ lê thün	8 8 4 5 6	stroll (in the) jungles with	5 6 7
မူ ထိုၼ် တူဝ် † ၵျ ႁွပ်။ ‡	mû thün tô lüng hôp	12 11 10 9	Chauphâhôm (and) met a	8 9 10
ပႃလင် ၶိုၼ် ယိုဝ် ကႃ ထုၵ် ကႃ	Pâlang khü yü kâ thôk kâ	13 14 15	wild pig. Pâlangkhü fired	11 12 13 14
တိၼ် မႆ မူ ထိုၼ်။ မႃ တႆ သီ	tin mai mû thün mâ tai si	19 18 17 16 20 21	(and) hit the wild pig	15 16 17
ပႆ ကႃ။ သၢင် ၶႃ ၸမ် သီ	pai kâ sâng khâ châm sî	22 24 23 24-a	on (the) leg, but (the	18 19
ၶိုတ် ကႃ။ ၸဝ် ၽႃ ႁွမ်	khüt kâ Chau phâ hôm	25 26	pig) not dying fled. They	20 21 22 23
ယိုဝ် ကႃ ထုၵ် ကႃ ၼုၵ် ၶင်	yü kâ thôk kâ nûk khang	27 28 30	both tracking overtook	24 24a 25
မႆ။ မိုဝ် ၼႆ မူ ထိုၼ် မႃ	mai mü nai mû thün mâ	29 31 33 32 34	(it). Chauphâhom fired	26 27
တႆ သီ လူဝ် မႃ။ ပႃလင် ၶိုၼ်	tai sî lô mâ Palang khü	35 36 37	(and) hit (it) in the ribs;	28 29 30
ယေ ¶ ပႆ ကႃ ၸဝ် လႃ ႁွမ်	yê pai kâ Chau phâ hôm	38 39	then the wild pig not dying	31 32 33 34 35
ယေ ¶ မႃ ‖ ၼႆ ပႆ သီ မူ ထိုၼ်	yê mâ nai pai sî mû thün	40 41 43 42	charged. Palangkhü fled,	36 37 38
			(but) Chauphâhôm fail-	39 40
			ing to fly the wild pig rip-	41 42 43 44

* *Kâ*, bare root of verb *go*, used for past time.
† *Tô* is a numeral expletive; ၵျ is an abbreviation for *lüng* = one.
‡ Here again the bare root of the verb is used for the past tense.
¶ *Yê* is apparently used here as an explanatory particle.
‖ *Mâ* = not; *nai* = get, *i.e.*, miss attaining, fail.

ပႆ ၵႃ။ မိုဝ်
pai kâ mü
44 45

ပႆ ၸဝ် ၽႃ ႁွမ် မႆ ၼႆ ပႃ
pai Chau phâ hôm mai nai Pâ-
46 47 46

လင် ၶိုဝ် လုၵ်* တီ ၵႆ မႆ
lang khü lûk tî kai mai
48 49 50

ယိုဝ် မႃ ထုၵ် ၵႃ ႁူဝ် မႆ
yü mâ thôk kâ hô mai
51 52 55 54

မူ ထိုၼ်း တႆ ၵႃ ဝႆ လင် ၼႆ
mû thün tai kâ wai lang nai
53 56 57 58

ၸဝ် ၽႃ ႁွမ် ၵေႃ တႆ ၵႃ။
Chau phâ hôm kaw tai kâ
59 60 71

ped (him). While (the pig) (was) ripping Chauphâhôm, Pâlangkhü from afar fired (and) hit the pig in the head (and) (it) died (and) after this Chauphâhôm likewise died.

Shooting Story No. 3.

One day two men, one of them named Chaungî the other Chaukoi, went into the jungle together.

Chaungî said, companion, I am afraid! Chaukoi replied don't fear! I am strong, whatever comes I will cut and stick it.

Then a large bear came towards them from inside the jungle, and Chaukoi fled at once and climbed into a tree. Chaungî was unable to climb therefore hid in a thicket. If he had not hidden the bear would have killed him.

ဝၼ်း လိုင်။ ၵူၼ်း သွင် ၵေႃ†
Wan lüng kôn săng kô
2 1 4 3

ႁူမ် ၵႃ‡ ထိုၼ်း။ ၸိုဝ် သွင် ၶႃ
hôm kâ thün chü săng khâ
7 5 6 10 9

One day two men went (into) the jungle together, their two names being one

---

* *Lûk mai* = from.

† *Kô* is a numeral expletive used with human beings.

‡ *Kâ*, bare root of the verb *go*, used here for past tense, *vide* page 41 of Grammar.

ၸမ် ၵုဝ်* လုင်း ၸဝ်ႈ ငီ
Cham kô lüng Chau ngî
11 12 13

တင် ၵုဝ်* ၸဝ်ႈ ၵွႆႈ၊ ၸဝ်ႈ ငီ ဝႃႈ
tâng kô Chau koi, Chau ngî wâ
14 15 16 17

ၵေႃ ၸဝ်ႈ ၵၢဝ်ႇ ၵေႃ ဢူး ၸဝ်ႈ ၵွႆႈ
kô chau kau kô û Chau koi
18 19 21 20 22

ဝႃႈ တီ ၵေႃ ထႃ သင်၊ ၵၢဝ်ႇ
wâ tî kô kâ sang kau
23 25 26 24 27

ႁႅင် ဢူ ၵႃ သင် မႃမႃ ၵေႃ†
hêng û kâ sang mâ mâ kaw
29 28 30 31 30

ၵၢဝ်ႇ တီ ၽၼ် တီ တိင် ၼႂ် ပီ
kau tî phan tî teng maü pî
32 33 34 35 36 38 37

ၵေႃ တႃ၊ မိူဝ် ၼႆႈ လုၵ်း ၼႂ်
kô tâ mü nai lûk naü
39 40 41 42

ထိုၼ် မႆႈ‡ မီ လွင် တူဝ်¶ လုင်း
thün mai mî lông tô lüng
44 43 47 46 45

မႃမႃ ၵၼ် ပႃ သၢင် ၶႃ မႆႈ‖
mâ mâ kan pâ sång khâ mai
48 49 51 50

မိူဝ် ၼႆႈ ၸဝ်ႈ ၵွႆႈ ဢွၼ် တင် ပႆႇ
mü nai Chau koi ån tang pai
52 53 55 54

ၶိုၼ် တူၼ်မႆႈ ၵႃ၊ ၸဝ်ႈ ငီ
khün tôn mai kâ Chau ngî
56 57 58

ၸမ် ၶိုၼ် တူၼ် မႆႈ မႃ ပိၼ်
cham khün tôn mai mâ pen
61 61-a 61-a 59 60

Chaungî, the other Chaukoi. Chaungî said, companion, I am afraid! Chaukoi said (you) what will fear! I am strong, whatever comes I will cut (and) will stick, don't you be afraid. Then from inside of the jungle a large bear came towards them both; then Chaukoi fled at once (and) climbed a tree. Chaungî (was unable to climb a tree therefore (he) hid in a thicket;

13 14 1
16 17 18
19 20 21 22
23 24 25
26 27 28 29 30
31 32 33 34
35 36 37 38
39 40 41 43
43 44 45 46
47 48 49 50
51 52 53 54
55 56
57 58 59 60
61 61-a 62
63 64 65

---

* *Kô* is a numeral expletive used with human beings.

† *Kaw* belongs to *kâ sang*; *kâ sang kau* = whatever.

‡ *Mai* belongs to *lûk*; *lûk naü mai* = from inside of.

¶ *Tô* is a numeral expletive.

‖ *Mai* belongs to *kanpa*; *kanpa mâ* = in direction of.

လႆ ပိုၼ် ၼႆ ယုံ ၼႃ မႆ မိပ် သီ
lai pü[62] nai yûm[65] nâ mai[64] mep sî[63]
ဢူ ၵႃႈ* သင် မၼ် မႃ မိပ်
û kâ sang[66] man[67] mâ[69] mep[70]
ၸမ်† မီ တီ ဢွၵ်ႉ တႆ ၼမ်ႉ‡
cham[68] mî[71] tî[72] au[73] tai nam.

supposing[66] he[67] had[68] not[69] hidden[70] the bear[71] would[72] have killed[73] (him).

---

* *Mep sî* = having hidden ; *û ka* = remained ; *mep sî û kâ* = remained hidden.

† *Cham* is a particle denoting supposition.

‡ *Nam* is a particle of assertion.

VOCABULARY.

I have given the bare root of verbs in the following vocabulary, and I may add that there is no complete formal distinction between nouns, adjectives, and verbs. Each in its root is indistinguishable from the others.

English.	Khâmtî.	Remarks.
Able (possessing sufficient physical or mental power for the accomplishment of some object).	ပၼ် (pen) ...	*Pen* also means to become, happen.
About (near, in time, &c.).	ၶၼ် (khan) ...	ၵႃတၵ်=*á ták* is also used.
Above (higher in place).	ၵႃၼိုဝ် (kâ nü)	Also means up stream.
Abuse, *v.*	ပႂ် (pau)	Pronounced with a rising inflection of voice.
Accompany, *v.*....	လွႆ (loy)	Also means in company of.
Accused, *n.*	တြႃလျိၵ်(trâ lyẹk)	
Adze, *n.*	ၶၼ် ၸၵ် khân châk.	
After, *a.*, *adv.*, and *prep.*	ၵႃႇလင်(kâ lang) ; ဝႆႇလင် (wai lang).	

English.	Khâmtî.	Remarks.
Again (once more), *adv.*	ၶုၼ် ၼႃ ၵဝ် (khün nâ kau).	သမ် (*sam*) also used.
Age, *n.*	ဢႃသၵ် (â sâk).	
Ago, past, *adv.* or *a.*	ထူၼ်ယဝ် (thôn yau)	*Yau* is a completive particle used to form a past perfect tense.
Agree (yield, assent).	ၸူ (chû).	
Aground, *adv.*	ၶင် (khâng) *or* ပိတ် (pet).	
Air, wind, *n.*	လူမ် (lôm)	Often used in conjunction with *pau* = to blow.
Alike (without difference, of like kind, species, &c.).	တူၵဝ် (tû kau) *or* တူတူ tû tû.	လႃ တေႃ တူ *lâ tô tû* is also used.
Alive, fresh, *a.*....	ၼိပ် (nîp).	
All, *a.*	တင်မုင် (tâng müng) *or* တင် လႆ (tang lai) *or* တင်လုင် (tang lûng).	တင် ဝၼ် (*tang wan*) = all day. တင် ၶုၼ် (*tang khün*) = all night.
Alligator, *n.*	ငုၵ် (ngük).	
Alone, *a.*	ၼႆ (nai)	ၼႆ သင် (*nai sang*) is more emphatic.
Also, and, *adv.* and *conj.*	ၵေႃ (kô).	
Always, *adv.*	ၵူမူ (kû mü).	
Amidst, among, between.	ၶုင် ၵင် (khüng kâng).	

English.	Khâmtî.	Remarks.
Angry, wrathful	ၶႃ ၸႃ (khâ châ)	ႁဵတ် ၸႃ (*het châ*) to rage.
Animal, *n*.	ၼိုဝ် မိုဝ် (nü mü)....	This word has not the same wide meaning that the English word animal has.
"Anna," four pice.	ေသြႃ (srô).	
Another (in addition to, one more, &c.).	တင် (tang)	
	ငဝ် ၵွ် တင် တူဝ် ယင် ဢူ ngô kau tang tô yang û	= I have another cow.
Ant, *n*.	မူတ် (môt).	
Anus, *n*.	ႁူၶီ (hû khî)	*Hû*=hole, *khî*=dung excrement.
Artful, *a*.	လိမ် (lêm).	
Arm, hand, *n*.	မိုဝ် (mü).	
Armpit, *v*.	ၵႃလေဝ် (kalî).	
Arrive, *v*.	ထိုင် (thüng).	
Arrow, *v*.	လိမ် (lim).	
As, like, similar to, *conj*.	ၼင် (nang)	Often used in conjunction with the adjective=ၼႃၵၼ် (*nâ kan*)=similar.
Ash	တွ် (tau).	
Ask, enquire, *v*.	ထမ် (thâm)	Often used in conjunction with the root verb ႁူ (*hau*)=give.

English.	Khâmtî.	Remarks.
Awake, *a.*	ထုၼ် (tün).	
Axe, *n.* ...	ၶၢၼ် (khân).	
Bachelor, widower, *n.*	ပုင်မႆ (pô mai).	
Back, *n.* ...	လင် (lang).	
Bad (not good), *a.*	ၼုင်ၼီ (n'nī) *or* မႃ ၼီ (mâ ni).	*Lit.* not good.
Bag, *n.*	ထုင် (thông).	
Bait (for fishing), *n.*	ယုင် (yü).	
Bamboo, *n.*	No generic word, each bamboo has its name.*	

* **Names of different kinds of Bamboo.**

Khâmtî.		*Assamese.*
မႆ လၢင် (mai † sâng)	... ...	Jati.
မႆ ႁုၵ် (mai † hôk)	... ...	Kâkô.
မႆ လၢင်ၼမ် (mai † sâng nàm)	... ...	Bûlûkà.
မႆ ၼႆ (mai † nai)	... ...	Bâzol.
မႆ ပု (mai † pôk)	... ...	Tâpô.

† *Mai*=wood, also material of succulent plants, parts of shrubs not hardened, and ligneous.

English.	Khâmti.	Remarks.
Bear, bring forth, *v.*	ၽေ (phê) *or* ၽွႃ ႁၢၼ် ၼႃ (phwâ han nâ) *or* ယင် (yâng).	

Examples.

မႃ ငႃ မေ ၸဝ် မႃ ႁႃ လုၵ်
Mâ ngâ mê Chau mâ hâ lûk
5 2 1 4
ၽေ ၵႃ *or* ၽေ လုၵ် ၵႃ
phê kâ phê lûk kâ
3
or ယင် ၵႃ *or* ၼႆ ၵႃ
yang kâ nai kâ

Chaumahâ's wife had a child yesterday.
1 2 3 4 5

မႂ် ၽေ ဢလႂ် မႆ *or* ဢလႂ်
Mau phê âlaü mai âlaü
2 3 1
မႆ ႁၢၼ်* ၼႃ *or* ဢလႂ် မႆ
mai hau nâ âlaü mai
ပဵၼ် † ၵုၼ်
pen kôn.

Where were you born?
1 2 3

English.	Khâmti.	Remarks.
Bank, of river	ၽင် (phâng) *or* ႁိမ်ၼမ် (him nam).	*Phâng* means precipitous side (of river) and *him* the edge or side (of river).
Bark, *v.* ...	ႁဝ် (hau).	လဝ် (*lau*) is also used
Barrel (of gun), *n.*	ၵွင် (kång) *or* ပျွင် (pyång).	
Basket (carried by men), *n.*	ဢိုၼ်ၽႆ (n'phai).	
Basket (carried by women), *n.*	ဢိုၼ်ပႃ (n'pâ).	
Bat (small kind), *n.*	ဢိမ် (en).	
Bat (large kind), *n.*	ပိင်လိင် (pengleng).	
Bazaar, *n.*	ၵတ် (kat).	

* Literally where did you see face?
† *Alaü mai pen kôn* = where did you become man?

English.	Khâmtî.	Remarks.
Bear, *n.*	မိ (mî)	Pronounced with a rising inflection of voice.
Beam, *n.* ...	ၶိုဝ် (khü)	
Beard, *n.*	ၼုတ် (nôt).	
Beat, *v.*	ပေႃ (pô).	
Because, cause, *conj.*	လႆပိုဝ်ၼႆ (lai p ü nai).	
Bed, *n.*	တီၼွၼ် (tî nån)	*Ti*= place, spot ; *nan*= sleep.
Bee, *n.*	ၽိုင် (phüng).	
Before (previous in time), *adv.*	ၵႃၼႃ (kâ nâ) *or* ၵၼ်ၼႃ (k a n nâ).	အွၼ်တင် (ån tâng) preceding, in time, *prep.*
Before (in front or presence of), *prep.*	ၶင်ၼႃ (khâng nâ).	
Before (just now) (Assamese *a thô ni*).	ၼ်ၵိုဝ်ၵႆ (n'kai) *or* မႃၵႆ (mâ kai.)	These words may mean (like the Assamese *a tho ni*) a very short time before, or several hours.
Beg, ask for, solicit, &c., *v.*	ယွၼ် (yån.)	
Behind (later in time, &c.).	ၵႃလင် (kâlang) *or* ဝႆလင် (w a i lang).	
Believe (credit), *v.*	ယုံ (yûm.)	
Believe, suppose, imagine.	ၶၼ်တိုဝ် (khan taü).	
Belly, *n.*	တွင် (tång).	
Bengal, *n.*	ၵြႃ (Kra)	Every place below Assam is called *Kra* ; for instance, an Englishman is called *Kra phük* or white Bengali !

English.	Khâmtî.	Remarks.
Bengali, *n.* ...	ၵြႃၼၵ် (kra nâk)	*Nâk*=black.
'Bheel,' *n.* ...	ၼွင် (nång).	
Bind (confine, restrain, &c.), *v.*	ၾုၵ် (phûk).	
Bird, *n.* ...	ၼုၵ် (nôk).	
Bite, *v.* ...	ၵပ် (kâp).	
Bitter, *a.* ...	ၶုံ (khûm).	
Black, *a.* ...	ၼမ် (nam) *or* ၼၵ် (nâk).	Pronounced with a rising inflection of voice.
Blind, *a.* ...	တႃမွတ် (tâ måt)....	*Tâ*=eye.
Blood, *n.* ...	လိုတ် (lüt).	
Blow, *v.* ...	ပဝ် (pau).	
Board, *n.* ...	ပိၼ် (pen).	ႁူဝ် (hô)=bow (*Lit.* head) ႁင် (*hâng*)= stern, pronounced with, a rising inflection of voice.
Boat, *n.* ...	ႁိုဝ် (hü).	
Boatman, *n.* ...	လုၵ်ႁိုဝ် (lûk hü)	တမ်ငႃ (*tam ngâ*)=Dum.
Body, *n.* ...	တူဝ် (tô).	
Boil, *v.* ...	တုံ (tôm).	
Bone, *n.* ...	ၼုၵ် (nûk).	
Book, *n.* ...	ပပ် (pâp) *or* လိၵ် (lik).	
Borrow (take loan of), (money), *v.*	ယုံဢဝ် (yûm au)...	*Au*=take.

English.	Khâmtî.	Remarks.
Both (the one and the other).	တင်သွင် (tang sång).	
Both (*i.e.*, we two)	ႁႃ (hâ).	
Both	သွင်ၵႃ (sång khâ)	Used in speaking *of* two persons.
Both	သွင်ၶိုဝ် (sång khü)	Used in speaking *to* two persons.
Bough, *n.*	ၵႃမႆ (khâ mai).	
Boundary	ၼိူၼ် (nen).	
Bow, *n.*	ၵူင် (kông).	
Box, *n.*	တိၵ် (tek).	
Boy, *n.*	တူဝ်ဢွၼ် (tô ån).	
Bracelet, *n.*	ဝိၼ် (wen).	
Brain, *n.*	ၵႄၵိၵ် (ke kå).	
Brass, *n.*	တွင် (tång).	
Break, by violence or spontaneously, *v.*	ႁၵ် (hâk)	*Hâk* applies to the breaking of things having length.
Break, *v.i.*	ၽေ (phê).	
Break, *v.t.*	ဢဝ်ၽေ (au phê).	
Break, string, cane, rope &c.	ၶတ် (khat).	
Breast, *n.*	ၸေ (chê).	
Breast nipple, *n.*	သူပ်ၸေ (sôp chê)	*Sôp*=mouth, *sôp chê* =mouth of breast.
Bridge, *n.*	ၶေႃ (khô).	
Brick, *n.*	ဢူတ် (ût)	*Ût* also means a camel in Khâmtî.
Bring, *v.*	ဢဝ်မႃ (au mâ).	
Broom, *n.*	ယူပတ် (yû pat).	

English.	Khâmtî.	Remarks.
Brother (elder)....	ပီ (pî).	
Brother (younger).	ၼွင် (nång).	
Brother-in-law....	လုင်တႃ (tûng tâ).	
Buffalo, *n.*	ၵႂၢႆ (khâi).	
Bugle, *n.*	တူတ် (lût)	Blow bugle=*pau pau tût*.
Build (house), *v.*	ပုၵ် (pôk).	
Bullet, *n.*	မၵ်ၸႃ (mak châ).	
Bundle, *n.*	ပၼ် (pan).	
Burma ...	မၼ် (Mân).	
Burn (as a fire)	ၽႆႈႁိုင်(phai hüng)	
Burn (destroy by fire).	ၸွတ်ၽႆ(såt phai).	
Burn (be on fire), *v. i.*	မႆၽႆ (maï phai).	
Bury, *v.*	ၽင် (phang).	
Busy (occupied with employment).	ၶၵ် (khak).	
But, *conj.*	တုဝ်ဝႃ (to wâ) *or* ထုဝ်ၼႆဢူၵေႃ (to nai û kå).	
Butter, *n.*	ထုဝ်ပတ် (thô pat).	
Buttock (rump), *n.*	ၵိမ်ၵုၼ် (kem kôn).	
Buy, *v.*	သိုဝ် (sü).	
Calf of leg, *n.*	ပွင်ၵၢၼ်(pång kan).	
Call, *v.*	ႁွင် (hång).	
Call, give alarm, shout out loud for help.	ဢီဝ် (î û).	

English.	Khâmtî.	Remarks.
Candle (made locally of wax), *v.*	ယိမိ (sî mî).	
Cane, *n.*	ဝႆ (wai).	
Cap (for gun), *n.*	မွက်တွင် (måk tâng).	*Mak*=' *chûngá* ' *tang* =brass.
Cards, *n.*	ၽႆ (phâi)	Made of ivory, horn, or wood; 32 in a pack.
Carry (in front), *v.*	ဢုံ (ûm).	
Carry (on back), *v.*	ပႃ (pâ).	
Carry, on shoulder as gun, &c., *v.*	မျက် (myek).	
Cart, for bullocks, *n.*	လိင် (lêng).	
Castrate, *v.*	တွၼ် (tân).	
Cat, *n.*	မိဝ် (mi au).	
Censure, blame, &c., *v.*	ၸႃ (châ).	*Chá* also means to rage at.
' Châng '	ႁင် (hang) *or* ၸင် (châng).	
Change, *v.* (substitute for).	လႆ (lai).	
' Châpurî '	ပင် (pâng).	
Charge (as an animal), *v.*	လုဝ် (lô).	
Cheap (not dear), *a.*	ၶၼ်မွ (khan mau)	*Khan*=price; *mau*= light.
Cheek, *n.*	ၵိမ် (kem) *or* ၵမ် (kem).	
Chest	ႁုဝ်ၸႂ် (hô chaü)....	*Hó chaü* also means heart.
Child, *n*	တုဝ်ဢွၼ် (tô ân) *or* လၵ်ၶႃ (lakkhâ).	
Chillie, *n*	မႃၽိတ် (mâ phit).	

English.	Khâmtî.	Remarks.
Chin, *n* ...	ကၢင် (kâng).	
China (country)	ၶေ (khê).	
'Chudder,' a native thin shawl.	ၽႃမႂ် (phâ mai).	
Cigar, *n.* ...	သိလိတ် (selit *or* silit).	
Claw, *n.* ...	လိပ် (lep).	
Clean, *v.* ...	ပွတ် (påt).	
Climb, ascend, *v.* (go up stream).	ၶိုၼ် (khün).	
Cloth, *n.* ...	ၽႃ (phâ).	
Cloud, *n.* ...	မွၵ် (måk).	
Coat, *n.* ...	သိုဝ် (sü).	
Coarse, thick, &c., *a.*	ၼႃ (nâ).	
Cohabit, *v.* ...	ဢဝ်ၵၼ် (au kan).	
Cold (catarrh), *n.*	ဝတ် (wat).	
Cold (not hot), *a.*	ၵတ် (kat).	
Cold (suffering from absence of heat).	ၼဝ် (nau).	
Cold season ...	မိုဝ်ၼဝ် *or* ၼီ (mü nau *or* nî).	*Lit.* when cold or nice.
Collect (gather into one body or place), *v.*	(håm) *or* ၵုမ် (kûm).	*Håm* is a transitive and *kûm* an intransitive verb.
Come (a moving hitherward), *v.*	မႃ (mâ).	
Come back, *v.* ...	ပွၵ်မႃ (pôk mâ).	
Comb, *n.* ...	ဝီ (wî).	
Companion, *n.* ...	တႆၵုဝ် (tai kô).	

English.	Khâmtî.	Remarks.
Complaint, *n.* ...	တြႃ (trâ) ...	Complaint တြႃၼေႃ (*trâ nó*).
Complete, not deficient.	ꩬုံ (kûm) *or* ထုၼ် (thôn).	
Consult, oracle, *v.*	မၢဝ် (niau) ...	*Paman*=man who consults oracles.
Converse, *v.* ...	တၢၼ်ꩬၢၼ် (tân kân) *or* မွၼ်ꩬၢၼ် (mon kân).	*Kan* is a reciprocal particle.
Cooked (not raw), *a.*	ꩬုꩡ်ယဝ် (sûk yau).	
Cooking-pot, *n.*	မေႃ (mô).	
Cool (moderately cold), *a.*	ယိၼ် (yen).	
Correct, right, precise, *a.*	ထုꩬ် (thûk) ...	မၢၼ် (*man*)=true is also used.
Cotton, *n.* ...	ꩬုၺ် (kouy) ...	Pronounced *kui*=cultivated cotton.
Cough, *n.* ...	ဢႆ (ai).	
Count (enumerate).	ဢၢၼ် (ân).	
Country, *n.*	မိုင် (müng).	
Cow, *n.* ...	ငူဝ် (ngô).	
Cow-house, *n.* ...	ၵွꩬ်ငူဝ် (khåk ngô).	
Cover (any article, *v.*	ꩡႃ (châ *or* ႁုံ (hôm).	
Crack, *v.* ..	တိꩬ် (tek).	
Crow, *n.* ...	ꩬႃ (kâ).	
Crow, *v.* ...	ၶၼ် (khan).	
Crooked, *a.* ...	ငွꩬ် (ngåk).	
Cross, river bridge, &c., *v.*	ၶံ (khâm).	
Cry (as human being), *v.*	ႁႆ (hai).	

English.	Khâmti.	Remarks.
Cry (as an animal), *v.*	ꩭင်ꩫ် (hångtai)	ꩡျိၵ်ႉ (*kyek*) to bark as a deer, or roar as a tiger.
Cubit, *n.* ...	ꩬွၵ် (såk).	
Cucumber, *n.* ...	တိင် (teng).	
Cup, for drinking.	ၵွၵ် (kåk) ...	ဝၼ် (*wán*) Assamse 'bâtî.'
(Glass for drinking).	ဝၼ်ꩬိင် (wânseng)	
Custom, *n.* ...	ထုင် (thûng).	
Cut, *v.* ...	မၵ် (mâk) ပတ် pat.	*Mák* means to cut with a downward blow, *pat* with a drawing movement.
Cut, wood, *v.* ...	တိပ် (tep).	
Cut, rice, *v.* ...	ပတ် (pat).	
Cut, jungle, *v.* ...	တိ (tî).	
Cut, string, cane, &c.	တတ် (tat).	
Cut down tree or bamboo, &c.	ပံ (pam).	
Cut boat, *v.* ...	ꩧၼ် (phan).	
Dacoit, *n.* ...	ၵုၼ်ꩡုၼ် (kôn chôn).	
Damp, *a.* ...	ယိၵ် (yik).	
Dance, *v.* ...	ၵႃ (kâ).	
'Dao' *n.* ...	ꩧႃ (phâ).	
Dark (not light), *a.*	ၼပ်ꩬိင်(nap sing).	

English.	Khâmtî.	Remarks.
Daughter, *n.*	လုက်သ်ꩬ် (lûksau).	
Daughter-in-law, *n.*	လုက်ပ်ꩬ် (lûk paü).	
Dawn, early morn, *n.*	ကင်လွ် (kâng laü).	
Day, *n.*	ဝꩫ် (wan). *	

* The days of the week in Khâmtî are—

ဝꩫ် တြၢင် ကၢꩫွ် (Wan trâng kânôy) ... ... Sunday.
ဝꩫ် တြၢ တၢꩫၢ (Trâng kâ nâ) ... ... Monday.
ဝꩫ် ဢင်ကၢ (Âng kâ) ... ... Tuesday.
ဝꩫ် ပုက် တၢꩭူ (Pók tâ hû) ... ... Wednesday.
ဝꩫ် ꩹ျၢ သၢပၢတေ် (Kyâ sâ pâ tê) ... ... Thursday.
ဝꩫ် သွက် ꩹ျၢ (Sak kyâ) ... ... Friday.
ဝꩫ် ꩡၢꩫေ် (Chânê) ... ... Saturday.

N.B.—Sunday is the first day of the week.

The Khâmtî day is divided into eight periods, namely,—

ꩫိုဝ် လိုꩫ် (mü lüng) ... Time between daybreak and sunrise.
သွင် ꩫိုဝ် (sang mü) ... About sunrise.
သံ ꩫိုဝ် (sâm mü) ... Sunrise to 10 A.M.
သီ ꩫိုဝ် (si mü) ... Midday.
ꩭၢ ꩫိုဝ် (hâ mü) ... Noon to 2 P.M. (about).
ꩭုက် ꩫိုဝ် (hôk mü) ... 2 P.M. to 4 P.M. (about).
ꩡိတ် ꩫိုဝ် (chet mü) ... 4 to 6 P.M. (about).
ပိတ် ꩫိုဝ် (pet mü) ... About sunset.

English.	Khâmtî.	Remarks.
Daytime, light, *n.*	ကၚ်ဝၼ်(kâng wan)	
Today, *n.* ...	မႃၼႆ (mâ nai).	
Yesterday, *n.*, &c.	မႃငႃ (mâ ngâ) ...	As last moon, last Saturday, next before present.
Day before yesterday, *n.*	မႃသုၼ် (mâ sûn).	
Dead, *a.* ...	တႆယွ် (tai yau).	
Deaf, *a.* ...	ႁူၼွၵ် (hû nôk).	
Dear (in price), *a.*	ၶၼ်ၼၵ်(khan nak)	Nak=heavy.
Debt, *n.* ...	ၼီ (nî).	
Decay, *v.* ...	ၼွၵ် (nåk) ...	Pronounced with a rising inflection of voice on the *k*.
Deceive, inveigle, *v.*	လွ (lau).	
Deep not shallow, *a.*	လုၵ် (lûk).	
Deer flesh, *n.* ...	ၼိူ (nü).	
Deficient, *a.* ...	ယွံ (yåm).	
Desire (wish), *a.*	ၶႃ (khâ)	
Descend, *v.* ...	လူင် (lông).	

English.	Khâmtî.	Remarks.
Dew, *n.* ...	ၼႝ (nai).	
Diamond, *n.* ...	ၸိင် (sêng).	
Die, *v.* ...	တႝ (tâi).	
Different (unlike), *a.*	တိၵျႃ (ti khyâ).	
Difficult (not easy), *a.*	ယပ် (yap).	
Dig, hole, *v* ...	ၶုတ် (khût) ...	ၸၵ် (*chák*)=dig, *sás.*
Direction (line or course upon which anything is moving).	ၵၼ်ပႃ (kanpâ).	
Dirty (not clean), *a.*	ႁင် (hang) *or* ၸမ် (cham).	ႁိူၼ် ဢၼ် ႁင် (*hün an hang*)=house dirty.
Dismiss, send, or drive away, &c., *v.*	ႁေႃ (hô).	
Distribute, *v.* ...	ပၼ် (pan) *or* မိင် (mêng).	
Dissatisfied, *a.* ...	ၸႂ်ၼ်တႝ (chaü n'tai).	*Lit.* mind dies not. Assamese *mon na maré.*
Dive, *v.* ...	ၼမ်ႁေႃ (nam hô).	
Divide, a portion, *v.*	ပၼ် (p a n) *or* မိင် (mêng).	*Méng* uttered with a rising inflection of voice.
Dog, *n.*	မႃ (mâ) ...	*Mà* uttered with a rising inflection of voice.
Do, execute, make, &c., *v.*	ႁိတ် (het).	
Door, *n.* ...	ပႃတူ (pâ tû).	

English.	Khâmtî.	Remarks.
Down stream, under, below, &c.	ကါတွိ (kâ taü).	
Up stream, above, &c.	ကါၼိုဝ် (kâ nü).	
Dowry (reward paid for a wife), *n.*	ကါမေ် (kâ mê) ...	*Lit.* price (*kâ*) of wife.
Dream, *v.* ...	ၽၼ်ႁၢၼ် (phan han).	
Drift, flow as a river, &c.	လႝ (lai).	
Drink, also eat, *v.*	ၵိၼ် (kin).	
Drop, *n.* ...	မိတ် (mit).	
Drum, *n.* ...	ၵွင် (kång).	
Drum, beat— ...	ႁႝ (hai) ...	*Ai* pronounced very short.
Drum, sound of, or gun fired, rumble of thunder, &c.	ၼင် (nang).	
Dry, *a.* ...	ႁိင် (hêng).	
Dry, *v.* clothes 'chang,' &c.	တၢၵ် (tâk).	
Dry season, *n* ...	မိုဝ်ၼီ (mü nî) ...	*Lit.* when good.
Dry fish or meat on 'chang' above fire.	ယင် (yång).	
Drunk, *a.* ...	တႝလွ် (tai lau)...	*Tai*=die, *lau*=liquor.
Duck, *n.* ...	ပိတ် (pet).	
Dumb, *a.* ...	မါဢါ (mâ â).	
Dung, excrement, *n.*	ၶီ (khî).	
Dust, *n.* ...	ၽုၼ် (phûn) ...	Pronounced with a rising inflection of voice.

English.	Khâmtî.	Remarks.
Each, *a.* ...	ၵူ (kû).	
Ear ...	ပိင် ႁူ (ping hû).	
Earring, *n.* ...	ၵိၼ် ႁူ (ken hû).	
Earth, soil, dry land, *n.*	ၼိၼ် (nin) *or* လင် ၼိၼ် (lang nin).	
Earthquake, *n.*	ဢိင် သၼ် (ing san).	
Earthern vessel for carrying water, *n.*	ဢိင် (êng) ...	*Êng* is also used for a brass *kala* or *kolos.*
East, *n.* ...	ဝၼ် ဢွၵ် (wan åk)	ဝၼ် = sun, ဢွၵ် = emerge.
Easy, not difficult, *a.*	ငႆ (ngai).	
Eat, *v.* ...	ၵိၼ် (kin).	
Egg, *n.* ...	ၶႆ (khai) ...	Pronounced with a rising inflection of voice.
Eight, *a.* ...	ပိတ် pet.	
Elapse, pass by as time.	ထုၼ် (thôn).	
Elbow, also cubit, *n.*	သွၵ် (såk).	
Elephant, *n.* ...	ၸၢင် (châng).	
Elephant, probo-scis of—	ငွင် (ngăng).	
Emerge, *v.* ...	ဢွၵ် (åk).	
Empty, *a.* ...	ပဝ် (pau).	
Enough, *a.* ...	ပေႃ ယဝ် (pô yau).	
Enquire, *v.* ...	ထၢမ် ႁႂ် (thâm haü).	
Enter, go or come in, go on, fit, &c., *v.*	ၶဝ် (khau).	

English.	Khâmtî.	Remarks.
Escape, from any danger, *v.*	လွတ် (lắt) ...	In the sentence 'the fish got off the hook,' *lắt* would be used.
Escort, accompany as safeguard, give honourable or ceremonius attendance to, *v.*	သုင် (sông).	
Evening *n.* ...	ပင်ၶမ် (pâng khâm).	
Every day, always, *adv.*	ကူ မိဝ် (kû mü).	
Everywhere, *adv.*	ကူ တီ (kû tî) ...	တီ = place ကူ = each.
Exactly ...	မၼ် (mân mân).	
Exceedingly, very much, in a great degree, *adv.*	လုင် (lông).	
Expert, experience, *n.*	ယမ် (yâm).	
Explain, *v.* ...	ပိၼ်ႁႂ် (pen haü).	
Extinguish, *v.*...	ဢဝ် မွတ် (au mắt).	
Eye, *n.* ...	တႃ (tâ) ...	*Tá* is generally preceded by ႁွႆ = *hőy*; *hőy* is a numeral particle used in enumerating round things.
Eye-brow, *n.* ...	ငၼ် တႃ (ngắn tá).	
Eye-lash, *n.* ...	ၶုၼ် တႃ (khôn tá).	
Face, *n.* ...	ၼႃ (ná) ...	Sudden cessation of voice on *ă*.
Fall, *v.* ...	လုံ (lôm) *or* တွက် (tôk).	*Lóm*=fall from up, right position; *tők* =fall from above.

English.	Khâmtî.	Remarks.
False, *a.* ...	ၸိတ် (phet).	
Famine, general want of provisions, *n.*	ဢုပ် (üp).	
Far (not near) ...	ꩲႆ (kai).	
Fast, quickly, *adv.*	ၶၼ် (khan khan) *or* ꩡဵဝ် (cheô).	
Father, *n.* ...	ပေႃ (pô) *or* ꩡဝ် (chau).	*Chau* is respectful.
Father-in-law, *n.*	ပေႃ ꩡဝ် (pô chau).	
Fathom, *n.* ...	ဝႃ (wâ). ...	Voice rests on the *a*.
Fat, not thin, *a.*	ပီ (pî).	
Fault, error, *n.*	ၸိတ် (phet).	
Fear, *a.* ...	ၵေႃ (kô).	
Feather, *n.* ...	ၶုၼ် (khon).	
Feed, rear, *v.* ...	လဵင် (lêng).	
Feel, have a sense of, know, *v.*	ႁူ (hû).	
Female, *n.* ...	ပႃယိင် (pâying).	
Female organ, *n.*	ႁီ (hî).	
Fence, of bamboo, *n.*	တင်ၶႃ (tâng khâ).	
Fetch, bring, *v.*	ဢဝ်မႃ (au mâ).	
Fever, *n.* ...	ၶႆ ၼဝ်. (khai nau)	*Lit.* cold (*nau*) sickness.
Few, not many....	ꩡၼ် လိုင် (chån lüng).	
Field, spot where things are grown, *n.*	ႁႆ (hai). ...	*Lit.* equivalent to Assam '*bam khet.*'

English.	Khâmtî.	Remarks.
Fierce, savage, violent, *a.*	ꩭႝ (hâi) ...	*Hai* is used for individuals, as a violent man.
Fight, with fists, *v.*	ၸဝ်ꩡၼ် (pô kan) *or* ထုၵ် (thôk).	ꩡၼ်= wrestle (*kan kan.*)
Fill, put into, insert, *v.*	သႂ် (saü) ...	*Saü pha tek*=put into jail.
Find, light upon accidentally, *v.*	ၵဵပ်ꩫႝ (kep nai).	
Find, by search, *v.*	ꩭႃꩫႝ (khâ nai)...	*Kha*=search; *nai*=get.
Fine, pecuniary penalty for an offence, &c., *n.*	မႂ် (maü).	
Finger, *n.*	လဵဝ်မိုဝ် (leo mü).	
Finished, done, used up, &c., *a.*	မွတ်ယွႆ (môt yau).	
Finished, ended, terminated, *a.*	ယွႆ (yau yau).	
Fire, *n.* ...	ၽႝ (phai) ...	ယင်ၽႝ (*yang phai*)= *chang* above fire-place.
Fire, to light, *v.*	ꩡပ်ၽႝ (chap phai)	
Fire, gun, *v.*	ယိုဝ် (yü).	
Fire, destroy by, *v.*	သွတ်ၽႝ (sât phai).	
First (ordinal of one), before anything else in time or space, *adv.*	ဢွၼ်တင် (ân tâng) ဢွၼ်ၼႃ (ân nâ).	
Fish, *n.* ...	ပႃ (pâ) ...	ပိၵ် (*pik*)=fin, also bird's wing.
Fish, with net, &c., *v.*	ꩭႃပႃ (khâ pâ).	

English.	Khâmti.	Remarks.
Fish, with rod and line, *v.*	ပွႆမိတ် (poi met)...	*Poi* means to free, let loose, and *met* means a hook.
Fish-hook, *n.* ...	မိတ် (met).	
Fist, *n.* ...	ကံမုဝ် (kâm mü).	
Five, *a.* ...	ႁႃ (hâ).	
Flame, *n.* ...	လိၼ်ၽႆ (lin phai).	
Flat, *a.* ...	မိပ် (mep).	
Flea, *n.* ...	မတ် (mat).	
Flesh, meat, *n.* ...	ၼုဝ် (nü).	
Flint (for gun), *n.*	ႁိၼ် (hin) ...	*Hin* merely means a stone.
Float, *v.*	ၽူ (phû).	
Flood, inundation, *n.*	ထုံ (thûm).	
Fly, *n.* ...	မိင်မုၼ် (meng môn)	*Meng* is the generic term for most flying insects, beetles, &c.
Fly, gad, *n.* ...	လိုၵ် (lük).	
Fly, *v.* ...	မိင် (meng).	
Flower, *n.* ...	မွၵ်ယႃ (måk yâ).	
Fog, *n.* ...	မွၵ် (mäk).	
Follow, pursue, *v.*	ႁုပ် (hüp).	
Fool, *n.* ...	ပိၼ်မႃ (pen mâ).	
Foot, *n.* ...	တိၼ် (tin) ...	*Tin* means leg and foot combined.
For, *prep.* ...	ႁင် (hang) ...	*Hang kau pachau*=for myself.
Force, compel, *v.*	ဢႃၼိင် (âneng).	
Forehead, *n.* ...	ၼႃၽၵ် (nâ phâk).	
Forget, *v.* ...	လုံ (lûm).	

English.	Khâmtî.	Remarks.
Formerly, in time past (indefinite), *adv.*	မိုဝ်ၼၼ် (mü nan)...	မၢင်ငႃပုၼ် (*mangâ pün*) also used.
Foreigner, *n.* ...	ၵုၼ်တင်မိုင် (kôn tâng müng).	*Kôn*=person ; *tâng*= another ; *müng*= country.
Foreigner, stranger, *n.*	ၵုၼ်တင်မၼ် (kôn tâng mân).	*Mân*=village.
Four, *a.* ...	သီ (sî).	
Fowl, *n.* ...	ကႆ (kai) ...	Uttered with a rising inflection of voice.
Fowl, kept for breeding.	ၽၼ်ကႆ (phan kai)	
Friend, *n.* ...	ကေႃၸဝ် (kô chau).	
Frighten, by, starting out from hiding place, &c., *v.*	လွက် (låt).	
Frog, *n.* ...	ၶဵတ် (khet).	
From, *prep.* ...	လုက် (lûk) ...	Usually used in conjunction with *mai.*
Fruit, except plantains, *n.*	မက် (mak).	
Full, *a.* ...	တဵမ် (tem).	
Gain, profit by trading, *a.*	ဢႃၽျႃ (âphyâ) *or* ဢႃမိတ် (âmet).	
Gain, win, to achieve by effort, or exertion, *v.t.*	ပေ (pê).	
Germinate, *v.i.*	ငွက် (ngåk) ...	Å little broader than in word for crooked.
Get, procure, obtain.	ၼႆ (nai) ...	*Ai* pronounced somewhat short.

English.	Khâmtî.	Remarks.
Get up, from lying or sitting position, *v.*	လုၵ် (lûk).	
'Ghat,' *n.* ...	တႃꩫံ (tâ nam).	
Gild, overlay with a thin covering of gold, paint, &c., *v.*	ဢုၵ် (ük).	
Ginger, *n.* ...	ၶိင် (khing).	
Girl, *n.* ...	လုၵ်ပႃယိင် (lûk paying).	
Give, *v.* ...	ႁႂ် (haü).	
Give back, return, *v.*	ၶိုၼ်ႁႂ် (khün haü)	
Glad, pleased ...	ꩡုံ (chôm).	
Go, *v.* ...	ၵႃ (kâ).	
Go away, depart, *v.*	ၶႆ (khâi).	
Goat, *n.* ...	ပေယႃ (pê yâ).	
God, *n.* ...	ၽြႃ (phrâ).	
Guatama, *n.* ...	ၵေႃတႃမႃ (Go tâ má).	ꩡဝ်ၽြႃ (Chaü phrâ) also used.
Goitre, *n.* ...	ၶေႃပွင် (khô pång)	*Lit.* neck swelling.
Gold ...	ၶမ် (khâm).	
Goldsmith, *n.* ...	ꩡင် ၶမ် (châng khâm).	
Gong, *n.* ...	ယမ်တွင် (yâm tång) small one.	ယမ်လုင် (*yâm lông*) = large gong (*lông*) = large.
Goose, *n.* ...	ပိတ်ႁၢၼ် (pet hân).	
Grandfather, father's side, *n.*	ပူ (pû).	

English.	Khâmtî.	Remarks.
Grandfather, mother's side, *n.*	ပူၼႂ် (pû nai).	
Grandmother, father's side, *n.*	ယႃ (yâ).	
Grandmother, mother's side, *n.*	ၼႂ် (nai).	
Grandson, *n.* ...	လၢၼ် (lân.)	
Granddaughter, *n.*	လၢၼ်သွ် (lân sau).	
Granary, *n.* ...	ယေၶွ် (yê khau)	(*Khau* = dhan).
Grasshopper, *n.*	သီတိၼ် (siten).	
Grass, *n.* ...	ၾွႆ်ယႃ (phôy yâ)	It really means rank grass.
Grave, *n.* ...	ထင် (thâng) ...	*Lit.* a large hole.
Green, *a.* ...	ၶိဝ် (khêô).	
Ground, take ground as a boat, &c., *v.*	ၵင် (khâng).	
Ground, land, *n.*	ငၢၼ် (ngân) *or* ၵင် ၼွႆ် (kâng noi).	(Assamese *bàm.*)
Guest, *n.* ...	ပီ ၼွင် (pî nâng).	
Gum, *n.* ...	ႁိုၵ် (hük).	
Gun, *n.* ...	သီ လတ် (sî lat) *or* သႃ လတ် (sâ lat).	
Hail, *n.* ...	မႃ ႁိၵ် (mâ hek).	
Hair, of head, *n.*	ၾုံ (phôm) ...	ၵွ်ၾုံ (*kau phòm*) knot of hair worn on top of head by Khâmtîs.
Hair, of body, *n.*	ၶုၼ် (khòn).	
Half, *n.* ...	ၾႃ ၶိုင် ၵင် (phâ khüng kāng).	
Hand, *n.* ...	ၾႃ မိုဝ် (phâ mü).	

English.	Khâmtî.	Remarks.
Hand, right, *n*....	မုဝ် ပႃ ၶႃ (mü pâ khâ).	*Pa kha* and *pásai* apply to leg, side, &c.
Hand, left, *n*. ...	ပႃ သၢႆ (pâ sai)...	
Handfull, open	ဢုင် မုဝ် (ông mü).	
Handfuls, two...	ၵွပ် မုဝ် (kâp mü).	
(Fistful) ...	ၵံ လိုင် (kam lüng)	*Kam*=fist; *lung*=one,
Hang, suspend, dangle, *v*.	ႁွႆ (hoi) *or* ယၢၼ် (yân).	*Hoi* means to fasten in a manner which will allow of free motion upon the point or points of suspension. To decorate by hanging pictures on an idol, &c.
Happy, contented, *a*.	ပဝ် (pêô).	
Hard, tough as food meat, *a*.	ၶိင် (khêng).	
Hat, *n*. ...	မုၵ် (môk) *or* မႃ ႁုဝ် ဢွၵ် (mâ hôt äk).	ၽႃ ႁုဝ် =*pugri* (phâ hô.)
Hatchet, *n*. ...	ၶၼ် (khân).	
Hawk, *n*. ...	ယႃ ႁုင် (ya hong).	
He, *pron*. ...	မၼ် (man).	
Head, *n*. ...	ႁုဝ် (hô) ...	Pronounced with a rising inflection of voice.
Headache, *n*. ...	ႁုဝ် ၵပ် (hô kâp) *or* ႁုဝ်ၸဵပ် (hô chep.)	ၶႆႁုဝ် (*khai hô*) also used.

English.	Khâmti.	Remarks.
Headman (of village).	ပၢ ၵေၵ် (pâ kê) *or* ၸဝ် မၢၼ်· (c h a u mân).	
Hear, apprehend, or take cognizance of by the ear, *v.*	ၼႆ ႁိၼ် (nai hin).	
Heart, *n.*	ၵၢၼ်ႁေႃၸၢၼ် (kân hô chan).	
Heavy, not light, *a.*	ၼၵ် (nak).	
Help, *v.* ...	ၸွႆ (choi).	
Herd, crowd, *n.*	ၾုင် (phûng).	
Here, *adv.* ...	မႆ (mai).	
Hide, secrete, *v.*	ဢဝ် လပ် မေပ် (au lâp mep) *or* လၵ် သုင် (lâk süng).	
Hide, keep oneself out of sight, *v.*	လပ် မေပ် (lâp mep).	
High, tall, &c., *a.*	သုင် (sûng).	
Hill, *n.* ...	ၼွႆ (noi).	
Him, *pron.* ...	မၼ်း မႆ (man mai).	
Hit, reach object aimed at, *v.i.*	ထုၵ် (thûk) ...	*Thúk* also means touch, come in contact with; also fit, hit off person, also means must.
Hire, price paid or contracted to be given for temporary use of anything, *n.*	ႁိင် (hêng).	

English.	Khâmtî.	Remarks.
Hire, give in hire	ယုံ (yûm) *or*	*Yum* means give or take hire of something which has to be returned.
Hire, take hire....	ၵူ (kû).	*Ku* means give or take hire for which a substitute is given as money, share, &c.
Hoe, *n.*	ၶော (khô)	Pronounced with a rising inflection of voice.
Hoe, *v.*	ၶော ၸၵ် (khô châk.)	
Hole, through anything, *n.*	ႁူလင် (hû lâng).	
Hole, *n.*	ႁူ (hû).	
Hold, keep in the grasp, *v.*	ပၼ် (pan) *or* တိုဝ် (tü).	
Hollow	ၵူင် (kông).	
Honey, *n.*	ၼမ်ၽိုင် (nam phüng)	*Lit.* bee water.
Hoof, *n.*	ၵိပ် (kip).	
Horn, *n.*	ၶဝ် (khau).	
Hot	လိုတ် (lüt).	
Hot season, *n.*	မိုဝ်ႁိုဝ် (mü hü).	
House, *n.*	ႁိုၼ် (hün).	
How, in what manner, *adv.*	ႁီလိုဝ် (hî lü) *or* ႁီၼိုဝ် (hî nü).	Used in conjunction with adverbial suffix သီ (*si*).
How many, much.	ၶႃလဝ် (khâ laü) *or* ၵီ (kî).	
Hundred, *a.*	ပၵ်လိုင် (pâk lüng).	
Hungry, *a.*	တင်မႆ (tâng mai).	

English.	Khâmtî.	Remarks.
Husk rice, *v.*	တံၶွ် (tam khau).	
Husband, *n.*	ၸေႃ (phô).	
I, *pron.*	ၵွ် (kau).	
If, *conj.*	သၢင် (sang) သၢင်ဝႃ sang wâ).	*Sang* is used as an emphatic particle with personal and other pronouns.
Ill, any bodily ailment, *a.*	ၶႆ (khai).	
Image, idol, *n.*, imitation of any person or thing.	ႁၢင် (hâng).	
Immature, *a.*	ႏုံ (nûm).	
Indian-corn, *n.*....	ၶွ် ၽႃ (khau phâ	
Industrious, *a.*....	ၶၵ် (khak).	
Ink, *n.*	ၼံမုၵ် (nam mük)	
Insect, *n.*, only applicable to those that crawl.	မွင် (mông).	
Inside, within, *n.*	ၵႃၼႂ် (kâ naü) or ၼႂ် (naü).	
Intrigue (with female), *v.*	ႁၢၵ်ၵၼ် (hâl kan).	*Lit.* mutual liking.
Inundate, overflow.	ထုံ (thôm).	
Investigate, *v.*	တႆ (tai).	
Iron, *n.* ...	လဵၵ် (lêk).	

English.	Khâmtî.	Remarks.
Island, *n.* ...	ငၢၼ်ကၢင် (n g â n kâng).	Assamese *mâjúli.*
Itch, *n.* ...	ႁိတ် (hit).	
Ivory, *n.* ...	ငႃၸၢင်(ngâ châng).	
Jack-fruit, *n.* ...	မႃလင် (mâ lang) *or* မၵ်လင် (maklang).	*Mak*=fruit.
Jackal, *n.* ...	မႃၼိၼ် (mâ nin) ...	*Mâ*=dog ; *nin*=earth.
Jacket, coat, &c., *n.*	သိူဝ် (sü).	
Jump, *v.* ...	ဝဵၼ် (wen).	
Jungle, *n.* ...	ထိုၼ် (thün).	
Just now, a short time ago.	မႃၵႂ် (mâ kai) ...	Assamese *athôni.*
Keep, take care of, *v.*	ၵဵမ် (kem).	
Keep quiet (Assamese *mane mane thâk*).	ထဵတ် (tet).	
Kick, as human being, *v.*	ထိပ် (thip).	
Kick, as animal, *v.*	ပိတ် (pit).	
Kill, *v.* ...	ဢွၵ်တၢႆ (au tâi).	
Kind, loving, *a.*	ႁၵ်ႉ (hâk).	
King, *n.* ...	ၸဝ်ၾႃ (chau phâ)	ၼၢင်ၾႃ (*nâng phâ*) = queen.
Kiss, *v.* ...	ၸုပ် (chûp).	

English.	Khâmtî.	Remarks.
Knee, *n.* ...	ႁဝ်ၶဝ် (hô khau).	
Kneel, *v.* ...	ၶုပ်ႁဝ်ၶဝ် (khûp khau).	
Knife, blade, *n.*	မိတ် (mit).	
Knife, handle, *n.*	လံ (lam).	
Knot, *n.* ...	ၵူ (kû) *or* ၶၢတ်တၵ် (khât tak).	
Knot, in wood, *n.*	တႃမႆ (tâ mai) ...	*Ta*=eye; *mai*=wood.
Know, understand, possess experience of, can.	ၸၢင် (châng).	
Know, to be acquainted with, recognize, &c.	ထွင် (tâng) ...	ႁူ (*hû*) also used.
Labour, work, *n.*	ဢႃမူ (â mû).	
Labour, *v.* ...	ႁဵတ်ဢႃမူ (het â mû).	
Ladder, *n.*, wooden or bamboo steps leading up to house.	ႁွၵ်ၵႃလႆ (hôk kâ lai).	
Lame, *a.* ...	တိၼ်ႁၢၼ် (tin hân).	
Land (Assamese *bâm*).	ၵၢင်ၼွႆ (kâng noi).	
Language, statement, narrative, &c., *n.*	ၶၢမ် (khâm).	
Large, big, bulky, *a.*	ယႂ် (yaü).	
Last, hindmost, nearest in time, next, &c.	ၵႃလင် (kâ lang).	

English.	Khâmtî.	Remarks.
Last year, *a.* ...	ပီကႝ (pî kai).	
Last month, or moon, *a.*	လိူၼ် (lün) *or* ၸိူၼ်မၢင်ၢ (nün mângâ).	
Late, *a.* ...	လႃ (lâ) *or* ၼၢၼ် (nân).	
Laugh, *v.* ...	ၵူဝ် (khô) ...	Pronounced with a rising inflection of voice.
Lay egg, *v.* ...	ၶႝ (khai).	
Lay hold, *v.* ...	ပၼ် (pan).	
Lazy, *a.* ...	ၶၼ် (khân).	
Leech, *n.* ...	တၵ် (tâk).	
Lead, *n.* ...	ၸိူၼ် (chün).	
Leaf, *n.* ...	ၵႂ် (maü) ...	တွင် (*tảng*)=large leaf, known to Assamese as *kò pàt* used to eat off, or tie up things in.
Leak, *v.* ...	ႁေႃ (hô).	
Lean, rest against, *v.*	ဢိင် (ing).	
Leave, depart from, *v.*	ၽၵ် (phâk).	
Leave off, abandon, relinquish work, *v.*	ၽႃ (phâ) ...	လႃၵႃ leave off talking.
Leave, quit home or village, emigrate, *v.*	ၶႝ (khâi) ...	ၶႝ ႁိူၼ် (*khâi hün*) = quit house. ၶႝ မၢၼ် (khâi mâṇ) = quit village.
Leisure, *n.* ...	ပႝ (pau).	

English.	Khâmtî.	Remarks.
Leg, *n.* ...	တိၼ် (tin).	
Lend, give loan of.	ယုံ ႁႂ် yûm haü.	
Leopard, *n.* ...	သိုဝ်ၸုံ (sü chûm).	
Less, not so much, *adv.*	ယွံ (yâm).	
Let go, release, *v.*	ပွႆ (poi).	
Letter, *n.* ...	ၽိုၵ်လိၵ် (phyek lik).	
Lick, *v.* ...	လေ (lê).	
Lie down, sleep, *v.*	ၼွၼ် (nân).	
Lift, raise, *v.* ...	ယုၵ် (yôk).	
Light, agent or force in nature by action of which upon organs of sight, objects from which it proceeds are rendered visible.	ငဝ် (ngau) ...	ငဝ်ၼိုၼ် (*ngau nün*) moonlight ငဝ်ဝၼ် (*ngau wan*) sunlight ငဝ်ၽႆ (*ngau phai*) firelight.
Light, not dark, *n.*	လိင် (lêng).	
Light, not heavy, *a.*	မဝ် (mau).	
Lightning, *n.* ...	ၽႃမိပ် (phâ mep).	
Like, approve of, covet.	ထုၵ်ၸႂ် (thûk chaü).	
Like, noting, resemblance, *a.*	ၼႃၵၼ် (nâ kan).	
Lip, *n.* ...	ပိင်သူပ် (ping sôp)	*Sôp*=mouth.

English.	Khâmtî.	Remarks.
Liquor, local, *n.*	လဝ် (lau) ...	လဝ်ႁိုဝ် (*lau hü*) is word for our distilled liquor; *hü* means condensed liquid.
Listen, hearken, *v.*	ထွံ (thâm).	
Little, small quantity, *a.*	ꩡွၼ် (chăn chăn) *or* ꩡွၼ်ၜိုင် (chăn lüng).	
Litttle, small in size, or extent, *a.*	ဢွၼ် (ăn) *or* လိၵ် (lêk).	
Little while, *adv.*	ꩡုပ်ၜိုင် (chô lüng)	ၵျိပ်ၜိုင် (kep lüng) also used. It means a shorter time.
Liver, *n.*	ပုံ (pûm).	
Load, burden carried at both ends of, bamboo or stick across shoulder.	ႁပ် (hâp).	
Load gun, *v.* ...	သတ် (sat).	
Loin, *n.* ...	ငိင် (ngeng).	
Loin cloth, *n.* (dhoti).	ၽႃၼွႆ (phâ noi).	
Long, in length, *a.*	ယဝ် (yau).	
Look, examine, inspect, *v.*	လႅမ် (lem).	
Loom, *n.* ...	ၵီႁုၵ် (kî hûk).	

English.	Khâmti.	Remarks.
Loose, not light, *a.*	လုံ (lôm) ...	As a loose coat or bracelet, ယႃ (*yâ*) = not rigid as the rope is not tight.
Lose, *v.* ...	ꩭႝ (hai).	
Loss, injury, damage, *a.*	ꩬုံ (sûm).	
Louse (head louse).	ꩭဝ်ႋ (hau).	
Louse, *v.* ...	ꩭဝ် လိမ် (hau lem)...	*Lem*=look, examine.
Low, near the ground, not tall, *a.*	တံ (tam).	
Low ground ...	ၵွံ (khåm) *or* ꩭုံ (khûm).	
Maggot, *n.* ...	ꩫွၼ် (nån).	
Man, male, *n.* ...	ပႃꩡႝ (pâ chai).	
Male organ, *n.* ...	ၵွႝ (khoi).	
Manipuri (native of Manipur), *n.*	ၵေꩬေ (Kêsê).	
Many, much, numerous, &c., *a.*	ꩫံ (nam nam).	
Marry (wife), *v.*	ဢဝ်မေ (au mê) ...	*Au*=take, *mê*=female.
Master, owner, *n.*	ꩡဝ် (chau).	
Mat, *n.* ...	ၽုၵ် (phôk) *or* ꩬတ် (sat).	
Matter, *pus*, *n.*...	ꩫံꩫွင် (nam nång).	

English.	Khâmtî.	Remarks.
Matter, that with regard to or about which anything takes place.	ပိၼ် (pen).	
Mature, seasoned, *a.*	ၵေ် (kê).	
Measure, *v.* ...	တိက် (tek).	
Medicine, *n.* ...	ယႃ (yâ).	
Meet, come together by approach from an opposite direction, *v.*	ႁုပ် (hôp).	
Melt, *v.*, silver, gold, and lead.	ꩡုမ် (chüm).	
Micturate, *v.* ...	ယိဝ် (yêô).	
Midday, *n.* ...	ဝၼ်တိင် (wan teng).	
Middle, midst, *adv.*	ၶိုင်ၵၢင် (khüng kâng).	
Midnight, *n.* ...	တိင်ၶိုၼ် (t.eng khün).	
Milk, *n.* ...	ၼမ်ꩡေ် (nam chê).	
Mine, *pron.* and *a.*	ၶွင်ၵဝ် (khång kau).	
Mistake, error ...	ၽိတ် (phit).	
'Mithon,' *n.* ...	ပၢင် (pâng).	
Miss, fail to hit, *v.*	ၼ်ထုက်(n'thôk)	*Lit.* not hit.
Mix, form by mingling, *v.*	ၶုၼ် khôn).	

English.	Khâmtî.	Remarks.
Money, silver, *n.*	ငိုၼ် (ngün).	
Monkey, *n.* ...	လိင် (ling).	
Moon, month, *n.*	ၼိုၼ် (nün), *or* လိုၼ် (lün).	
Moon, full, *n.* ...	လိုၼ်လမ် (nün lâm) *or* လိုၼ်မွၼ် (lün môn).	†*Lam* and *mon* mean round.
Moon, new, *n.* ...	လိုၼ်မႂ်ႇ (lûn maü)...	*Maü*=new.
Moon, light, *n.*	လိုၼ်လိင် *or* ငဝ်လိုၼ် (lün lêng) *or* (ngau lün).	
More, used with an adjective to form the comparative degree.	လိုမ်သီ (lüm si).	
More, something, other and further, *n.*	ၶိုၼ်ၼႃၵွ် (khün nâ kau).	ဢိၵ် (*ik*) also used.
Morrow (next nearest in time), *n.*	မႃႁွၵ် (mâ hôk).	
Morrow, day after, *n.*	မႃႁိုဝ် (mâ hü).	
Mosquito, *n.* ...	ယုင် (yûng).	
Moth, *n.* ...	မိင်မီ (meng mî).	
Mother, *n.* ...	မေ (mê).	
Mother-in-law, *n.*	မေၸဝ် (mê chau).	

English.	Khâmtî.	Remarks.
Mount, get upon, or into, *v.*	ၶီ (khî).	
Mouse, *n.* ...	ၼူ (nû).	
Mouth, *n* ...	သွပ် (sôp).	
Mouth, of river, *n.*	သွပ်ပင်ၼမ် (s ô p pâng nam).	
Much, great in quantity or amount, *a.*	ၼမ်ၼမ် (nam nam).	
Much, to a great degree or extent, *adv.*	ၵွႝၵင် (koi kăng) *or* ၵႃႁဵင် (kâ hêng).	The adverb လွင် (*lông*) = very also used.
Mud, *n.* ...	တုၵ် (tük).	
Must, physical, and moral necessity, *v.*	ဝႃ (wâ) *or* တီၼႂ် (tî nai).	
Naga (inhabitant of Naga hills), *n.*	ၶင် (Khâng).	
Nail, finger or toe, *n.*	လဵပ် (lep).	
Naked, nude, *a.*	ပွႆ (pôy).	

English.	Khâmtî.	Remarks.
Name,* *n.* ...	ၸိုဝ် (chü).	
Narrow (not wide), *a.*	ႁိပ် (hip) *or* တိပ် (tip).	
Navel, *n.* ...	ပုလီ (pû lî).	
Near, not remote, *a.*	ၵႂ် (kaü) ...	The adverb nearly, almost, within a little, as he is nearly dead, is made by using the conjunction *nang* = as.
Near, only a litte distance. (in the vicinity of) *adv.*	တႆ (tai) *or* တႆၶင် (tai khâng).	

* As with Singpho families so with Khâmtis, boys and girls are named according to seniority by a fixed rule which never varies, thus—

Boys.

First is called ...	ဢႆ	(*ai*)
Second is called ...	ငီ	(*ngî*)
Third is called ...	သမ်	(*sâm*)
Fourth is called ...	သႆ	(*sai*)
Fifth is called ...	ငဝ်	(*ngô*)
Sixth is called ...	ၼုၵ်	(*nok*)
Seventh is called ...	ၸိတ်	(*chet*)

After the seventh boy the next is called after the numerals, *pet*, *kau*, or *sip*, &c., &c.

Girls.

First is called ...	ယေ	(*yê*)
Second is called ...	ဢီ	(*î*)
Third is called ...	ဢံ	(*âm*)
Fourth is called ...	ဢႆ	(*ai*)
Fifth is called ...	ဝေါ	(*wô*)
Sixth is called ...	ဢုၵ်	(*ôk*)
Seventh is called ...	ဢိတ်	(*et*)
Eighth is called ...	ဢိတ်	(*êt*)
Ninth is called ...	ဢုတ်	(*ût*)

No names after the ninth for girls.

English.	Khâmtî.	Remarks.
Neck, *n.* ...	ေၵႃ (khô).	
Necklace, *n.* ...	ပွႆ (poi).	
Needle, *n.* ...	†ၶိမ် *or* ၵမ် (khem).	
Neither ...	Made by using particle ေၵႃ (kô) in conjunction with a negative verb.	*Vide* examples in Grammar.
Necessary, requisite, *a.*	ႁင် (hâng).	
Nest, *n.* ...	ႁင်ၼုၵ်(hang nôk)	*Nŏk*=bird.
Net, *n.* ...	ေၶ် (khê).	
Never, at no time, *adv.*	Made by using *mâlaü* (=when) in conjunction with *kŏ* (=even) and a negative verb.	
New, not old, *a.*	ၵႂ် (maü).	
Next, following	မႃႁုၵ် (mâhôk)	*Lit.* tomorrow.
Night, *n.* ...	ၵင်ၶိုၼ် (kâng khün).	
Night, to-, *n.* ...	မႃၼႆ (mâ nai khün).	*Mâ nai*=this.
Morrow, to-, *n.* ...	မႃႁုၵ် (mâhôk khün).	

English.	Khâmtî.	Remarks.
Nine, *a.* ...	ၵွ် (kau).	
Noise, sound of any kind, *n.*	ယိင် (sêng) ...	Pronounced with a rising inflection of voice.
Noise, clamour, din, *a.*	ꩨိၵၼ် (mô kan) *or* ၶင်ၵၼ်(khang kan).	
North, *n.* ...	ၼႃႁင် (nâ hång).	
Nose, *n.* ...	ႁူၼင် (hû nang).	
Nostril, *n.* ...	ႁူႁူၼင် (h û h û nang).	
Not yet, *adv.* ...	ꩫိပ်ႝ (n'pai).	
Nothing, *n.* ...	ၵႃ ꩬင် ၵေႃ မႃ ယင် (ka s a n g kô mâ yang).	*Lit.* what even exists not.
Now, *adv.* ...	ငႝ (ngai.)	
Now-a-days, *adv.*	ဝင်ငႝ (wông ngai).	
Oil, for eating, *n.*	ၼံမၼ် (nam man).	
Oil, for burning, *n.*	ၼံမိၼ် (nam men) ...	Kerosine-oil is called nam men. It means *Lit.* smelling-water !
Old, not new, *a.*	ၵွ် (kau).	
Old, aged, *a.* ...	ထွ် (thau) ...	ၵေၼ် (*ke*)=mature.

English.	Khâmti.	Remarks.
On, above, *prep*.	ကႃၼိုဝ် (kâ nü)	Used in conjunction with locative case particle *mai*.
Once, *adv*.	ပွၵ်လိုၚ်း (påk lüng) *or* ပၼ်လိုၚ်း (pân lüng).	
One, *a*.	ဢႃ လိုၚ်	
Only, merely, *adv*.	ၼႆ (nai).	
Open, lift off cover from anything, *v*.	ပုတ် (pût).	
Open (unconfined) space.	ပၚ် (pâng)	Pronounced with a rising inflection of voice.
Or, *conj*.	Made by using ကႆ (*kai*) a particle denoting vague probability.	
Orange, *n*.	မၵ် ငေ (mak ngê) *or* မႃ ငေ (mâ ngê).	
Order, command, *n*.	ဢႃ ၶၚ် (âkhâng) *or* ဢႃ မိၚ် (â ming).	ႁႂ် (*haü*) give command.
Other, second of two, *pron*. and *a*.	တၚ်ဢၼ် (tâng an).	
Others, people in general.	ပိုၼ် (pün).	
Otter, *n*.	မွၼ် (môn).	
Orphan (child who has lost one or both parents), *n*.	တိမ် ၽႃ (timphâ).	

English.	Khâmti.	Remarks.
Ought, behooveth, is proper, &c., *v.*	ထုၵ် (thük).	
Our, *pron.*	ၶင်တူ (khång tû).	
Outside, *a.* ...	ၵႃၼွၵ် (kâ nåk).	
Overflow, inundate, *v.*	ထုမ် (thôm).	
Overtake, come up with, &c., *v.*	ၶုတ် (khüt).	
Own, *a.*	ပႃၸွ် (pâ chau).	
Paddle, *n.*	မႆၽႆ (mai phai) *or* ၽႆတၵ် (phai tâk).	
Paddle, row, &c., *v.*	ဝၵ် (wâk).	
Pain, hurt, wound, &c., *n.*	ၸဵပ် (chêp).	
Pair, of animals, *n.*	ပင် (pång)	*Páng* is only used for animals.
Pair, of other things, *n.*	ၵုပ် (kôp) *or* ၵူ kû).	
'Panji,' *n.*	ၶၵ် (khâk)	ပၵ် (*pák*) to fix or plant same in ground.
Paper, *n.*	ၸေ (chê).	
Parrot, *n.*	ၼုၵ်တိတ် (nôktet).	
Part, fragment, piece, &c.	တွၼ် (tân)	သိၵ် (*sik*) also used.
Past, in time gone by.	မိုဝ်ၼၼ် (mü nan).	
Past, beyond, further than, *prep.*	ပုၼ် (pôn).	

English.	Khâmtî.	Remarks.
Pay respects, homage, with joined hands extended in front.	ပႆ (pai).	
Peacock, *n.*	ၼုၵ် ယုင် (nôk yûng).	
Peck, pick up with beak, *v.*	တွတ် (tât	*Tát* means also to strike as a snake.
Perspiration, *n.*	ႁိူဝ် (hü)	Pronounced with a rising inflection of voice.
Pestle, *n.*	ၸၵ် (sak).	
Petticoat, *n.*	ၸိၼ် (sin) ...	(Assamese *meklá.*)
Person, human being, *n.*	ၵုၼ် (kôn).	
Pick up, *v.*	ၵဵပ် (kep.)	
Picture, *n.*	ႁၢင် (hang).	
Pierce, penetrate as bullets, spear, &c., *v.*	မၢင် mång).	
Pig, tame, *n.*	မူ (mû)	Pronounced with a rising inflection of voice.
Pig, wild, *n.*	မူထိုၼ် (mû thün)...	*Thün* = jungle.
Pigeon, *n.*	ၵႃၵေ (kâ kè),	
Pillow, *n.*	မၼ်ႁူဝ် (mân hô)	*Man*=raise, *hô* head.
Pinch, *v.*	ယၵ် (yak).	
Pine-apple, *n.*	ၵိင်ႁမ် (kêng håm).	
Pipe, *n.*	မူ ယႃ (mû yâ) *or* မူဝ်ယႃ (mô yâ).	

English.	Khâmtî.	Remarks.
Place, spot, *n.*	တီ (tî).	
Plain, level, even, flat (as applied to land), *a.*	တီပိင် (tî peng).	
Plank, *n.*	ပိၼ် (pen) *or* ၽိၼ် (phen).	*Pen*=small plank; *phen*=large plank.
Plant *v.* (set in ground for growth).	ပုၵ် (pûk)	*Púk* applies to seeds sown singly as well as to plants.
Plantain, *n.*	ၵွႆ, (kôy).	
Plate, brass, *n.*	ၽေ (phê)	ပၼ်း (*pân*) plate made of wood or earth.
Play (children's), *v.*	လိၼ် (len).	
Pleased, glad	ၸုမ် (chôm).	
Plough, *n.*	ထႆ (thai).	
Plough, *v.*	ထႆ (thai).	
Pocket, in coat, *n.*	ထုင်သိူဝ် (thông sü)	*Sü*=coat.
Point, sharp end of anything, *n.*	ပႆ (pai).	
Point, with finger, *v.*	ၸီ (chī).	
Poison, *n.*	ၵွင် (kång).	
Poke fun at, *v.*	ယွၵ် (yåk).	
Pole, for boat, *n.*	မႆႉထေႃ (mai thô).	
Pole, boat, *v.*	ထေႃ (thô).	
Poor, indigent, *a.*	ၽၼ် (phân).	
Porpoise, *n.*	ပႃ ၸၢင် (pâchâng) *or* ပႃၶႃ (pâ khâ).	

English.	Khâmtí.	Remarks.
Post, *n.*	ꩬွ် (sau).	
Potato, *n.*	မၼ် * (man)	မၼ်ကြႃ (*man krâ*)=imported potato (*krâ*=Bengal).
Pour out, or away, *v.*	လုဝ် (lô).	
Pour (liquid) into anything, *v.*	ꩬႂ် (saü).	
Powder, *n.*	ယမ် (yâm).	
Pregnant, *n.*	ꩬွၼ် (sån).	
Present, gift, donation, *n.*	ꩬူ (sû).	
Pretty, handsome, attractive, &c., *a.*	ꩬိၼ် (sen).	
Previously, *adv.*	မႃငႃပုၼ် (mâ ngâ pûn) *or* မိုၼၼ်ပုၼ် (mü nan pûn).	
Price, value, worth, *n.*	ၵႃ (kâ) *or* ꩤၼ် (khan).	
Promise (verbal), *n.*	ꩬိင် (seng).	
Puberty. *n*, ...	ဢွၵ်.ꩬွ် (åk sau)	*Pen sau* is more usually used; *pen*=to become; *sau* = young woman.
Pull, draw by force, *v.*	တုတ် (tüt).	
Pull down, demolish, house, *v.*	ယႃႁုၼ် (yâ hün).	
Punishment, *n.*	ꩡႃဝတ် (châ wat).	
"Punkah" (hand) *n.*	ဝီ (wî).	

*မၼ် really means a yam.

English.	Khâmtî.	Remarks.
Purportless, *a.*, for nothing particular.	မႃကႃ (mâkâ)	Assàmese *e n ê k e*, as *enêke ai san*.
Push, *v.*	ၸႆ (sai)	Pronounced with a rising inflection of voice.
Put upon, lay down upon anything, *v.*	တင် (tang).	
Put down, lay down, *v.*	ဝႆ (wai).	
Put on, wear, *v.*	သုပ် (sûp) *or* ၼုင် (nŭng).	*Sŭp* means to put on anything with a hole in it.
Putrid, decomposed, *a.*	ၼဝ် (nau).	
Quarrel, *v.*	ၼၼ် ကၼ် (nan kan)	*Kan* is a reciprocal particle.
Quick, speedy, *a.*	ၶၼ် (khan khan).	
Quickly, *adv.*	ၸိဝ် (chêô) *or* ၶၼ် သိ (khan khan sî).	
Quiver, *n.*	မၵ် (måk)	*Măk* means a *chunga.*
Raft, *n.*	ပေ (pê).	
Rage, anger, *v.*	ၶႃ ၸႃ (khâ châ).	
Rain, *n.*	ၽုၼ် (phôn).	
Rain, *v*	ၽုၼ် တုၵ် (phon tôk).	*Tôk*=to fall.
Rainbow, *n.*	ႁုင် ၵိၼ် ၼမ် (hung kin nam).	
Rapid, *n.*	ႁတ် (hat).	

English.	Khâmtî.	Remarks.
Rat, *n.*	ၷူ ဢူၼ် (nû ûn).	
Raw, also alive, *a.*	ၷိပ် (nip).	
Read, *v.*	ၸၢတ် (phat).	
Reach, arrive at destination, *v.*	ထုင် (thüng).	
Ready, prepared, *a.*	မေ (mê).	
Reap, *v.*	ပတ် ၵွႃ (pat khau).	
Rear, bring up, *v.*	လဵင် (lêng).	
Receive, obtain, *v.*	ၷႂ် (nai).	
Recognise, *v.*	တွင် (tång).	
Reign (time during which king or queen governs), *n.*	ၸေႃ (chô).	
Red, *a.*	ၷိင် (neng).	
Remain, stay, tarry, *v.*	ဢူ (û) *or* သွႃ (sau).	
Remain, stay behind while others go, also that which is left undone as work, &c., *v.*	ၵိုတ် (küt)	Also, means deficient, short.
Remind, *v.*	ဢွၵ်ၸႂ် (åk chaü).	
Repair, *v.*	မေ (mê).	
Repay, money or things borrowed (liquidate), *v.*	သႂ် (sâi).	

English.	Khâmtî.	Remarks.
Reply, *v.* ...	တွပ် (tåp).	
Require, want, *v.*	ႁင် (hâng).	
Reside, *v.*	ဢူ (û).	
Return, go again to some place, *v.*	မိုဝ် (mü).	
Return, turn back, *v.*	ပွၵ် (påk).	
Return, give back, *v.*	ၶိုၼ်ႁႂ် (khün haü).	
Rhinoceros, *n.* ...	ꩡုင် (chông).	
Rib, *n.* ...	ၼုၵ်ၶင် (nûk khâng).	
Rice (husked paddy), *n.*	ၶွ် ပိုၵ် (khau pük).	
Rice, unhusked (paddy), *n.*	ၶွ် သၼ် (khau sân).	
Rice (cooked) ('what'), *n.*	ၶွ် သုၵ် (khau sûk).	
Rich, affluent, possessing property, *a.*	မိ (mî) *or* သႃထေ် (sâ thê).	
Ring, *n.* ...	လၵ်ꩡွပ် (lâk chåk).	
Ring tree, *v.* ...	မၼ် (man) *or* ၵိင် † (keng).	
Ripe, *a.* ...	သုၵ် (súk) ...	† *Sûk* also means cooked.
Rise, get up, *v.*	လုၵ် (lûk).	
River, *n.* ...	ၼမ်ၶေ (nam khê) *or* ၶေၼမ် (khê nam).	
River, rise in—	လွင် (lång).	

English.	Khâmtî.	Remarks.
River, fall in—	ႁိင် (hêng) ...	*Heng*=dry.
Road, path, *n.* ...	တင် (tâng) *or* ၵုၼ် တင် (khon tâng).	Our broad roads are called တင်တိၼ် (*tang ten*).
Roadway that by which one passes or progresses.	တင်ၼွႇ (tâng noi)	Would be used in the following sentence: Did you come *by* road or *by* boat?
Roast, meat, fish potatoes, &c., *v.*	ၸိ (chî).	
Roof, of house, *n.*	လင်ၶႃ (lang khâ).	
Room, *n.*	ၶွၵ် (khåk).	
Root of tree, &c., *n.*	ႁၵ် (hâk).	
Root, take, *v.*	ႁၵ်ၸိပ် (hàk chep)	
Root, strike, *v.*.....	တိၵ်ႁၵ် (têk hàk).	
Rope, string, cane, &c., *n.*	သႂ် (sai) ...	Pronounced with a rising inflection of voice.
Rotten, *a.*	ၼွ် (nau) ...	Anything that smells.
Round, *a.*	လွံ (låm).	
Rub, *v.* ...	လုပ် (lùp).	
Rubber, *n.* ...	ယင်ႁုင် (yâng hûng).	
Rubber tree, *n.*	တုၼ်ႁုင် (tôn hûng)	
Run, *v.* ...	လိၼ် (len).	
Run away, flee, *v.*	ပႂ် (pai).	
Rupee, *n.* ..	တြႃ (trâ).	

English.	Khâmtî.	Remarks.
Rump, *n.* ...	ၵုၼ် (kôn).	
Rust, *n.* ...	ၶီႈၶၼ် (khî khan).	
Sacrifice, *v.* ...	ႁဵတ်ၽီ (het phî)...	*Phi*=good, or evil spirit.
Salt, *n.* ...	ၵိူဝ် (kü).	
Saltpetre, *n.* ...	ယိမ်ၼိပ် (yâm nip)	*Lit.* raw powder.
Salute, greet, *v.*	ပႆ (pai).	
Same, like corresponding, &c., *a.*	တူတူ (tû tû) *or* တူၵၼ် (tûkan).	
Sand, *n.* ...	သႆ (sai).	
Sandbank, *n.* ...	ပႃသႆ (pasai).	
Satisfied, *a.* ...	ၸိူဝ်တႆ (chaü tai).	
Say, affirm, recite, *v.*	ဝႃ (wâ).	
Scar, cicatrix, *n.*	တိုင် (tüng).	
Scissor, *n.* ...	ၵိမ်ၶုမ် (kîm khôm).	
Scold, *v.* ...	ၼၼ် (nan) *or* ၸႃ (châ).	
Scratch, as a tiger, cat, *v.*	ဝၵ် (wâk) *or* ၶၼ် (khân).	
Scratch, as human being, *v.*	တိုၼ် (tün).	
Search, seek, look for, *v.*	ၶႃ (khâ).	
Search, house, &c. (by order), *v.*	သွၵ် (såk).	

English.	Khâmtî.	Remarks.
Seat (of wood), *n.*	တင် (tang) ...	Anything for sitting on is called *tang* (*i.e.*, anything raised off the ground).
See, percieve by the eye, *v.*	ႁၼ် (han).	
Seed, *n.* ...	ႁွႝ (hôy).	
Seed, for propogating, *n.*	ၽၼ် (phan).	
Seer (weight), 2 lbs., *n.*	တွၵ် (tåk).	
Seize, grasp, lay hold of, &c., *v.*	ၸေဢဝ် (se au).	
Sell, *v.* ...	ၶႝ (khâi) ...	Pronounced with a rising inflection of voice.
Send, dispatch, *v.*	ပွႝ (poi).	
Separately, apart, singly, *adv.*	ႁင်ၽႂ်ႁင်မၼ် *or* ၵွႝႝ (hang phaü hang man).	(*Koi koi*).
Sepoy (soldier), *n.*	လုၵ်ႉသိုၵ် (lûk sük).	*Sük*=war.
Seven, *a.* ...	ၸဵတ် (chet).	
Sew, *v.* ...	ယပ် (yâp)	
Shade, *n.* ...	ႁူမ် (hôm).	
Shadow, *n.* ...	ငဝ် (ngau ...	Pronounced like word for light.
Shake, tree, &c., *v.* ...	ၶွၼ် (khân).	
Shallow, not deep, *a.*	တုၼ် (tûn).	

English.	Khâmtî.	Remarks.
Shame, *a.*	ဢႆ (âi)	*Ai* (pronounced exactly the same) also means steam.
Share, *n.*	ꩡႃ (châ).	
Sharp, having thin edge, or sharp point, *a.*	ၾႆ (phai)	သဵမ် (*sem*) also meas pointed, sharp point.
Shield, *n.*	ၵိူၼ် (ken).	
Shoe, boot, *n.*	ၶဵပ်တိၼ်း (khep tin).	
Shoot, *v.*	ယိုဝ် (yü).	
Shop, *n.*	ꩡေႊ (chè).	
Short, not long, *a.*	ပွတ် (pât).	
Short, not tall or high, *a.*	တံ (tam)	As a short man, or tree, &c.
Short, deficient, *a.*	ယွံ (yâm) *or* ꩫိုၼ် ၵုံ (n'kûm).	
Show, exhibit, *v.*	ꩡီ (chî).	
Shut, door, box, or any thing with lid, *v.*	ႁပ် (hâp).	
Shoulder, *n.*	ႁုဝ်ၶိူၼ် (hô khên)	*Hô* pronounced with a rising inflection of voice.
Sick, ill, indisposed, *a.*	ၶႆ (khai).	
Silver, *n.*	ငိုၼ်း (ngün).	
Silversmith, *n.*	ꩡၢင်ငိုၼ်း (châng ngün).	

English.	Khâmtî.	Remarks.
Since, before this, or now, *adv.*	ပုၼ် (pûn).	
Sing, *v.* ...	မေႃၶမ် (mô khâm).	
Sister, *n.* ...	ပီသဝ် (pî sau) ၼွင်သဝ် (nâng sau).	*Pi sau*=eldest; *nàng sau*=younger.
Sister-in-law, *n.* (husband or wife's sister).	......	Same as sister.
Sit, *v.* ...	ၼင် (nang).	
Sit, incubate, *v.*	ငမ် (ngam).	
Site, locality, situation, *n.*	ယၢၼ် (yân).	
Six, *a.* ...	ႁူၵ် (hôk).	
Skin, *n.* ...	ၼင် (nang) ...	Pronounced with a rising inflection of voice.
Skin, flay, ...	လွၵ် (lâk).	
Sky, *n.* ...	ၵင်ၾႃ (kâng phâ).	
Slap, strike with open hand, *v.*	တပ် (tâp).	
Slave, *n.* ...	ၶႃ (khâ) ...	Voice rests on the *ā* a little.
Sleep, lie down, *v.*	ၼွၼ် (nân).	
Slippery, *a.* ...	မုၼ် (mûn).	
Slowly, *adv.* ...	လွႆ" (loi loi).	
Small, not large, *a.*	ဢွၼ် (ân).	
Smell, *v.* ...	မိၼ် (men) *or* ႁွမ် (hâm).	*Men*=bad smell; *hàm*=good smell.
Smoke, *n.* ...	ၶွၼ်ၾႆ (khân phai).	

English.	Khâmtî.	Remarks.
Smoke, pipe, or cigar, *v.*	လုတ် (lût).	
Snag *n.* ...	ၶၢၼ် (khân) ...	Pronounced with a rising inflection of voice.
Snake, *n.* ...	ငူ (ngû).	
Sneeze, *v.* ...	တၢꩡမ် (kâ châm).	
Snore, *v.* ...	ꩫၢၼ်ၶုၼ်(nân khûn).	
Snot, *n.* ...	ꩫမ်မုၵ် (nam môk).	
Snow, *n.* ...	မွႆ (môy).	
Soft, not hard, *a.*	ဢွၼ် (ôn).	
Sole, of foot, *n.*	ၸၢတိၼ် (phâ tin).	
Solicit, ask for, *v.*	ယၢၼ် (yân).	
Some one, *n.* ...	ၽူၵႆ (phaü kai).	
Somehow, in some manner, *adv.*	ႁိၼုဝ်သီၵေႃ (hî nü sî kaw).	
Sometimes, *adv.*	မၢလႂ် (mâ laü) *or*	
Something, *n.* ...	ယေပၼ် (yê pân pân).	
Somewhere, *adv.*	ဢၢလႂ်မႆၵေႃ (â laü mai kaw).	ꩫၢမႆ ၵေႃ (*namai, kaw*) also used.
Son, *n.* ...	လုၵ်ꩡႆ(lûk chai).	
Son-in-law, *n.* ...	လုၵ် ၶွႆ (lûk khôy).	
Soon, presently, in a short time, *adv.*	မၢꩡမ် (mâ cham).	Often pronounced *ma jam!*
Sore ...	တိꩡိပ် (ti chep)...	*Lit.* pain, or hurt spot.

English.	Khâmtî.	Remarks.
Sort, class, caste, *n.*	ၸၼ် (phan).	
Sour ...	သုံ (sôm).	
Sound ...	သိင် (sêng).	
South, *n.* ...	ပႝၸၼ် pai chân).	
Sow, *n.* ...	မူမေ် (mû me).	
Sow (plánt by strewing), *v.*	ဝၼ် (wân).	
Span, *n.* ...	ၵိုပ် (khüp).	
Spark, *n.* ...	မိင်ၸႝ(ming phai).	
Sparrow, *n.* ...	ၼုၵ် ၸွၵ် (nôk châk).	
Spawn, *n.* ...	ၶႝပႃ (khai pâ)	*Pà*=fish.
Speak, converse, *v.*	တၼ် (tân).	
Spear, *n.* ...	ႁွၵ် (hâk).	
Spear, pierce, stab, *v.*	တိင် (têng).	
Spectacles, *n.* ...	မၼ်တႃ (mân tà)....	*Lit.* eye-looking glass.
Spider, *n.*	ၵုင်ၵွ (kûng kau).	
Spider, web, *n.* ...	ယူၵုင်ၵွ (yaü kûng kau).	
Spin, *v.* ...	ယိတ်, (yêt).	
Spinning-wheel, *n.*	ၵုင် (kông).	
Spine, *n.* ...	ၼုၵ်ပေလင် (nûk pê lang).	*Nük*=bone; *pe*= 'mårôlî' and *lang* = back.
Spirit, *n.* ...	ၸီ (phî).	

English.	Khâmtî.	Remarks.
Spit, eject from mouth, *v.*	ထွၵ် (taü) *or* ၸိတ် ၼမ်လႆ (chit nam lai).	
Spittle, *n.* ...	ၼမ်လႆ (nam lai).	
Spleen, *n.* ...	ပင် (pâng).	
Split, wood, *v.* ...	ၽႃ (phâ).	
Spoon, wooden or otherwise, *n.*	ၸုဝ် (chô).	
Spread, mat, or cloth, *v.*	သိုဝ် (sü).	
Sprout, push out new shoots.	ၼုဝ် (nô).	
Stand up, or remain for a while, tarry, *v.*	သွၵ် (sau).	
Stand, anything upright.	တင် ဝႆ (tang wai) at a slant ဢိင် (ing).	
Stalk, approach an animal by stealth, *v.*	ငမ် (ngâm).	
Star, *n.*	ၼွၵ် (nau).	
Steam, *n.* ...	ဢႆ (ai).	
Steep, ascending or descending with great inclination, *a.*	ၸၼ် (chan).	
Step-father, *n.*...	ပေႃ ပုတ် (pô pût)	Step-daughter and step-son called daughter and son respectively.
Step-mother, *n.*	မေ ဢွၼ် (me ân).	

English.	Khâmtî.	Remarks.
Step upon, *v.* ...	ယိပ် (yêp).	
Stern of boat, *n.*	ꩭင် ꩭိုပ်(hâng hü)	*Lit.* tail of boat.
Stick, *n.* ...	ၼႂ် တွႝ (mai tau).	
Stick, fix in, set, *v.*	ပၵ် (pâk).	
Sticky, gluey, *a.*	ၼိပ် (nêo).	
Sting, *n.* ...	ယိၼ် (sên).	
Sting, nettle, *n.*	ၼံၸၼ် (ṇâm phân)	
Stone, *n.* ...	ꩭိၼ် (hin).	
Limestone, *n.* ...	ꩭိၼ် ယုၼ် (hin sûn)	
Stool, evacuate, *v.*	ၶိ (khî).	
Stoop, *v.* ...	ꩶုံ (kôm).	
Stop, arrest the progress of, hindrance of, operation, action, or speech, &c., *v.*	ပိၸႃ (pî phâ).	
Straight, not crooked, *v.*	ၼၼ် (nan).	
Strangle, by hanging, *v.*	တႝ ၵိတ် (tai ket).	
Straw, stubble, *n.*	ၸိုင်. ၼႃ (phüng nå).	
Strike, *v.* ...	ပုပ် (pô).	
Stroll, wander on foot, *v.*	လေ (lê).	
Strong, possessed of strength, *a.*	ꩭိင် (hêng).	
Strong, intoxicating, *a.*	ၶိၼ် (khên).	

English.	Khâmtî.	Remarks.
Subsequently ...	ကႃ လင် ၼၼ် (kâ lang nan).	*Lit.* after that.
Substitute successor, *n.*	ပုတ် (put).	
Suck, *v.*	ႁုတ် (hût).	
Suffice, to be enough or sufficient, *v.*	ပေႃ (pô).	
Sugarcane, *n.*	ဢွႆ (oi).	
Sulky, *a.*	ၶြႃ (khra).	
Sulphur, *n.*	ကၼ် (kân).	
Sun, *n.*	ဝၼ် (wan).	
Sunrise, *n.*	ဝၼ်ဢွၵ်(wan âk).	
Sunset, *v.*	ဝၼ် တုၵ် (wan tôk).	
Sunshine, *n.*	ၽႃ ၼဵတ် (phâ net).	
Surround, *v.*	လွမ် (lâm)	*Âm* pronounced a little shorter than in word for round.
Suspect, *v.*	ပိၼ် (pin) *or* ထုမ် (thüm).	
Swallow, *v.*	ဢုၼ် (ün).	
Swell, *v.*	ပွင် (pâng) *or* ၵႂ် (kaü).	*Pång* = protuberance + kaü = swelling from a blow.
Sweet, *v.*	ဝၼ် (wân).	
Sweep, *v.*	ပတ် (pat).	
Swift, *a.*	ၶၼ် (khan).	
Swim, *v.*	လွႆ (loi).	
Sword, *n.*	ၼပ် (nâp)	Same in Singpho.

English.	Khâmtî.	Remarks.
Taboo, *v.*	ၵံ (kam).	
Tail, *n.*	ႁၢင် (hâng) ...	Pronounced with a rising inflection of voice.
Take, receive, *v.*	ဢဝ် (au)	*Au* is also the instrumental case prefix, also causal prefix.
Take out, *v.*	ဢဝ် ဢၵ် (au âk)	*Au* here is a causal prefix.
Take, by force, or against wish.	ႁိမ် ဢဝ် (him au).	
Take, off clothes, undress, *v.*	လၢၼ် (lân)	*Lan* means to take off anything.
'Tâmâshâ,' singing, playing, dancing, &c.	ပဵဝ် (pêô).	
Taste, *v.*	ꩡိမ် chim.	
Tattoo, *v.*	သမ် (sam).	
Tea *n.* ...	ၼိင် (ning).	
Teach, also learn, *v.*	သၢၼ် (sân).	
Teacher, *n.*	ပႃ သၢၼ် (pâ sân) *or* သိရႃ (sîrâ).	
Tear, *n.*	ၼမ် တႃ (nam tâ).	
Tear, separate by violence, *v.*	တုၼ် (tün).	
Tell, inform, acquaint, *v.*	လၢၼ် (lan) *or* ၶႆ (khai).	
Temple, *n.*	ꩡၢင် (chăng)	Priest, *n.*, ꩡဝ်မုၼ် (chau môn).
Ten, *a.*	သိပ် (sip).	
Tendon, ...	ဢဵၼ် (ên).	

English.	Khâmtî.	Remarks.
Testicle, *n.*	ꩭံ (ham).	
Than, *conj.*	ၶိူၼ် (khên).	
That, *dem. pron.*	ဢႃ ၼၼ် (ânan).	
Thatching grass, *n.*	ၶႃ (khâ) ...	Voice does not rest on the *a* like in the word for slave.
Them, *pron.*	ၵဝ်မႆ (khau mai).	
Then, at that time, *adv.*	မိုဝ်ႉၼႆ (mü nai).	
Then, in that case, *conj.*	ၼႆ ၵႃ ယေႃ (nai kâ yê) *or* သိၼႆ ၵႃ ယေႃ (sî nai kâ yê).	ၵႃၸမ် (*ka cham*) may be substituted for ၵႃ ယေႃ
Thence, *adv.*	လုၵ်ၼၼ် (lûk nan).	
There, *adv.*	မၼ် (man)	ပုၼ် (*pun*) there, some distance off.
Therefore, *adv.*	လႆ ပိုဝ် ၼႆ (laipü nai) *or* လႆပိုဝ်ၼႆ သိ (laipü nai sî) *or* လႆလင်ၼႆ (lai lang nai) *or* ၵပ် ပိုဝ်ၼႆ (kâp pü nai) *or* ပိုဝ် ၼႆ (pü nai) *or* လႆၼႆ lai nai).	
They, *pron.*	ၵဝ် (khau).	
Thick, not thin, *a.*	ၼႃ (nâ) *or* ထိ (thi)	A thick stick would be a large stick in Khâmtî.

English.	Khâmtî.	Remarks.
Thick, close, crowded in space, *a*.	ထိ (thi).	
Thief, *n*.	ပႃလၵ်ႇ (pâlâk).	
Thieve, steal, *v*.	လၵ်ႇ (lâk).	
Thigh, *n*.	ၶႃ (khâ)	Pronounced with a rising inflection of voice.
Thin, not thick, *a*.	မၢင် (mâng)	Not dense, close, ၶၢင် (*háng*).
Thin, not fat, *a*.	ယွမ် (yám).	
Things, goods, *n*.	ၶိူင် (khüng).	
Thirst, *n*.	ၶႃ ၵိၼ်ၼမ် (khâ kin nam).	*Lit*. desire to drink water ၶူဝ် ႁိင် (khô héng), *lit*. dry throat also used.
This, *dem. pron*.	ဢႃ ၼႆ (â nai).	
This much	ၶႆ လိူင် (khai lüng).	
That much	ၶၼ်လိူင် (khan lüng)	
This side	ပႃမႆ (pâ mai).	
That side	ပႃမၼ် (pâ man).	
This year ..	ပီၼႆ (pi nai).	
This month	ၼိူၼ်ၼႆ (nün nai).	
Thorn, *n*.	ၼမ် (nám).	
Thousand, *a*.	ႁိင် (hing).	
Thread, for weaving, *n*.	မႆ (mai).	
Threaten, menace, *v*.	လွၵ်ႇ (lăk).	
Throat, *n*.	ၶူဝ် (khô).	
Throw, *v*.	ထိမ် (thim).	

English.	Khâmtî.	Remarks.
Throw away, quit, *v*.	ၵွတ် (khåt).	
Thumb, *n*.	ꩫေမိုဝ် (mê mü).	
Thunder, *n*.	ၾႃ ၸေတ် (phâtê)	Crash prior to rumbling, rumbling.
Thus, in this, or that manner, *adv*.	ၾႃၼင် (phâ nang) ၼင်ငႆ (n a n g ngai) *or* ၼင်ၼႆ (nang nai).	
Tick, *n*.	ႁိပ်ႁၵ် (hip håk).	
Tickle, *v*.	ၸုင် ၵႃရီ (chûng kârî).	
Tie up, fasten, *v*.	ၾုၵ် (phûk).	
Tie up, hair, *v*.	ၵွႆ (kau).	
Tiger, *n*.	သိုဝ် (sü)	Pronounced with a rising inflection of voice.
Tight, not loose, fitting close, *a*.	ၵပ် (kap).	
Tide, jade, &c., *v*.	ၼွႆ (nôy).	
To, *prep*.	မႆ (mai) *or* တီ (tî).	
Tobacco, *n*.	ယႃ (yâ).	
Toe, large, *n*.	ꩫေ တိၼ် (mê tin).	
Toe, others, *n*.	လဵဝ် တိၼ် (lêô tin).	
Together, in company, *adv*.	ႁူမ် ၵၼ် (hôm kan).	
Tongue, *n*.	လိၼ် (lin).	
Tooth, *n*.	ၶဵဝ် (khêô).	
Toothache, *n*.	ၶဵဝ် ၸဵပ် (k h ê ô chep).	
Top, *n*.	ၶင် (khâng).	

English.	Khâmtî.	Remarks.
Torch, *n.*	ၶေ ၽႆ (khè phai) *or* ၽုၼ်ၶေ (phûn khê).	
Tough, *a.*	ၶိင် (kheng)	*Lit.* hard.
Towards, in the direction of, *prep.*	ၵၼ် ပႃ (kanpâ).	
Town, *n.*	တပ် (tâp).	
Track, foot print, *n.*	ႁွႆ တိၼ် (hoi tin).	
Track, *v.*	ၸၢမ် (châm).	
Trade, *v.*	ၵႃ (kâ).	
Trader, *n.*	ပႃ ၵႃ (pâ kâ).	
Transplant, dhan, *v.*	သၢမ် (sâm).	
Transplant, small plants, *v.*	ပုၵ် (pûk).	
Tree, *n.*	တုၼ် မႆ (tôn mai).	
Tremble, *v.*	သၼ် (san).	
Trouble; annoyance, vexation, inconvenience, &c., *a.*	ၸမ်ၸိုဝ် (cham chaü).	
Trousers, very wide, worn by Shans, *n.*	ပင် ပိ (pâng pî).	
Trousers, like ours, *n.*	ၶုၼ် (khôn).	
Truly, exactly, *adv.*	မၼ် (mân mân).	
Try, examine judicially, *v.*	ပိတ် (pet).	
Trunk, of tree, *n.*	ငဝ် (ngau).	

English.	Khâmtî.	Remarks.
Turn round, face, *v.*	ဝိꩫ (win).	
Turn round, body altogether, *v.*	ပꩫ (pan).	
Tusk, whether elephant, pig, dog, tiger, &c., *n.*	ငႃ (ngâ).	
Turban, *n.*	ၽႃ ႁူဝ် (phâ hô).	*Lit.* head cloth.
Turtle, tortoise, *n.*	တဝ် (tau)	There are two kinds, namely, တဝ်ပိၵ် (*tau pik* တဝ် ၵပ် (*tau kȧp*).
Twelve, *a.*	သိပ်သွင်(sip sȧng).	
Twice, *adv.*	သွင် ပွၵ် (sȧng pȧk).	
Twins, *n.*	လုၵ်ၽႃ (lûk phâ).	
Twenty, *a.* ...	သဝ် (sȧu).	*Lüng* is usually suffixed to denote a single (one) twenty.
Two, *a.*	သွင် (sȧng).	
Ugly, not comely, *a.*	မႃသိꩫ (mâsen)	*Lit.* not comely.
Umbrella, *n.*	ၸွင် (chȧng)	Same in Singhpo.
Uncle, father's younger brother, *n.*	ပေႃ လုင် (pô lông).	
Uncle, father's eldest brother, *n.*	ပေႃ ဢဝ် (pô au).	
Uncle, mother's eldest brother, *n.*	ပေႃလုင် (pô lung).	

English.	Khâmtî.	Remarks.
Uncle, mother's younger brother, *n.*	ၼိုပ် ꩡဝ် (n' chau).	
Under, below, *adv.* and *prep.*	ကႃ တႂ် (kâtaü).	
Understand, *v.*	တင် (tâng).	
Unnecessary, needless, not wanted, *a.*	ၼိုပ် တပ် (n' tâp).	
Urine, *n.*	ယိဝ် (yêô).	
Unripe, also uncooked, *a.*	ၼိပ် (nip) ...	Also means alive.
Unfasten, untie, *v.*	ကိ (kî) *or* ကေ (kê).	
Until, *prep.*	ကႃ (kâ) ...	Sudden cessation of voice on *â*.
Uproot, tear up by root, *v.*	ထုၺ် (thóy).	
Upset, boat, *v.*	လုံ (lôm) ...	Only applicable to upsetting of boat.
Upside down, topsyturvy.	ၽုၼ် (phûn).	
Up stream, *adv.*	ကႃ ၼိုင် (kâ nü)	ႁူဝ် ၼမ် (hô nam), *lit.* head of water also used.
Use, or exert force, *v.*	သႂ်ႁႅင် (saü heng).	
Vegetable, *n.*	ၽၵ် (phak).	
Vein, *n.*	မၵ် လိုတ် (m â k lüt).	
Very well (used eliptically).	ၼိ (ni).	

English.	Khâmtì.	Remarks.
Very, exceedingly, in a great degree, *adv.*	လုင် (lông) *or* ၸဵဝ် (pheau).	ဢဵဝ်ႁဵင် (*auheng*) ꩀႃ ႁဵင် (*kā heng*) are used as adjectives and are apparently equivalent to the English adjective 'more.'
Village, *n.*	မၢꩫ် (mân).	
Vomit, *v.*	ႁၢၵ် (hâk).	
Vulture, *n.*	ꩫၢင်တႃ (nang tâ).	
Wait, tarry, stay for, *v.*	ထႃ (thâ).	
Wake, rouse from sleep, *v.*	ပုၵ် (pôk).	
Walk, move along on foot, *v.*	ၽႆ (phâi).	
Wall, of house, *n.*	ၽႃ (phâ) ...	Pronounced with a rising inflection of voice.
Want, need, *v.*	ႁၢင် (hâng)	
War, *n.*	သိုၵ် (sük).	
Warm, *a.*	လိုတ် (lüt).	
Warm, make hot, *v.*	ဢုၼ် (ûn).	
Wash body bathe, *v.*	ဢၢပ်ꩫမ် (âp nam).	
Wash clothes, *v.*	သၢၵ် (sâk) *phā*= clothes.	*Sāk suk*=wash hands or face.
Wash pots, plates, *v.*	လၢင် (lâng).	
Wasp, *n.*	တိူၼ် (tên).	
Water, *n.*	ꩫမ် (nam).	

English.	Khâmtî.	Remarks.
Water, clear, *a.*	လိင် (lông).	
Water, turbid, *a.*	ၵုၼ်း (khûn).	
Waterfall, *n.* ...	ၼမ်တုၵ်တင် (nam tôk tâng).	
Watch, guard, also attend in sickness, *v.*	ပႂ် (paü).	
Watch, be on look out as for a wild animal, *v.*	ႁေ (hê).	
Wax, *n.*	ၶီႉၽိုင် (khi phüng)	*Lit.* bees' excrement.
Weak, not strong, *a.*	ႁႅင်းမႃႇယင် (hêng ma yang).	*Lit.* possessed of no strength, without strength.
Weed, *n.*	ၽွႆႇယႃ (phôy yâ).	
Weed, *v.*	ထွႆႇ (thôy).	
Weave, *v.*	တေႃႇႁုၵ်း (tô hûk).	
Weigh, v.	ၶိင် (khing).	
West, *n.*	ဝၼ်းတုၵ်း (wan tôk)	*Tŏk*=to fall.
Wet, containing water, *a.*	ယမ် (yam).	
Wet, moisten with water, *v.*	ဢဝ်ယမ် (au yam).	
What, *interrog. pron.*	ၵႃႇသင် (kâsang.)	
What sort or kind.	ၽၼ်းလႂ် (phan laü).	*Lit.* what *jat*?
Whatever, *pron.*	ၵႃႇသင်ၵေႃႈ (kâ sang kaw).	

English.	Khâmtî.	Remarks.
When, at the time that, *adv.*	မိုဝ် (mü).	
When, at what time, *adv.*	မႃလႂ် (mâ laü).	
Whence, *adv.*	လုၵ်ၼႃမႆ (lûk nâ-mai).	
Where, *adv.*	ၼႃမႆ (nâ mai) *or* ဢႃလႂ်မႆ (â laü-mai).	
Which, *interrog. pron.*	ဢႃလႂ် (â laü).	
Whistle, *v.*	ထိဝ် (thio) လိၼ် (lin).	
White, *a.*	ၶႂ် (khau) *or* ၽိူၵ် (phük).	
Whiteant, *n.*	ပုၵ် (pôk).	
Who, *interrog. pron.*	ၽႂ် (phaü).	
Who know	ပႃထူ (pâthû).	
Whose	ၽႂ် (phaü).	
Whole	တင် (tâng).	
Why	ႁဵတ်းသင် (het-sang).	
Wide, not narrow, *a.*	ၵၢင် (kâng).	
Widow, *n.*	မေႈမႆ (mê mai).	
Widower, *n.*	ပေႃႈမႆ (pô mai).	
Wife, woman, *n.*	မေႈ (mê).	

English.	Khâmtî.	Remarks.
Wild, not tame, only applies to buffalo, *a.*	ႁေ (hê).	
Win, gain by success, in competition of contest.	ပေ (pê)	Also means win money.
Wind, *n.*	လုံ (lôm).	
Wing, *n.*	ပိၵ် (pîk).	
Wipe, *v.*	ၸိတ် (chet).	
Wish, desire, *v.*	ၶႃ (khâ).	
With, in company with, along with.	ထင် (tang).	
With, instrument, means, *prep.*	ဢဝ် (au).	
Woman, female, *n.*	ပႃယိင် (pâying).	
Womb, *n.*	ၸွၼ် (sår)	
Wood, for burning, *n.*	ၽုၼ် (phûn).	
Wood, substance of trees.	မႆ (mai).	
Work, labour, *n.*	ဢႃမူ (â mû).	
Worm, earth, *n.*	တိုၵ်ၼိၼ် (tük nin)	*Nin*=earth.
Worm, instestinal, *n.*	တိုၵ် (tük).	
Wound, a hurt, an injury, *n.*	တိၸိပ် (ti chep)	*Lit.* hurt spot.
Wrist, *n.*	တႃမိုဝ် (tâ mü).	
Write, *v.*	တိမ် (tîm).	

English.	Khâmtî.	Remarks.
Writer, *n.*	ပါတမ် (pâtem) *or* ၸူတမ် (phû tem)	
Wrong, not right, *a.*	မါၼီ (mâ nî).	*Lit.* not good.
Yam, *n.*	မၼ် (man).	
Yawn, *v.*	ႁဝ် (hau).	Pronounced with a rising inflection of voice.
Year, *n.*	ပီ (pî).	
Yes, affirmation and consent, *adv.*	ၸဝ် (chaü).	
Yesterday, *n.*	မါငါ (mâ ngâ).	
Day before yesterday, *n.*	မါသုၼ် (mâ sûn).	
Yet, up to present time, *adv.*	တုၵ်ၸမ်ငႆ (tôk chem ngai).	
Yoke, *n.*	ၵႆၼိင် (khai neng)	*Lit.* red of egg.
Yolk, of egg, *n.*	ဢိၵ် (êk).	
Young, of animal, *n.*	လုၵ် (lûk).	Also used with reference to human beings.
Young man, *n.*	ပါၼမ် (pâ nam).	
Young woman, *n.*	ပါသဝ် (pâ sau).	

G. B. C P. O.—No. 6946—B. S. 15-11-98—400.